THE CATHOLIC SPIRIT
IN
MODERN ENGLISH LITERATURE

The Catholic Spirit
IN
Modern English Literature

BY

GEORGE N. SHUSTER, *1894-*

"Yet ever and anon a trumpet sounds
From the hid battlements of eternity."

FRANCIS THOMPSON.

Essay Index Reprint Series

BOOKS FOR LIBRARIES PRESS, INC.
FREEPORT, NEW YORK

First published 1922
Reprinted 1967

LIBRARY OF CONGRESS CATALOG CARD NUMBER:

67-26785

PRINTED IN THE UNITED STATES OF AMERICA

To

FATHER CARRICO

OF NOTRE DAME

FOREWORD

Modern literature is largely made up of deliberate, if somewhat ornate, pamphleteering. It is a great written debate between the exponents of different ways of living and looking upon life. Never before have solutions so divergent been offered to the riddle of human destiny and never have the protagonists been more belligerent. We all feel that the older English letters were concerned with an established point of view; that, while Spenser was an Anglican and Milton a Puritan, their human creed, their idea of man, was substantially the same. But the pressure of these latter days has lain heavily on every kind of art; and literature has been forced to voice the protest or the defense of a multitude of individuals deriving their strength from sources which have very little in common. In many ways the influence of this state of affairs has been evil and has led to recklessness and perversity in the statement of opinion, as well as to the abandonment by a large portion of the reading public of anything like standards, not only of judgment but even of taste. On the other hand, there are many who as a result of the modern upheaval have grown quite tired of eccentricity and faddishness; who are convinced as men otherwise circumstanced could scarcely be convinced, that some basic philosophy is needed to save art from ruinous futility.

No other constructive force that has come into English literature during the nineteenth century is nearly so important as the Catholic spirit. By this I mean the Catholic way of living and of looking upon life; the understanding of the Christian traditions of European civilization, the acceptance of the principles upon which those traditions were based, and confidence in their efficacy in modern life and letters. Of necessity this spirit is concerned with the Middle Ages from which modern England broke away, but its concern is not limited to lucarnes, alchemists, and Knights Templars. It is worth noting that a man may refuse (though it happens unfrequently) to recognize the supremacy of the Pope and still possess the Catholic spirit; that he may recognize that supremacy without having the spirit. What cannot be dispensed with is a sense of fellowship with the religious force which built up Europe from the ruins of Rome, which maintained certain principles of human liberty and dependence on God, and which taught the Truth without which Beauty is either a corpse or an evil spirit. It will be the purpose of this little book to indicate how the Catholic idea gained power in England and how it went about using that power in literary art. The achievement to be considered is really too large for adequate treatment in so small a space, but I shall make no long apology for that.

In fact, the surprising thing is the general indifference which has been manifested in critical circles to this really phenomenal wealth of energy. It is, I suppose, sheer inability to understand an alien point of view which has led the author of a popular manual to assert that Newman's conversion was the result of a feverish interest in ritual, and which has inspired the strangely myopic section on the Cardinal in the "Cambridge History of English Literature." I believe that the time has come when the reading public generally will find useful a franker and more coordinated statement of the workings of the Catholic spirit than it has been able to find. People go far in their inspection of principles nowadays, and will not be inclined to discountenance as narrow a tradition that was once broad enough to create the manifold reality of Europe and that has meant much to the England and America of our time. Catholics, of course, have an especial motive for knowing more of the expression given to their views by literary genius. In school and out of it there ought to be for them a way of getting a bird's-eye view of the situation.

I have tried to work in the spirit of filling this demand. The present book is devoted to the public rather than to the scholar and aims to convey a general impression rather than to enumerate a wealth of minute, if erudite, details. A good many books on literature, it often seems, are quite unliterary. Whenever possible an attempt has been made to give an idea of an author's personality and work without aiming directly at criticism; but proportion and common-sense both require some consideration of the relative importance of writers. Mistakes have undoubtedly occurred. Well, let them stand while we go to the business of a survey of modern Catholic letters, frankly, with no view of partisanship, and above all, with Pascal, on our knees.

CONTENTS

CHAPTER   PAGE

FOREWORD vii

I THE DAYS OF LOST TRADITION 1

II KENELM DIGBY AND THE DISCOVERY OF THE PAST 15

III THE PERSONALITY OF NEWMAN 33

IV NEWMAN THE THINKER 56

V NEWMAN THE ARTIST 73

VI LEADERS AT OXFORD AND CAPTAINS OF THE CHURCH 88

VII POETRY AND THREE POETS 104

VIII FRANCIS THOMPSON THE MASTER 127

IX INHERITORS 147

X RUSKIN, PATER, AND THE PRE-RAPHAELITES 166

XI THE CHRONICLERS OF CHRISTENDOM. . . 187

XII ROBERT HUGH BENSON AND THE AGING NOVEL 208

XIII THE ADVENTURES OF A JOURNALIST: G. K. CHESTERTON 229

XIV THE ADVENTURES OF A HISTORIAN: HILAIRE BELLOC 249

XV THE VOICE OF IRELAND 268

XVI THE AMERICAN CONTRIBUTION 294

XVII LITERATURE AND THE VISTAS OF THE CATHOLIC SPIRIT 317

ADDENDA 352

xi

THE CATHOLIC SPIRIT

IN

MODERN ENGLISH LITERATURE

THE CATHOLIC SPIRIT IN
MODERN ENGLISH LITERATURE

CHAPTER ONE

THE DAYS OF LOST TRADITION

"The return of civilization to religion is like the return of the energy stored in coal to the heat of the sun."

D. MEREJKOWSKI.

THE Catholic Spirit has been, and is, hard at work in modern English literature. By "Catholic" is meant here nothing sectarian or narrowly controversial, but instead the broad, traditionally Christian outlook upon life which through many centuries moulded European society into all but its ultra-modern forms. It antedated the agnostic and it superseded the pagan; it was both the enemy and the lover of Rome. Although inherently artistic, it condemned art for its own sake. We shall not try to account for it or to make an apology for what is so obvious that it has been ignored. Catholic art raised every structure worth looking at that has been built since the days of the Parthenon and the Capitol; wrote the "Divina Commedia," the "Morte D'Arthur," and, to some extent at least, the plays of William Shakespeare; and erected, finally, a social order in which the art of living was possible. There was nothing wooden or pedantic

1

about it anywhere, but instead a surprising vitality, as of old Adam forgetting his age: yet it stood like a rock on two points—belief in God and in Man. Theology and politics were written into its poetics. No workman in whom the Catholic Spirit breathed would have admitted that religion can be excluded from life and art. Christianity sent thousands of its representatives to death for a Roman holiday; it carried armies over pestilential wastes to the conquest of a blighted town; it was everywhere alarmingly reckless of life: but it tried honestly to make that life worth the trouble. Woman believed and was honored; the slave was freed and the king became a slave. And from one end of Christendom to the other, the *Miserere* ended in a chorus of laughter.

Gradually that spirit died out of the world and its sacred temples were profaned. During nearly four hundred years of English history it was reviled and spit upon, and then it returned, disguised at first, cautiously showing its face to friends until it had once more the right to sit in the market-place. It entered into the literature of England, wherever men lived again in the past of Christendom, wherever souls yearned for the faith and blessed peace that were symbolized by the spires of Lincoln and Canterbury, wherever the spell of modern pessimism was broken by sacramental mirth. Occasionally the hovels of the poor were shaken, and it got inside the gates of Oxford. Poets were thrilled with the rich music of mediæval life, and thinkers battled with modern thought, clad in the armour of the schools. The world was shaken with memories and though many were heedless or distrustful or filled with rancour, those who loved them

were given new courage and new vigour. They chanted
songs that had long been forgotten and voiced hopes
that had been changed into despair. While the world
about them reeled in the din of its delusion, they stood
serene; and when they wept their tears were pure.
But they themselves shall tell the story of how they
came to know the splendid continuity of Christendom,
its interest in the fate of man, its trust in God.

That excellent knight, Sir Thomas More, who laid
his head on the block during the first year of Henry's
usurpation, had been saddened with the vision of evils
which were to come over an England that had long
been popular and merry and Christian. "Your shepe,"
he said, thinking of the growing tendency to oust the
tenants from land that could be used for grazing,
"that were wont to be so meke and tame, and so smal
eaters, now, as I heare say, do become so great devow-
erers and so wylde, that they eate up and swallow
downe the very men themselves." Sir Thomas did not
live to witness the full rapacity of those sheep or of
the wolves that went about in their clothing. He did
not see the fiendish greed that would consume every
bulwark in which the common man took refuge: the
sacking of merciful monasteries, the bitter tyranny of
kings and queens with lust in their bowels and blood
in their eyes, the hunger and sickness of millions for
whom there would be at length no refuge but the slavery
of industrial towns, or the final darkness that would
sit heavily on England's soul. He died in testimony to
the past, and mindful of his serenity we shall hasten
over the days of the democratic downfall, merely noting

how every principle which the religious conscience had set up in defense of the poor was spurned; how the artistic impulse that had made of life a beautiful and holy thing was torn from the hearts of men; and how, at last, the very memory of the older Faith and the older Happiness was beaten into the dust by warriors' horses, the silken trains of courtesans, and all that musty paganism which is as brutal as it is proud. Verily, these were sheep that "swallowed downe the very men themselves" and they were remembered again and again, till even the gentle and goodly Tom Hood cursed them in his lyric verse. The middle years of the century into which that poet was born were indeed the days of the lost tradition, when England that had been gay was sad, and the throne of Edward a pedestal for gain.

The eighteenth century was sallow, stale. Over all of Europe walls began to crack, buttresses to sag. The humanistic solvent of the Great Revolt had steadily undermined the authority of the Church, but it was a long while at work before society began everywhere to decay. Clergy and nobility were, in the higher ranks at least, separated from the people by the new egoism of wealth; the sacred marks of consecration were not on their souls. France especially was restless. Under the thrusts of Voltaire, whose acrid pen was never at rest, tradition began to totter; and the false but fierce philosophy of the Encyclopedists stood out strong by comparison. Then, Rousseau, the watchmaker's son of Geneva, made the world believe that his drugged dreams of a perfect social order were capable of realization. Rousseau not only discovered a world by his writings, but conquered it also; and the already

unstable structure of Bourbon society was doomed.
In vain would his Lordship call for "Order" while he
doubled the tithes; crass convention was at the death-
grapple with radical vision. Add to this a new and
widespread skepticism in matters of religion, and you
will understand the eighteenth century soul. There
were, at first, the French critics and dreamers; there
was at the end the great Goethe, who is like a glass
of Burgundy in a pint of Rhenish wine—both native
and exotic. Everywhere the sufficiency of human reason
was candidly assumed, and "Unknown" was subtly written over the name of God.

England, however, with much less to conserve was
vastly more conservative. There was little demand
for a change of political régime. What religion remained was firmly welded with the State, and the State
was powerful, even though it would have to battle with
revolutionary colonists in all its domains. Almost as
if by design, the classes for whom reading was possible
developed a code of genteel utilitarian morals slightly
diluted with aristocratic sentiment. Aristotle came
into his own and both the "Poetics" and the "Ethics"
were consulted with some gusto. Except for the manly
squirearchy of Fielding there is little in eighteenth century fiction which contains the substance of democratic thought. In general the novelists understood
only one worth-while thing, laughter, and this the pre-
modern Englishman seldom forgot. The representative
thinkers followed the French lead to its ultimate conclusion and were either relentlessly Scotch or stubbornly
British. The unstable epistemology of John Locke,
the staid, cold skepticism of David Hume, the bitter
and cruel politics of Hobbes, were adaptations of

French thought to the more conservative attitude of an insular public; it seemed that men would gradually abandon, for the sake of a callous phrase, what remained of the decent philosophy of their fathers. History, which is philosophy in action, was courted by a brilliant pagan who appreciated fully the historic importance of the Gospel's success over the mandates of the Emperors. "It was at Rome, on the 15th of October, 1764," says Gibbon, "as I sat musing amid the ruins of the Capitol while the barefoot friars were singing Vespers in the temple of Jupiter, that the idea of writing the decline and fall of the city first started to my mind." His "Decline and Fall" was a gorgeous and stately tyrant who closed the doors to the mediæval narrative for many years, and supported the impression, not yet dead, that the science of history must confine itself to ancient and modern times. What a mass of nonsense about "dark ages" and "mummery" and "ignorance" was used to blanket the fires of the most amazingly active and speculative era in human annals! Instead we got the private scandals of Medes and Parthians, Roman bankers and prehistoric fossils; "progress" and "evolution" and "freedom" and a hundred other perversions of common nouns, which the most prevaricating of mediæval annalists would have been ashamed to use.

Again it was a man from the midst of the people who rallied all that was most charitable in the friendly world of letters; and Doctor Johnson, brusque of figure and mellow of heart, guided the Irish Goldsmith as well as any man could. Johnson made a thousand errors in judgment and taste, but he was the only person in the land who understood what the author of

"The Deserted Village" and "The Vicar of Wakefield" was worth. For that delightful vagabond remembered the death-cry of the poor, despoiled of property as well as freedom, and faced the hard syllogisms of Adam Smith with simple fact. One of the truths which humanity can never part with is that *laissez-faire* will never do; and if in Goldsmith's songs of a dying peasantry there runs the wail of a dirge, it was something to have sung it in the teeth of commercial pride. Johnson's other good deeds were numerous and his heart was right; he was the Englishman at his level best.

In still another way Art made a final stand. Poetry, forever vibrant and untamed, forgot the taunts of Pope and the smooth controversy of Dryden and murmured some of the old hymns. Gray, Warton, Percy, Chatterton—all of them caught glimpses of ancient chivalry lost on haggard moors and set down something of what they had seen. A certain ploughman, whose name was Robert Burns, told more of human nature than the professors in his country had dreamed of. But through all of these and through the visions of Blake, the virulence of Byron, and even the nature-worship of Wordsworth, the face of Rousseau looked out, bathing in the smiles of Ceres, lost in the morning dew. They could not alter the fact that Europe had been built at the foot of the Cross and that its faith was dead. Old Triton and his horn were silent, indeed; chimney arose on chimney, loom next to loom, and around them were built the shambles of the new serfs. There was precious little religion left, just as there was no great freedom. The old stories of the Saints were derided; pilgrims no longer went to the rifled tomb at Canterbury, or clerks to Oxford. The former place was asleep and the latter was drinking port. A people that had been forbidden to utter the Virgin name of Mary was taught the monstrous fetish of the virgin-queen.

Meanwhile the peasant struck in France and the King went down. In his stead the minions of the new philosophy settled themselves in the judgment seat, the guillotine struck off heads with a kind of voluptuous cruelty, and men gathered in the temples to worship the goddess of reason. When the butchery had finally ceased and the standards of Napoleon had been furled forever, a new religious fervour was born out of the hearts of tired men. Chateaubriand in France, Görres and Chamisso in Germany, and Manzoni in Italy began to look back upon the bright days of Christendom and to hunger for the things of the soul. It seemed for a time that the powerful missionary spirit of Art had returned, but the destruction had been too complete. Wonderful things were accomplished in the face of odds; but the sadness of the romantics was only too prophetic, only too profoundly real.

England escaped political revolution and the people continued in their silence. Instead, the spirit of change, of Liberty, entered into literature and uprooted its conventions, despite the beautiful pathos of Edmund Burke. There was the atheistic rebellion of Shelley and Byron, Godwin and Mary Woolstonecraft: English Voltaires and Rousseaus respectively, lashed into fury by the cant of the prevailing civilization. And then, far greater and more influential than any of these, appeared the perennially virile Sir Walter, enchanted spectator of a thousand vanished tournaments, delightful magician of trysts and trappings, knights and fair ladies, of the whole picturesque life of the olden time. But though he sent all the world into a feverish study of heraldry, he was unconcerned with the soul of Christendom, the spirit which had created these thousand rapturous symbols for its inward joy. Bluntly, Scott was neither democratic nor spiritual, though his influence made in the end for both qualities throughout Europe. The people were best represented by a strange and violent journalist whose copy brought him eventually into Parliament, but never far away from his folk. In his "History of the Reformation" William Cobbett emphasized one tremendous matter which the student of the period had generally neglected —the spoliation of the poor. Through him was voiced, with a passion often boorish enough, their protest, which the philosophers and historians had apparently forgotten.

When Victoria came to the throne, the English had practically settled down to a smug admiration for trade. The girl-queen governed an Empire larger— and more cruel—than Cæsar had dreamed of. This Empire had forgotten nearly all the traditions of Englishmen, being immensely more interested in the heathen. Commerce was god, and commerce implied a territorial policy, military force, and a continuous debate in Parliament over the subjugation of the Irish or the Hindus. Such an enormous scheme had little to do with the public, although occasionally it would be pestered by a publicist. The mob stayed speechless, but it was a subject for conversation—a subject written in the miseries of a thousand industrial towns, in the crooked streets of London, in the quiet districts where men had

kept their freedom. But for all of this the powers
that ruled felt more or less contempt. That so good
and great a man as Lord Macaulay could be utterly
misled is significant of the times: he made his best
speech against workingmen and his best poetry about
Rome. It is not surprising either that Lord Mon-
mouth, when talking of the established religion, should
have felt the emotions of Caius Julius. These matters
meant very simply that the popular institutions of the
past had been swallowed up in a gigantic utilitarianism
whose efficiency and refinement were utterly pagan.
The most Christian thing economics could do was to
use a French phrase; education confined itself to teaching wealthy boys how to quote Virgil and how to
despise their neighbors; and the height of religious
fervour was to sing a song for the Queen.

An hour had come, however, when this apparently
fixed alignment would be violently assailed. First,
England awoke to the giant protest of Charles Dickens.
Here was a man, amazingly ignorant of ever so many
historical details, who read history correctly; who was
an optimist and yet a rebel; who walked the dirtiest
streets of London and shook with laughter while his
heart bled. Dickens' importance cannot be valued too
highly, for, although he created no disturbance, he
did create people—a mob of people whom nobody can
put down and nobody ignore. They broke through
the priggishness of the Victorian era as a hod-carrier
might disturb an ethical society. Still, after this
stupendous sermon on charity, the world went to din-
ner and to bed, a little more kindly, a little more restless, but essentially the same world.

Then there followed in quick succession a series of

surprising outbursts against the "progress" which
Macaulay had so highly complimented. John Ruskin,
angry with the interminable smokestacks and their
soot, inspected modernity by the light of Beauty and
found it decidedly shabby; for a while he contented himself with praising the art of the older time, but finally
he understood, nearly, that art cannot be dissociated
from life, and he even tried to restore civilization.
Ruskin's greatest hindrance was his education; somehow he never managed to look around it and see what
lay beyond. Next, a dyspeptic Scotchman, who prided
himself on "four walls" and some brains, discovered
the amazing mediocrity of his environment, measured
it by the rule of genius, and cursed it roundly. Carlyle
was a good and worthy man but with all these prescrip-
tions he did not even cure himself. The Positivists,
from George Eliot to John Stuart Mill, consoled themselves with an altruistic version of the new gospel, advo-
cated a thousand things which nobody would take,
and died wondering at the folly of the world. It remained to suggest Culture pure and simple, and this
Matthew Arnold did skillfully; but, though he has been
quite largely complimented by the professors, Mrs.
Grundy has lent a disdainful ear. George Meredith
examined society by the gleam of nature's dawn, and
Browning counseled vigour and exuberance. Thus one
by one the thinkers railed at John Bull, but that stolid
gentleman went on unperturbed.

The upshot of all this criticism was that the power
of reason came at last to its goal. It scrutinized the
bases of religious belief as matters quite independent
of its own needs; and with the great catapult of Evolution set the entire structure of popular theistic opinion

to tottering. Was it because man had become so like an ape that he was willing to concede that his ancestor was one? At least here was the paradox of reason equalling itself to Everything and consenting also to be Nothing. There came over England the final darkness: loneliness, the boredoom of being alone. Solidarity of intellectual effort was destroyed; step by step idiosyncrasy usurped the seat of originality and society pursued unbelievable philosophic tangents. The powers of the State increased, as the meaning of man was lessened. Force was worshipped either with frank rejoicing or with bitter acquiescence. And even tears were idle things, "from the depths of some divine despair."

As not the least of the energies loosened against the complacency of the English mood, the Catholic Revival appeared. Wherever the religious spirit was strong, whether in poet or preacher, there developed a concern with the beautiful faith of the past, with its sacraments and saints, with its manifest confidence in the voice of God. Almost in the twinkling of an eye, the members of a creed that had long been despised as impotent and ridiculous stood with their loins girt for battle and recruited some of the most brilliant minds of Britain. Whereas there had been no great Catholic apostle in the country since the days of Campion and More, a dozen now moved the hearts of men; whereas the poetry of the old religion had been silent since Crashaw, singers took up the Catholic lyre with abounding and brilliant gifts; and even the press, grown more tolerant, carried the defenders' voices to the ends of the earth. The challenge of the modern mind was accepted and even forestalled: the mission-

ary now coveted battle as he had once sought martyrdom.   Christendom, as the Great Tradition that
guarded the rights and guided the aspirations of common humanity, won crowds of men by its new exposi-
tions of the beauties of the faith and by the honesty
of its literary effort.   New voices stirred in shrouded
Ireland, and the testimony of Britain lent confidence
to the army of God that struggled in Europe.   The
issue between belief and denial has now become clear
everywhere, and the modern philosophers, who scoffed
at Christendom as something withered and outgrown,
have discovered its branches over their heads.   And
even the critics shall have to reckon with the Cross.

The story of the Catholic Spirit working in modern
English letters is at once the record of a movement
and the biography of strong men.   If literature be the
expression of great personalities considering general
truths, it is no less a series of flaming windows where
the colour of Life is broken and reflected under the
arches of towering minds.   We shall deal here with
many fascinating men; with books that have brought
answers to numberless hearts; with the victories and
failures of literary effort.   Most of all, however, we
shall deal with the Spirit which any of these men valued
more highly than life or success, their insight into and
love for the sanctity of their hope.   We shall scarcely
divine their purpose or their meaning unless we remember that, while facing the modern opponent where-
ever he appeared, they worshipped the beauty of the
past.   Behind them is the synthesis of mediæval life,
with the fervent symbolism of its cathedrals, the robust
nobility of its moral code, and the success of its
popular society.   They kneel at shrines at which for-

gotten artisans laid down the glory of their buoyant lives and before which pilgrim and Crusader, saint and king, begged forgiveness of their sins. They go into battle gayly, but their voices tremble with the melody of dead songs. Only, they believe that the old realities can be again a reasonable ideal, and they have faith in God.

BOOK NOTE

In addition to the works mentioned—More's "Utopia," Goldsmith's "The Deserted Village," Boswell's "Life of Johnson," Cobbett's "Reformation"—see the following: "The Present Position of Catholics," by J. H. Newman; "The Eve of the Reformation," by Dom Gasquet; "The Victorian Age in English Literature" and "Notes on Charles Dickens," by G. K. Chesterton; "A Social and Political History of Western Europe," by Carleton Hayes (2 vols.); "La Renaissance Catholique en Angleterre"—Vol. I.—by Paul Thureau-Dangin; "Memories," by Kegan Paul, and the later volumes of "The Cambridge History of English Literature." Of interest also are the "Lives" of Gibbon, by J. Cotter Morison, of Hume, by T. H. Huxley, and of Locke, by Thomas Fowler. The files of the *Tablet,* the *Dublin Review* and the *Catholic World* contain indispensable information not available elsewhere.

CHAPTER TWO

KENELM DIGBY AND THE DISCOVERY OF THE PAST

"Neither for gold nor for gifts did I undertake this book so great and difficult . . . only, I prayed that my book might be beautiful."

GAELIC MONK, XIITH CENTURY.

THE discovery of a romantic past and its application as a creative force in literature was due, beyond any doubt, to the genius of Sir Walter Scott. His festive mind, browsing amid heaps of ragged books which the generations immediately preceding had frowned upon, and searching the landscape of Scotland for the sites of chivalric prowess, admired the Christian Ages for their picturesque strength. Scott's neighbors had largely tired of the sour, matter-of-fact philosophy which had been provided for them, and read his tales with abounding delight. The virility of the Waverly Novels was a tremendous thing; on account of them new literary currents began to move in Europe generally, and America imbibed so much of their teaching that Mark Twain's diatribe on the chivalry of the South was by no means directed at an abstraction. Sir Walter, however, was quite content with the role of entertainer, and it was probably as much of a surprise to him as to anyone when a French disciple of Rousseau, François-René de Chateaubriand, followed him into the romantic past, accepted the old faith, and

15

published the first part of "La Genie du Christianisme" just as the bells of Notre Dame were ringing out again, after a silence of twelve years.

In this and in his subsequent defenses of the Catholic Spirit Chateaubriand missed something of the peace of God; as a French critic says, he "presents Christianity not as a safe port amidst the storm, but rather as the storm itself which would carry men into a new world." He had more than a little of the pose of an explorer who is enthusiastic over dim vistas in the distance, but quite sadly certain that he can never reach them. Following his guidance, the European literature of the nineteenth century exhausted the force, the melody, and the melancholy of the imagination, sometimes approaching religion, sometimes ending in bitter disenchantment. It was an unbalanced, an unsteady movement and one is not surprised that its last great disciple should have advised people to be "always drunken." But intoxication is, after all, better for the soul than mortal thirst.

He to whom England owes the first strong and deep presentation of the Spirit of the past, not in its external prettinesses only, but in its inner radiance, is a man whose name means little to the average modern reader; whose books have suffered the saddest of all defeats, obloquy at the press; but whose message has nevertheless brought memorable joy to those who have sought it out. Kenelm Henry Digby, the author of "The Broad Stone of Honour," "Mores Catholici," and "Compitum," master of the literature of dead centuries, and heritor of the spirit of Godfrey and St. Francis, is a name to love even if that affection involves sacrifice. Who can say that he has read through

this encyclopedia of Christian piety and charity, as
vast in its volume as the "Comedie" of Balzac, as
learned as Mommsen's "History"? Still, it was
through Digby that the Catholic Spirit entered once
more into English letters, got into Cambridge—where
men still follow the vision—and moved the pen of Ruskin.

His life was given to the ancient story with the
rarest filial devotion: he wrote not because men praised
or even read his work, but because he loved what he
had to say. Digby was the *Pius Æneas* of the past,
"the Fra Angelico," as Canon Barry says, "of Christian Apologetics." The newer books on mediævalism
are simply restatements or criticisms, sometimes force-
ful and popular in manner, of truths which he understood, of thoughts which he cherished, of facts which
he had gathered. Digby did more than study the history of Christendom; he saw it, lived in it with abandon, a master of its many moods, but sublimely and
constantly aware of its central theme. Perhaps the
greatest reason why he should be remembered is that he
was always himself without ever being selfish. There is
even a way in which he seems the complement of Dante:
he stirred the ashes, so that the fire of the great Floren-
tine might burn more brightly.

Long before Newman's voice aroused the soul of
Oxford, Digby had found his way into the Church,
having been baptized in 1825, shortly before the conversion of his lifelong friend, Ambrose Phillips de Lisle.
The change was due quite simply to his concern with
the past. Long before there had been a Sir Kenelm
Digby who returned from his travels abroad a Catholic,
a gentleman, and a defender of the Faith, even if a

somewhat unsteady one; the blood of Sir Thomas More,
that pattern of Christian knighthood, ran in the family.
Was it their spirit which lead the youthful Digby into
the Church? At least he went "their great and gracious
ways," mingling his historical studies with journeys
through all the Catholic lands until he had gathered
sufficient material for "The Broad Stone of Honour."
The first edition of this fine tribute to Christian tradition appeared while the author was still an Anglican,
but the changes made necessary by his religious conversion were slight. It seems almost that Digby was
born a Catholic, for the strength and humility with
which he practiced his religion throughout life are testified to by every page he wrote. In the midst of nearly
superhuman labour that was rewarded with comparative neglect, he preserved the modest poise of a gentle
saint for whom the final day of beatitude is the goal
of life.

The details of his career have been recently set forth
in a fine volume by Bernard Holland; we shall consider here only those matters which are indispensable
for a proper knowledge of Digby's work. He was born,
most probably, in 1797—the date seems uncertain—
and died at Kensington on March 22, 1880. Trinity
College, Cambridge, received him in 1815 as a candidate
for the degree in Arts, and he distinguished himself
by pulling "number seven" in Trinity's first famous
boat. Almost to the end of his life Digby preserved
a fondness for sport, and his books are dotted with enthusiastic references to swimming exploits, boating
on the Thames and elsewhere, mountain expeditions,
and outings in general. None the less, he devoted
himself assiduously to study, having profited by the

wise guidance of a splendid tutor, the Rev. Julius C. Hare, of Whewell. In those days anything smacking of mediævalism was quite generally derided, and Scholastic philosophy was scorned, without being, in the slightest way, known; yet it was along these forbidden paths that Digby came into the Church. Ambrose Phillips, the intimate companion mentioned previously, fostered Digby's bent; he was a man of very idealistic principles, who later spent his forces in trying to bring the Anglican High Church as a body to Rome. The later private life of Digby was rather tranquil. He was happily married and became the father of five children, enjoyed the friendship of numerous gifted men, but bore many a severe trial and lived for some time in dire financial straits.

His personality remained charming to the end of his eighty-two years, and in personal appearance he was most striking. Fitzgerald describes him as "a grand, swarthy fellow who might have stepped out of the canvas of some knightly portrait in his father's house." A more definite reminiscence is Mr. Holland's, "A chivalric figure, over six feet in height, strongly built, with dark hair and eyes, a fine forehead." One can easily fancy such a man going on those long voyages to remote and romantic places, which carried him through Spain and France, Austria and Germany, but it is not so easy to recall him bent over aged and archaic volumes, with the scent of midnight oil strong on his own folios. Only, those tomes, with their dim records of ancient glory, were for him more golden than doubloons and more rare than Inca gems. He was the hunter of priceless words which the pirates had buried, they thought, forever.

Let there be no misunderstanding of Digby's manner. Literature is quite largely a matter of style, and what shall we say of the method in which this prodigious man sought to put down his impressions? For every one of his books he made, indeed, a carefully unified plan which he took care to expound in the introduction, but which nobody could possibly follow through the maze of his writing. As he set down in language a single, ·sober thought, a thousand illustrations apparently crowded themselves into his pen, and he wrote out all of them, one after another, with an extraordinary disregard for sequence. The essays of Montaigne, which among other ancient writings may have served Digby for a model, are packed with quotations and examples, but these are always inlaid into the discourse with a Gallic nicety. Digby surpasses even Montaigne in the number and variety of his instances and saws, but, though they illustrate a point, they follow along helter-skelter, with a weird commingling of Greek and Latin, French and Old English, that is altogether amazing. What other writer would mass together a line from Cicero, Richard de Bury's curious instructions on the care of books, anecdotes of Blessed Thomas More, and legends of the Saints? His books are mosaics, most ingenious and sometimes most interesting, but always mosaics.

When his own English becomes master of a page or two, it is pleasantly archaic, with occasional striking turns, even epigrams, with which he says things that are as good as anything he quotes. Thus, in "Evenings on the Thames," this remark follows a formidable array of citations: "In fact, to have a taste for serene hours ·is to have a taste for heaven." Not even St.

Francis de Sales could have uttered a more admirable sentence! It is Digby's indomitable enthusiasm which carries him steadily along; all the details of his study seemed to him so valuable that he could not bear the loss of one of them, and his profound humility led him to believe, poor fellow, that the dictum of a saint or a chevalier was infinitely more important than anything which he himself might say. Digby has chapters on ecclesiastical art, as learned as, and perhaps truer than, Huysmans' "Cathedrale" but how very much more personal and effective the latter is! Had Digby been more of an egoist he would have earned greater fame, at the price of being a meaner man. As it is, the reader will scarcely grow interested in books like "The Broad Stone of Honour" unless his enthusiasm for the ages of faith is great, unless he possesses the spiritual loadstone which will coördinate these multitudinous details as Digby did, and unless he is charmed by the utter self-abandonment of a marvelously magnanimous man. A reader who meets these requirements could live happily on a desert isle with "Mores Catholici" for his sole companion.

Digby's writing, enormous though it is in volume, is singularly unified in theme. Predominantly the historian, he read the past by the light of a beautiful philosophy, which is saved from extravagant idealism by a deep consciousness of the reality of the Faith. His teaching is happiest when done by a sort of poetic pantomime, and when he ventures into abstractions there is likely to be a touch of bathos. Above all, Digby was a man, and no trait of writing is more prominent than his affection for the heroic character. "Mores Catholici" is a vast storehouse of information on mediæval life that lays, of course, no claim to the rigid impartiality of the modern monograph. In it Digby attempts to show that the Ages of Faith were exemplifications of the eight beatitudes, and that they built up the ideal state, from which later eras have unfortunately departed. With what affection he followed those wonderful years of the saint and the hero, years which the mass of men now think the creation of poetry or even darkness! Their songs were for him the symphony of the eternal unseen, fingering the hearts of men, and his joy in the melody was often nigh to tears. In the opening chapter of "Mores Catholici" Digby synthetizes all that he has to say in a glowing paragraph:

"The Middle Ages were ages of highest grace to men; ages of faith; ages when all Europe was Catholic; when vast temples were seen to rise in every place of human concourse to give glory to God, and to exalt men's souls to sanctity; when houses of holy peace and order were found amidst woods and desolate mountains, on the banks of placid lakes as well as on solitary rocks in the ocean; ages of sanctity which witnessed a Bede, an Alcuin, a Bernard, a Francis, and crowds who followed them as they did Christ; ages of vast and beneficent intelligence, in which it pleased the Holy Spirit to display the power of the seven gifts, in the life of an Anselm, a Thomas of Aquinum, and the saintly flock whose steps a cloister guarded; ages of the highest civil virtue; which gave birth to the laws and institutions of an Edward, a Lewis, a Suger; ages of the noblest art which beheld a Giotto, a Michael Angelo, a Raffaelo, a Dominichino; ages of poetry, which heard an Avitus, a Caedmon, a Dante, a Shakespeare, a Calderon; ages of more than mortal heroism,

which produced a Tancred and a Godfrey; ages of
majesty, which knew a Charlemagne, an Alfred, and
the sainted youth who bore the lily; ages, too, of England's glory, when she appears not even excluding a
comparison with the eastern empire, as the most truly
civilized country on the globe; when the Sovereign of
the greater portion of the western world applied to
her schools for instructors; when she sends forth her
saints to evangelise the nations of the north, and to
diffuse spiritual treasure over the whole world; when
heroes flock to her courts to behold the models of reproachless chivalry, and Emperors leave their thrones
to adore God at the tombs of her martyrs!"

Here, then, was the perfect civilization, the Kingdom
of God, for which Digby yearned. Through the scores
of chapters which follow he brings a wealth of testimony to establish every statement in his theme: the
activities of the Church, monastic life, building, missionary spirit, the effort for peace, the serene contemplativeness of philosophy and religion, are examined;
the State gives forth the secrets of its administration
over the poor and its concern for justice and charity
to all; private life makes known its beauties, its aspirations, and its joys, with here and there an allusion to
the misfortunes from which human toil can never be
free. Majestic voices repeat the guiding words of
Christendom, and the richest revelry is held at the
courts of worthy kings. Very rarely does the author
grow controversial, and then the combat is waged
sadly, gently, with that modern spirit which has rifled
the temples, which is so secure in its pride and possession, and so hollow in its faith. Throughout Digby's
familiarity with ancient and modern literature and his

historical erudition are surprising. "Mores Catholici" is like a review of an abbey library made by a scholarly saint to appease the hunger of wandering minds, or like a series of quaint windows, less brilliant than comforting, in which the artisan has written in allegory the story of the conquest of the Cross.

Kenelm Digby, however, became an historian only because he was a deeply religious thinker. Because he had found peace of heart in his studies, he somewhat naïvely imagined that others would adopt the principles of his belief if he told them what he had learned. Those principles are continually bobbing up in his work because they are the knots which tie his fleeting strands of fact together. The reader of "Mores Catholici"— a rare person whose acquaintance is to be cultivated— will have met with them often enough. It is best to look for them, however, in those books "whose study would delight the angels," as Ambrose Phillips de Lisle said, "The Broad Stone of Honour." Here the youthful, enthusiastic Digby wrote himself out in generous pages that glow with the anguish of lost chivalry, that are sweet and tearful as the memories of a long and cleanly love. "I shall but suggest things in imperfect sounds," he says modestly, with his heart set on "images of quiet wisdom, sanctity, and innocence: symbols of infinite love, of divine and everlasting peace, the daily sacrifice, the evening hymn, the sweet music of the pilgrim's litanee, the portals that open to receive the living to joy, and the dirge of requiem to supplicate rest and deliverance for the dead." Ancient chivalry was the realization of everything for which his soul yearned; it was kind to the lowly, for the Church had said, *Beati pauperes;* it obeyed "from the bottom of the heart, like a child"; it cultivated friendship, "that musical, poetic, religious word"; its courage was the self-sacrifice of the strong; and its hope was in God. It held the secret of eternal youth, for "how can he grow old who lives separated from all that is destined to decay, who unceasingly beholds the same bright altars and angelic forms which proclaim his own eternity?" Loyalty was the soul of knighthood, and Digby was intensely, almost desperately, loyal; he was one in spirit with Thomas More.

"The Broad Stone of Honour" is divided into four books: Godfridus lays down general views of chivalry, and says some thoughtful things about the art of government; Tancred considers the religion and discipline that prevailed during the Middle Ages; Morus answers the objections which modern thinkers have raised against the practice of knighthood; the last book, Orlandus, best and most interesting of all, presents a "detailed view of the virtues of chivalrous character, when it is submitted to the genuine and all-powerful influence of the Catholic faith." In a general way, Digby tried humbly to show that the Church of Christ, moulding the hearts of men, had given them a safe sanctuary from the blandishments and delusions of a pagan world. His philosophy was derived from the practice of a simple man; there is in it no subtlety, no "higher criticism, no Germanic phraseology. These things would probably have perplexed him if he had thought it worth his while to consider them at all.

The aching void in his soul had been filled with heavenly truth, and in the practice of kindly virtue he beheld the shining destiny of man. With Saint Augustine he was ready to say, "I am an old man and a

Bishop, but I am ready to be taught by a child"; but
he would probably have gone to sleep under a modern
professor. In a later book, "Compitum," Digby undertook to establish the difficult thesis that "all roads lead
to Rome." His road of Children, of Youth, of Travel-
ers, is easy enough to follow if one has already begun
the journey, but he was a poor apostle to those who are
hindered by intellectual difficulties. He went along
ancient paths of glory by the light of regal if abandoned stars, and was just as unable to lead the modern
spirit as he was half-unconsciously uninfluenced by it.
Noble treasurer of the words of God, he dwelt in a
splendid citadel where those who follow him will find
that "an angel has been charged to speak such words
to men."

The human, the lovable quality that softens the somewhat unearthly erudition of Digby is his inimitable
dreaming. How constantly, fervently, he seems to have
anticipated the beatific vision! Going through life in
the company of an imagination crowded with pictures
of a hallowed era, he lived in it as completely and genuinely as a sailor lives in his boat. It was useless to
tempt him with speculation, science, or gold, while he
felt under his feet the strong bulwarks against the
waves of the world. "From the disciple who believed
because he saw Our Saviour under a fig-tree," remarks
Orlandus, "to the latest examples of men who have
been added to the Church, speculation and knowledge
seem to have been little employed in the work of conversion; it has been accomplished by very different
means, the meeting of an old man on the seashore, the
answer of a child, or a dream." And in Digby's instance it was the last: a dream of sacred Faith master-

ing the bloody arena and the tomb; of majestic and
solemn temples alive with universal yearning for the
joys of heaven, and simple happiness in the beauty of
the world; of nature, itself a mighty cathedral alive
with multitudinous images aglow with the lavish colour
of God; and of man himself, ennobled and purified by
no mechanical process of "Evolution," but by the
stirring advance of his will to the battle-drums of
Saints.

Digby lived a religious existence which some people
find it impossible to understand. Only to those who
know the supreme loveliness of the road to perfection,
where childlike eyes are fixed on the merciful countenance of a divine Redeemer, will it seem natural and
worth while. The lofty mission of the Church, to heal
the wounds of society with inspired law and to crown
the humblest life with the sacramental kiss, was for
the author of "The Broad Stone of Honour" the only
consoling reality. He saw a thousand cloisters that
had long been razed, heard multitudes of dead Saints
chant the *Benedicite*, and encountered legions of
knights whose phantom shields bore the device of eternal honour. Splendid Christian! And for him, too,
at the sight of the desolation around him, there was reserved that sacred melancholy which is loved in heaven
because Jesus Himself had suffered it on the walls of
Jerusalem.

Let us not get the impression, however, that he lived
always among ruins. For Digby the Spirit of God
was a *dulce refrigerium*, a source of joy if not of hearty
laughter. He loved the minstrelsy, the merry-making,
and the hospitality of the olden time quite as much as
the dizzy road to heaven. All his books breathe the

tranquillity of calm human relationships, joy in nature, and fondness for domestic life. In some of his minor works, like "Evenings on the Thames," "The Children's Bower," and "The Lover's Seat" he tried to show how life could be made a graceful love story with a happy ending, rather than a tale told by an idiot. Digby explains that he seeks "the subtle essence of happiness, which is not to be found in recondite or exclusive activities but in common things." Like Wordsworth, he had followed Plato in his affection for the simplicity of nature. Not so many persons in these harrowed days of ours would, one must suppose, find his reflections on English country life interesting. Digby had little dramatic or even narrative instinct; at his best he possesses the fine, pensive quality of Walton, but at his worst he is almost stupidly pedantic. What he lacked for success in the discursive familiar essay was variety, lightness, that ounce of wit which makes the literary porridge savoury. He could not draw his mind from the enchantment of the past. "As one who beholds a beautiful picture," he says, "gazes till he ardently wishes to see it move . . . so every one who contemplates the noble images of reproachless chivalry must feel anxious that they be revived in the deeds of men." This was the sole concern of his long and devoted life.

Another charming characteristic of Digby's character was his intense delight in travel. During the course of his wanderings he must have seen most of the romantic spots in England and on the Continent. He speaks very rarely of large cities, and if an occasional notice of one is taken, he generally adds a phrase to indicate his disapprobation of its modern features.

Somewhere he even upbraids Doctor Johnson for having expressed a fondness for London. In the country, however, among either the wild beauties of nature or the remains of the ancient civilization, Digby is the ideal traveler, divining the inner radiance of the one or refashioning the other according to the legend of its antique glory. How appealing is his happiness when permitted to look upon some ruined monastery, castle, or shrine, whose renown was once as great as its present neglect! "On the high Alp of the Surinam Pass," he relates, "I found a little chapel with a bell . . . time would fail me to describe . . . the dark, fearful walls of Lusignan, near Poitiers; the wonderful architecture of the curious gates and Oriental halls of Granada, its courts of the lions emblazoned with the symbols of Mohammedan superstitions; the beautiful embattled heights of Johannisberg; the deep pool and gloomy towers of Bingen, and Lichtenstein with the sun setting over the Danube." There was a place for every mood.

"The Broad Stone of Honour" was inspired largely by a visit to Ehrenbreitenstein, mighty symbol to Digby of so much glory that had gone. It begins with a revel in nature. "We walked on a spring morning through the delicious groves that clothe the mountains of Dauphiny which surround the old castle of the family of Bayard"—and ends, or very nearly, with Petersborough, "rising out of the water like a pile of grotto work." In "Mores Catholici" there is a characteristically humble confession: "For my part, if I had never seen Altenrive or Vallombrosa, Camaldoli or St. Urban, the beauties of our loveliest scenery would not delight me as they now can do. I should see them with quite different eyes. The walls would not inspire any bright

consoling recollections, nor the deep forests, peace."
This present world was for Digby only a keyboard
from which he could draw at will "the giant melodies
of the past." Sometimes there is an outcry of pain,
never savage as in Heine, or rhetorically melancholic
as in Burke or Chateaubriand, but quaintly plaintive;
a child might have sorrowed thus for his mother. "How
many noble ruins, memories of the Gallic fury, have I
met in places that one might have thought far too
sequestered for its force to reach," he says; and again,
"Modern poetry has only one sound, 'like the wind
through a ruin'd cell.'"

Such are the marvelously beautiful though forgotten
books of the gentlest modern man who has followed
Christian knighthood. Kenelm Digby gave himself
more fully than even Sir Walter Scott to the romantic
vision; but he was less of a Don Quixote because he
took the Faith. Middle Age life was not for him
a mere matter of gorgeous plumes and pink-cheeked
damsels, but also of the cloister and the poor, above
all of the soul. One cannot but feel that he preserved
to the day of his death those "clouds of glory" in
which he was born. It may be quite true that he was
somewhat unpractical and that his knowledge of money
and banking was decidedly limited; but Barney New-
come was superior in this respect to the Colonel. If
in the years that come Digby's golden books shall by
some cruel alchemy be turned to dust, or rouse only a
faint gleam in the eyes of collectors, his character and
eagerness to serve must stand in mute testimony to
a Faith by which the world was once redeemed. It
was "for the real manna" that he grew mighty in
learning. His humility would have asked no larger

reward than that somewhere a youth reading one of his books should be stirred by the breath of the Past, or that some quiet thinker, turning the pages of "Mores Catholici" should have been reminded of the grandeur that was God's.

It would be a grave mistake, however, to believe that the effort of Kenelm Digby was entirely without fruit. His books, as Canon Barry observes, have taught teachers, who, like Julius Hare, have found in them priceless counsel. Wordsworth drew inspiration for a sonnet from "The Broad Stone of Honour," and Ruskin owed to it some of the artistic idealism which determined his career. Indeed, the author of "Modern Painters" confessed even another debt.[1] "The reader will find . . . every phase of nobleness illustrated in Kenelm Digby's 'Broad Stone of Honour.' The best help I have ever had—so far as help depended on the praise and sympathy of others in work—was given me when this author, from whom I first learned to love nobleness, introduced frequent references to my own writings in his 'Children's Bower.' " That is sufficient praise; but surely there are hundreds of less famous men whose lives have been enriched and whose steps have been guided by his labour.

Digby, the unforgettable, the magnificent dreamer! What better tribute could be paid to his memory than the epilogue which he himself affixed to the work of his youth:

"O that the poet were not just in saying, that this is now an age of selfish men, that life is drest for a shew, while the great events which old story rings seem

[1] Vol. IX, 361.

vain and hollow. O that some voice may raise us up again and give us virtue, that avarice and expense may be no more adored, but plain living and high thinking be again our glory. Had these rude and faint images of a faithful age been drawn by one who had indeed caught its simple spirit, he would not have let you depart without praying that you, who have followed him from the beginning to the ending would be pleased in charity to put him, who would rejoice to serve you, into your devout memento; that Almighty God might send him good deliverance while he was alive, and when he was dead and his body laid to the cold earth, when the darkness of age and death should have covered over both this book and him, through God's grace, his soule might enter Paradise. He would have prayed you all, if you heard never more of him, to pray for his soule."

BOOK NOTE

The works of Kenelm Digby are very difficult to obtain. Those of outstanding importance are "Mores Catholici," several times reprinted, "The Broad Stone of Honour," the last volume of which (Orlandus) has not, to my knowledge, been reissued since 1829, and "Compitum." "Evenings on the Thames" is worth looking into. Digby's verse, of which there is a great deal, is impossibly tedious. His erudition had ironed life out of any quatrains he might possibly make. The fine "Memoir of Kenelm Digby," by Bernard Holland, called forth several essays in review, the most noteworthy of which are those by William Barry in the *Dublin Review*, by Henry Lappin in the *Catholic World*, and by Paul E. More in the *Unpartizan Review*. All of these appeared during 1920.

CHAPTER THREE

THE PERSONALITY OF NEWMAN

"I also in all things please all men, not seeking that which is profitable to myself, but to many, that they may be saved."
                                                    SAINT PAUL.

THE upheaval of the sixteenth century bequeathed to the world that would embattle the Catholic Spirit a two-edged sword: one, the humanistic elevation of nature and consequent debasement of the supernatural; the other, the astringent, menacingly ascetic outlook of the Puritan. It was against the second of these that Kenelm Digby, poetic and eruditely romantic, lifted an unwieldy voice, even though the matter he dealt with was the comparatively definite and simple life of the past. Then there arose from the midst of the thinkers of Protestant England a man whose powers were resolutely devoted to conquering the first enemy and the future it seemed destined to rule; who would read the scrolls of the final atheistic laughter at God and write over them a palimpsest of Christian confidence; who would attempt to fathom the dark and complex soul of all time and set down his findings with the clearness of a logbook. Again, as the human embryo is said to mirror the growth of the race, so John Henry Newman, triumphing over modern thought by the victory gained within himself, has seemed to many a symbol of the intellectual development through which religiously unsettled moderns may have to pass.

There is little reason why we should insist here upon the greatness of Newman's influence. A dozen gifted minds have confirmed Disraeli's opinion that he was the most powerful religious thinker to appear in England during several centuries; and we have only to consider the amazing betterment in the position of English Catholicism during the last generation to realize how much, even in an outward way, was accomplished by the man who stirred Oxford. Everyone admits that he possessed a remarkable mind and quite unusual gifts of expression, but the world has rightly placed above even these the vigour of his personality. That is almost as firmly established a tradition as the genius of Napoleon. The elite of England were moved by the fervour and glory of his creed. Wherever he passed in that springtime of the Catholic revival, faith sprang up from the wayside; he was the sower of God, upon whom was the seal of election. Later, however, there came a time when his effectiveness seemed to have vanished, when his subtle, indefatigably cautious theology was doomed to be thought half-hearted allegiance by men at the controversial front, when his heart was wrung by denunciation, by sheer failure, until it seemed of little use in the world. The very triumphs of his later years were bloody from his wounds. The delicate steel of his own sensibility pierced him through.

But, whether men followed or opposed or silenced him, it was never forgotten that he was a religious teacher of tremendous significance. The active man might chafe at Newman's inaction; the pedant might try to make of him the kind of clever artist that he could understand; the short-sighted might accuse him of error or dishonesty; still, no one ever denied that he was, uniquely, Newman. A kind of marvelous *wholeness* distinguished his character and thought, a white light to be captured by no prism. The single apostolic purpose of his mission is evident from first to last, but the points at which it touches life are multitudinous and astonishingly varied. He considered existence from more points of view than any of the great Victorian novelists had known, but he never forgot the purpose of his examination. One feels in reading Newman that one's personal intellectual discoveries have been anticipated, that the Cardinal has been everywhere in spiritual geography, although he seems quietly to take it for granted that he should have been there and so to make nothing of it. In a sense, he is like a masterful major-domo, possessing the keys to all the chambers of the soul, even the darkest of which he has explored and aired and lighted up with a touch that betrays his watchful presence.

The universality of his mind's action images the scope of his personality. Newman's character is a mysterious blend of extraordinary qualities: to the study of experience he brought the rarest energy both of analysis and deduction; solitary, sensitive, mystically conscious of the scrutiny of God, he nevertheless read the souls about him with the same surety which distinguished his examination of himself; contemplative by nature, he still coveted, needed, action. His eye, glorying in the beauty of the world, was fixed sternly on its deepest, most ascetic, cravings. There is a sense in which Newman's appearance seems, also, a complement of his inner nature: no one ever looked more like a dignified old lady and no one was ever more of a man. Remember the "head of Cæsar" that Froude speaks of; the preacher at St. Mary's, Oxford; the stillness that followed his retirement, of which Dr. Shairp says, "It was as when, to one kneeling by night, in the silence of some vast cathedral, the great bell tolling solemnly overhead has suddenly gone still"; the pilgrim, going to St. Peter's in Rome, barefoot, praying for guidance, with deep furrows tightening their grip on his countenance; the Oratorian priest, secluded in the obscurity of Birmingham, teaching boys to enact Terence and himself to be patient; the Cardinal, finally, his aged face plaintive above the magnificence of the purple garments. Remember these things and as many more if you would read Newman correctly.

John Henry Newman was born in London on February 21, 1801, of a London banker whose wife traced descent from Huguenot *émigrés*. There was nothing to distinguish the family from the Victorian middle-class to which it belonged, excepting, perhaps, certain rather uncommon intellectual concerns. The life about them was tranquil and reticent, governed by the restraints, the conventions, and the practical virtues which characterized a society the individual members of which were more than a little eccentric, relatively unsocial. Religion was very far from being a dominant interest and, but for their diligent reading of the King James Version, men would have come near forgetting all about their souls. "He was a very philosophical young gentleman" is his sister's description of Newman at the age of eleven. "Philosophical" meant extraordinary reti-

cence, gentleness, aversion to the rougher games, quick
sensibility, and a taste for dreamy thinking. "Unknown influences" and "magic powers" interested him,
and it is not strange that at fifteen he experienced a
Calvinistic conversion from which he drew and retained the idea that "there are two and two only
absolute and luminously self-evident beings—myself
and my Creator."

Depth of religious experience in the soul of a youth
inordinately gifted is not unusual, but with Newman
eagerness of mind overcame a dangerous egoism and
dispelled the quietism of reverie. He could not help seeing the world, being interested in the world. His curiosity was skeptical, interrogative; and for a time he
sought the response to his query in Gibbon and Locke.
Nor had his religious instability vanished when, at Oxford, he turned from the study of law to enter orders,
and when he was, on a memorable day in 1822, elected
Fellow of Oriel College. The young Newman possessed
all the reflectiveness, the sincerity, and the gaucherie of
a great spirit rising out of an environment where it
has not been at home. It was Whately, the massive,
somewhat worldly logician, who first recognized the
talent of this forbiddingly introspective youth; it was
Whately who, addressing Newman as an equal, won a
temporary disciple for liberalism. Nevertheless, fascinated though he might be with the dialectic of his
master, Newman had now come into contact with the
world, and his omnivorous intellect was never any
longer at rest. More and more deeply conscious of the
Spirit of God, confident of a destiny, he set out on the
tireless search for Truth.

The growing mind of Newman proved unusually receptive and at the same time daringly original in the use it made of discoveries. No experience stirred him more deeply, perhaps, than the death of a favorite sister; he began to consider the material world illusory, to look for spiritual realities veiled by externals, in short, to read vastly more of Plato into his somewhat arid Christianity. With this there came naturally a new interest in the significance of personality. He began to feel strongly the power of love, and the circle of friends that formed at Oxford answered his appeal. First among these was Hurrell Froude, a fervent youngster who, like Digby, had drunk the wine of the Catholic Ages and sensed the feebleness of the prevailing creed, though his life was doomed to end before he had reached the goal. Then there was John Keble, at the height of his influence as a spiritual leader and renowned for the authorship of "The Christian Year." Keble's character was amiable and so was his religion, fed as it had been on the poetry of the older Anglican divines. To the warmth of this atmosphere, vibrant with enthusiasm, with the romantic aspiration for more generous beliefs, Newman's heart opened. It was clear that a part of Oxford, at least, had caught echoes of Chateaubriand and Walter Scott; and the ancient walls which had enshrined the scholars of Catholic England began once more to drink in whispers of Christendom.

But this coterie of men was far too sincere for dilettantism. Gradually their concerns left the domain of the purely speculative and turned practical: they felt a keen interest in the life of the primitive Church, where belief and action had obviously been less formal and intensely more vital than they were in modern England. What, at this particular stage of his life's

journey, were the actual aims of Newman? He was
no longer the mere philosopher, absorbed in the idea
of the creature's apprehension of the Creator, but a
man who had discovered the immeasurable realities of
love. Existence had become for him an urge to find
God in the world, to seek the body of doctrine and
symbol in which the Spirit had been expressed. Newman the idealist had passed; Newman the liberal realist
had been a transitory figure. Envisaging the realm
of his own thought, weighing with the most resolute
sincerity the worth of his own convictions, he now
began to penetrate the minds of others, especially of
those to whom religion made no marked appeal. Conscious for the first time of a mission to teach, he instinctively adopted the invaluable method of example.
"Know thyself" and "Know others" were twin and
constant stars. The power of the Oxford sermons, to
which men listened with bated breath, lay in the utter
sincerity of the preacher's experience, thinking, and
emotion. England had heard no such speech for centuries.

These Oxford sermons were the result of one of those
recurrent crises in Newman's life, in which his essentially contemplative mind encountered the shock of the
outer world. He had come to realize the necessary
existence of the Christian Church as the custodian
of the spiritual life bequeathed by the Saviour, and to
see that his countrymen were totally indifferent to
purity of doctrine and freedom of action in that
Church. Rather naïvely, he fancied that the return
of the Anglican Communion to the belief and practice
of the Fathers of the Church could be accomplished by
means of certain definite reforms. Then, gradually,

he awoke to the difficulties of the situation and to the
poverty of his own knowledge. What were the reasons
for believing? What had the Fathers taught? How
had the Church of England become the inheritor of that
teaching? Nothing could lessen the burning eagerness
of Newman to answer these questions. In his effort
to discover the reality of the Apostolic Church, he undertook tedious researches into the history of the
Arians. The total indifference of his mind to affairs
alien to this great spiritual quest is interestingly revealed in a letter written at the time in response to a
gentleman who wished Newman to address a popular
gathering. Loftily though kindly, he states that he has
nothing to say on the subject proposed, being "engaged
on a history of the Arians." In reality the interests of
his life were world-wide, but he never compromised with
his mission.

The time had come, however, when Newman's earnest
apologetics could no longer avoid the reality of Rome.
History revealed the continuous energy of the Papacy,
and Continental thought never overlooked the importance of its modern position. But he had been born
into the Church of England, had imbibed anti-Roman
views with mother's milk, and had learned to love the
sweetness and majesty of those early Anglican divines
who had never doubted the apostolic character of their
creed. And, therefore, while Newman might make increasingly larger concessions, he would not cease to
repudiate the dominion of the Popes. At this time
an important, seemingly Providential change in his
environment considerably modified his views. Having
endangered his health by too much study, Newman set
out with Froude on a cruise of the Mediterranean.

Catholic life impressed him very deeply: the cities he visited, the services he attended, the people he met, gave him a view of things that he had never before encompassed.   Nevertheless, his convictions stood firm against Rome, and he was shocked by what he believed superstition, as well as hurt, in his Victorian propriety, by the somewhat wanton relics of Renaissance art.   The best he could do was to cry out upon leaving, "O, that thy creed were sound!"   Returning to England he felt surer than ever of his mission, more aware of the "Kindly Light" that would lead him onward.

It was characteristic of Newman until the end not to understand the conservatism that safeguards institutional life.   No one was ever less of an egoist, and yet few men have been more absolutely individualistic.   His beliefs and practices were those which he found satisfactory in the light of his own experience; and the service that he yearned for was to render easy for others the way to the splendour and peace of God as vouchsafed to him.   And thus, while many Oxford men drew close to his doctrine, and the phrase "*Credo in Newmannum*" came to represent a definite creed, the vast machinery of the Church of England showed no unsteadiness.   Bishops, indeed, muttered a rather indistinct disapproval of the "Romanizing tendencies" manifest at Oxford; certain vicars in distant country parishes responded eagerly to the fervour of Oriel College; but the great mass of Englishmen viewed the matter with stolid unconcern.   There was, men said, a vague movement on foot within the Church; but it seemed very provincial, quite harmless.   And then, suddenly, the peace was broken by Keble's sermon on

"National Apostasy," which castigated the outspoken meddling of the State in the affairs of the Church, the issue being the suppression for political reasons of certain sees in Ireland. The spokesman received quick and courageous support. Newman was ready for battle now, and launched from the pulpit at St. Mary's a series of trenchant sermons that analyzed the depths of Christian doctrine, while the light of his own personality seemed to the intent audience a votive lamp given wholly to Truth. Disciples gathered, men listened in spite of themselves, and what had seemed only a theory suddenly lived in practice. Nevertheless, the energy of Newman did not rest here: the weapon of literature was at hand, and on September 9, 1833, he launched the first number of "Tracts for the Times."

Did he realize the significance of this undertaking? Probably not. An apostle now, conscious of divine leadership, he yearned and laboured solely for the renovation of the English Church. The tracts took up one by one the practices of Apostolic Christianity, and attacked vehemently the liberalism of most Anglicans. Keble, even Pusey—the authoritative and imposing theologian—wrote arresting discussions, but Newman remained the leader upon whom the destinies of the combat depended. He had not reckoned, however, with either of two things: the actual organization and character of the Church to which he belonged, or the possibility that he had not yet discovered the reality which he sought—the living, concrete institution which represented upon earth the majesty of God. The paradox upon which the Tractarian movement was based—though its leaders did not view it as a paradox—was that Rome, though it had best conserved the tradi-

tions of the Apostolic Church, was hopelessly wrong,
and that Anglicanism, which had forgotten those
traditions, was altogether right. Newman, wholly absorbed in the battle within himself for more light and
the outer battle of the apostle against the world, became
aware only gradually of this radical difficulty. At first
he solved it to his satisfaction by proposing a *via
media*, but events occurring in rapid succession proved
to his dismay that the *via media* was only an illusion.
There was the article by Wiseman on the Donatists,
showing that the Anglicans are perilously like those
unfortunate and forgotten heretics; there was the constant testimony of history to the deference with which
the Fathers had looked upon the Papal authority; and
finally the weight of the Anglican organization made itself felt in a series of heavy blows. Tract 90, interpreting the Thirty-nine Articles of the Book of Common Prayer in a Catholic sense, was discountenanced by
the Bishops; ecclesiastical sees were created for purely
political reasons; William George Ward was condemned for his book, "The Ideal of the Christian
Church"; and charges of heresy and treason were lev-
eled against the Tractarians as a body. Before the
overwhelming evidence against the paradox which he
now saw quite clearly, Newman yielded. He could
preach at Oxford no longer, he had built his house on
sand.

Littlemore, the retreat prepared during the splendour of his spiritual leadership, became his refuge in
the hour of pain. There remained one great problem
to solve, and, entering into semi-monastic retirement
with a few friends, he set about the task resolutely,
patiently, humbly. What is the visible power, the or-

ganization, to which divine Revelation has been confided? Is this a purely formal custodian, something like a manuscript library with a group of commentators, or is it a vital institution, almost a person, in which breathes the Presence of the Spirit of God? Newman had been seeking for years, somewhat unconsciously, the answer to this problem, but it had now become the sole concern of his life. The solution at which he arrived is "The Development of Christian Doctrine," a strikingly original discovery, and the supreme product, in all likelihood, of his thought. Time and effort were needed to abate his difficulties, to clear away his doubts, and to overcome his prejudices against Rome. But the angel of God had not stirred the waters in vain; quite suddenly he halted his pen at the end of the beautiful epilogue to the "Essay on Development," and then wrote the words, "*Nunc dimittis servum tuum, Domine, secundum verbum tuum in pace, quia viderunt oculi mei salutare tuum.*" On October 8, 1845, Newman was received into the Catholic Church by Father Dominic of the Passionists, and some time later was confirmed by Wiseman, who had carefully noted the progress of the movement from the beginning. What it had cost this convert to break from fond associations, from tried and beloved friends like Keble and Pusey, and from the church to which his strong early manhood had sworn the noblest allegiance, has left no furrow on the hard face of time; but when one walks through the altered Littlemore of today, or seeks out at Oxford the ways that Newman went, one remembers, as something great and sorrowful, the legend of his anguish and tears.

Even when due allowance for the restraints of affection has been made, it must be admitted that Newman's spiritual development was very slow. At the close of the forty-fifth year of his life, he stood on the threshold of an utterly new departure, however thoroughly his philosophy may have been formed. Nevertheless, although his powers of thought and concentration were most unusual, the hesitancy with which he reached conclusions was the natural result of his genius. This is beyond analysis, but its tangible characteristics are noteworthy. While he was fundamentally a mystic, a contemplative, who could have found under ordinary circumstances sufficient engrossment in the relation between his spirit and its Ultimate Destiny, Newman still, on the other hand, when once aroused to the actual, the real, tried to find in it everywhere the footprints of his ideal. The surprising many-sidedness of his gaze, the faculty for viewing things not as generalities but as collections of individuals, made him alive to almost numberless points of view, difficulties, lacunæ, and above all wilful sidesteppings of action. To make the individual realize the individuality of objective truth (or, as philosophers would say, to coördinate the one and the many) and act upon it, became the mission into which he threw all his powers. It needed the crisis of battle with the conventions and prejudices of surrounding society to call forth the full creative energy of Newman and to develop the flare of his intuition. And thus the Oxford Movement drew out a great share of his best work and enabled him, not indeed to overcome the organization with which he fought, but to escape from it unto Truth.

On May 30, 1847, Newman was ordained a priest, and shortly after resolved to establish an English

oratory under a modification of St. Philip Neri's rule.
Thus he came under the patronage of the simple and
kindly saint, the worth of whose example he was to
feel throughout life. The Birmingham Oratory was
opened in 1848, under bright and promising conditions,
though Newman himself felt old and weary, rather
strangely at ease in comparison with the rich activity
of his Oxford years. Henceforth his life would be
concerned with many things, but the broad principles of
his mental action would remain the same. His object
was still the arousal, the conversion, of the individual;
opposition would come, as always, from the organization to which he had belonged. Newman, though conservative, was utterly indifferent to conventions: he
could see no worth in words from which the living,
energizing thought had departed. Now during those
years of the nineteenth century the theological defense
of the Church was virtually a stubbornly armed resistance. The Catholic Spirit, resolutely entrenched behind traditional apologetics and philosophy, beheld
with dismay the rise of a multitude of heretical opinions, of revolutionary teachings, of naturalist dogmas,
which were the harvest of the great humanistic revolts
that had broken out in succession since the fifteenth
century. New views were, therefore, scrutinized rigorously, and Roman theologians took on much of the
character of military police, inclined to treat roughly
any apparition not obviously orthodox. This state of
affairs was brought home to Newman by the misunderstanding that greeted certain passages in the "Essay
on Development." He was to encounter it again and
again: the sternness of a struggle in which no quarter
was given scarcely respected the sensitiveness of a mind

that moved always above the battle. There was, however, an all-important difference between his attitude as a Catholic and his Anglican position. However much he might resent the curbing of his influence, the blindness of officials, or the constraints imposed by a too anxious authority, he never swerved in his allegiance or in his confidence that the difficulty would, in the end, be adjusted. In fact, these recurrent brushes with the outposts of the Catholic Spirit were really tocsins that summoned the best of his powers, tocsins to which he responded with the valour and self-sacrifice of a hero.

At no time in Newman's life did the fine mettle of his character prove itself more genuine than during the early days of his priesthood. Giving himself utterly to that missionary work he could do so well, and no less wholly to the needs of his young community, he strengthened himself also with meditation and prayer. The "Sermons to Mixed Congregations" and "Sermons Preached on Various Occasions," wherein the style grows steadily more eloquent and more serene, give an outward stamp to the satisfaction he drew from religion. Then the Gorham Case, a celebrated instance in which the authority of the English bishops had been brusquely ignored by the Privy Council, having provided the opportunity, he attacked Anglicanism directly in the ringing, unusually outspoken lectures which have since been entitled, "On the Difficulties of Anglicans." These were followed by some of his very best oratorical efforts, the addresses "On the Present Position of Catholics," which did much to quell the "No-Popery" outbursts, so easy to stimulate in a populace that does not understand. All of this controversial work is brilliant, witty, even satirical, but its chief distinction is the admirable deference with which Newman the convert treats the convictions of those who were once his brethren. He does not mince matters, but he meets deftly and lovingly those whom he has abandoned, holding even that the Anglican position is worth while as a bulwark against infidelity. Retrospective controversy is always a dangerous undertaking, and Newman's genius found the exact combination of courtesy and manliness needed for the task.

Naturally enough, he longed constantly for apostolic labour, for a position which would bring with it that vast influence upon souls which he felt able to exert. He would not have been human had he forgotten the glory of Oxford; he would not have been a man of God had he been willing to forgo a similar opportunity after Catholic truth had been vouchsafed him. Suddenly the idea of a Catholic University to be erected in Dublin was brought forth by Doctor Cullen, with the suggestion that Newman direct the enterprise. There seemed to be unlimited opportunities here of the sort which, when developed, leave their impress upon a whole society; there were also enormous difficulties and almost forbidding requirements. It was characteristic of Newman to see all of these things with exceptional clearness and to hope for success. Again he followed the light of his mission, trusting because "Peter had spoken" and could not have misjudged the issue, and again he failed to take into account the actual condition of the organization with which he would have to deal. Another Englishman would have halted upon considering the relations existing between

his country and Ireland, but Newman was beyond all
of that.   At the price of intense personal hardship
he traveled throughout the island, admired the people,
and expressed unqualifiedly his sympathy with their
national aspirations.   The introductory Dublin lecture, with its portrait of the amiable sharing of interests that had once distinguished England and Ireland,
was utterly sincere.   Unfortunately the University
was still-born; Cullen proved to be a narrow and officious prelate whose views, too small to merit any
earnest attention, tied Newman hand and foot; many
who had acclaimed the project most boisterously when
it was broached showed no practical interest in it as
a reality: and the impassioned hope, the noble vision,
of Newman's "Idea of a University" became great literature but no school in the concrete.   Again the
organization had triumphed over the serenity of a
great man's dream, and Newman came back to the
oratory wasted in health and quite broken in spirit—
a disillusioned man.

Failure began to haunt him.   The retirement in
which he now lived was more trying by far than the
traditional isolation of genius, for it was the result of
a virtual repudiation of his work and mission, a cast-
ing out of his thought as well-nigh unclean.   Envisaging the minds of thousands upon thousands of Englishmen, divining their spiritual needs and difficulties with
impartial realism, he saw with dismay that the appointed leaders of Catholic thought were considering
other matters.   His plan to make a new English version of the Scriptures was first encouraged and then
peremptorily snuffed out.   His resolve to aid young
Catholics at Oxford by establishing a mission there

was foiled, chiefly through Manning's agency. Finally, the position of conciliation which he assumed on the question of Papal Infallibility incurred opposition both from the belligerent supporters of an absolute Papacy—one of whom, W. G. Ward of the *Dublin Review*, declared that he should like a new bull each morning with his breakfast,—and from liberals who, like Capes and Lord Acton, had been influenced by Germanic criticism to the point where they very nearly denied the traditional authority of Rome. Newman's views on the Infallibility and the Temporal Power were quite generally misinterpreted, and Rome was led to consider him a lukewarm supporter, if not a positive enemy.

There is no room here for an examination of the controversy, but it may safely be affirmed that the real cause for all these difficulties lay in the contrasted temperaments of Newman and Cardinal Manning. The Archbishop of Westminster lacked breadth of vision and artistic power, but he possessed an energy in direction and a diplomatic skill quite military in character; scorning what he believed to be speculative heckling with all the brusqueness of a soldier, he strained every sinew in an effort to dominate the here and now. It is interesting to note that time has vindicated the views of Newman on these subjects which Manning frowned upon: our view of Papal Infallibility is, practically, Newman's, there is a mission at Oxford, and a new version of the Scriptures has been undertaken. On the other hand, the genuine service rendered by Manning is attested to by the soundness of his views on labour, his correct appraisal of Church administration, and his schemes for popular missionary work—all of them views alien, in their practical aspects, to the mind of Newman.

So deep was the humiliation of the great Oratorian, and so confined was he to the simple duties of a parish priest and rector of a boys' academy, that in 1860 his return to the Anglican Church was announced as probable, even imminent. He was, indeed, quite discouraged, but he put down these reports in a flaming letter which did not reveal, of course, the ascetic religious life from which he drew strength. Even though the sensibility that was interwoven with his poet's nature might have been bruised and beaten, though his mission to other minds might have been hampered, the inner Newman, the contemplative, the visionary, the man of religion, remained unaltered. *Il faut souffrir pour être beau;* and the aging priest, crushed by the hostility of his environment, was never more kindly, more fervent, more distinctly the seer. This was the Newman of the "Meditations," of "The Dream of Gerontius," of the myriad letters so instinct with sympathy and understanding. It was not, however, the creative Newman, master of controversy and convincing motive, the Newman who would appear only when contact with the outer world was large and free.

Then, at Christmas time, 1863, Charles Kingsley the novelist stated in *Macmillan's Magazine:* "The truth for its own sake has never been a virtue with the Roman clergy. Father Newman informs us that it need not be." At first the accused was disposed to view here only another petty annoyance, and contented himself with a protest. To this Kingsley paid little attention; in fact he issued a vigorous denunciatory pamphlet entitled, "What, Then, Does Dr. Newman Mean?"

This was plainly not the fruit of personal resentment, but aimed at pillorying an example, at making allegations of dishonesty that would apply to the Catholic priesthood as a whole. Newman was aroused to the full meaning of the issue and resolutely took up the cudgels of debate, all the better fitted by reason of his long rest. In a celebrated attack he rushed Kingsley off his ground and riddled the unfortunate pamphlet with something akin to fury. Then, in a number of articles written at white heat, where the swift thought and virility of emotion give English words an almost uncanny vitality, he told the intimate narrative of his soul. Kingsley was hopelessly crushed and left to stand naked and desolate before public opinion; and the universal recognition of Newman's success has scarce an equal in the history of controversy. The character of the Oxford Movement had been vindicated forever, and, no matter what opinions men might in the future hold concerning the Catholic faith, they could not decently or openly accuse its ministers of dishonesty. It is worth noting that the victory achieved by the "Apologia pro Vita Sua" was purely literary; that for the first time in his career Newman had gained a cause without the aid of oratory. This was to hold true of all his later work.

While England accepted joyfully Newman's vindication, his relations with extremists among Catholics did not become easier. So thorough a lack of prestige may have continued to sadden, but did not any longer curb him. In 1870 he began another purely literary mission, which when completed was called very modestly "An Essay towards a Grammar of Assent." Newman's objective here was a defense of the ultimate

grounds for reasonable faith, against which he saw
more and more clearly that the forces of skepticism
were beginning to move. His battle is with souls that
have lost themselves far away from the domain of
religious belief, who have, in fact, almost forgotten
what belief is like. Never had his thought, his charity,
his fervent missionary spirit, gone so far: and in the
subtle labyrinth of innermost human psychology he
struggled with the most tenacious and skillful of demons. The effort of this wrestling cost Newman more
energy than anything else he had undertaken, but his
success was immediate and sustained. Everyone recognized the importance and originality of the work, and it
won unstinted praise from even his Catholic opponents.
The shadow lay upon him still, but now it was of the
texture of twilight, not of the desolate night that had
seemed unending. Personally, he felt certain that his
work had been wrought in the grace of his Master.

The Church, it seemed to the aging priest, would
never trust him fully, and he was prepared to go down
to his grave in that atmosphere of faint suspicion
which to a zealous Catholic apostle is the most harrowing form of bondage. Then, almost in the twinkling
of an eye, there was wrought one of those profound
changes in the direction of the Church by which the
Spirit of God seems to guard her from decay, and Leo
XIII came from seclusion to the throne of Peter. He
had long been aware of Newman's importance, and
when a petition came from the leaders of English
Catholicism asking that their aged guide be elevated
to the Cardinalate, the Holy Father gladly acceded to
the request. The aged Oratorian understood well the
meaning of the dignity: "The cloud has been lifted

from me forever," was his grateful recognition. After the formal ceremony in Rome, May 12, 1879, he returned to his beloved Birmingham whence he stirred only on certain occasions. Serene, deeply interested in the rhythm of life throughout the world, he waited calmly for the end, which came after a brief illness, on August 11, 1890. On the pall over his coffin were embroidered the words he had chosen for his shield: *"Cor ad Cor Loquitur."* And, indeed, the numbers who attended his burial, the multitude of souls for whom he had been a patient spiritual father, felt that they summed up the blessed secret of his life.

No portrait of Newman can be complete, and this one is only a poor sketch. We will not close, however, without some attempt to indicate the little human things that stressed his individuality and made him lovable. He was, of course, an apostle first of all, with intense convictions and absolute purity of sentiment. Then, too, he was a poet, with all the delicate sensibility of an artistic nature born to the nuances of loveliness and pain. But though the affection he offered his friends was regally crowned by the greatness of his mission, though the majesty of his personality was felt by all who entered his life, he was also tender, solicitous, and charming. No letters to children are more delicately child-like than his; no debater was ever more magnanimous to his opponents; no friend ever stood nearer to a friend than he did to Hurrell Froude or Ambrose St. John. The light of the peace in his heart was unflinching. Nature he fathomed as deeply as Wordsworth; he divined with satisfaction the inner harmony of great art; music was his constant solace, and he played on the violin those great visions of Beethoven and Mozart to which his spirit responded with the gentleness of perfect understanding. "His soul was in his voice," says Canon Holland, "as a bird is in its song." Gifted with a ready, though delicate, sense of humour, he would occasionally run the rapier of satire through an unwary impertinence. He could even be sternly acrid and snub Monsignor Talbot, his officious though masked opponent in Rome, with something akin to the cruelty of vengeance. In many ways, of course, he remained a staid Victorian, but, more than any of his contemporaries realized, he was a daring innovator, the bearer of a new beacon, the apostle of tomorrow. The mystery of sanctification in his private life made of his career a rounded whole. In the words of Chaucer,

"Christus' lore and His apostles twelve
He taught, but first he followed it himselve."

CHAPTER FOUR

NEWMAN THE THINKER

"Shall we say that there is no such thing as truth and error, but that anything is truth to a man which he troweth?"

"GRAMMAR OF ASSENT."

T HE personality of Newman was, as has been said, a religious force; his thinking was quite simply the bulwark of that force, supporting it in the conflict with intellectual representatives of the skeptical world. Nowadays philosophy is largely academic, and its teachers are generally men who bring to a special branch of thought a vast erudition and a scarcely less vast disdain for practical interference in the spiritual affairs of the day. Newman, however, did not study the mind for its own sake, but because of faith; in analyzing the powers of the soul he sought to find battlements where religion could hold fast against the attacks of atheism in its most insinuating and plausible forms. He wished to show that, when all the hypotheses of skeptical science had been granted, there remained ample reason for a complete confidence in the truth of revealed religion. No opportunity was missed; by treatise, by sermon, by pamphlet, and by private correspondence he tried to lend to those in need of it the assistance which he had found so valuable during the conflict within himself. Newman's thought is moulded into a thousand shapes, hidden in

56

a thousand places; in none does it stand complete, but nowhere, also, does it stand alone.

Emphatically, the great Cardinal's thought was not in any sense of the word a patchwork. That which guided his mind always was a single apostolic mission, a rarely disturbed consecration to the things of the Faith. Looking upon the business of life as an intensely practical affair, where the great goal is harmony between creature and Creator, where the great rule of conduct is the Christian religion, he saw with dismay that the skeptic could plausibly deny the reality of both Creator and Christianity, or could, at least, affirm the essential intangibleness of both. Newman went through life a *Defensor Fidei*, and because his influence was handicapped by the lack of an adequate theory of knowledge, he set about to discover one. Because the differences between the primitive Church and its modern successor had not been satisfactorily accounted for, he constructed his doctrine of Development to reconcile old and new. Whenever he thought that an argument of his would meet an objection and dispose of it, he set that argument down. It is his purpose that gives to Newman's thought an admirable unity and a remarkable practicality, though in form it is diffuse. This unity is rendered more striking by the fact that no phase of modern thought escaped his notice, and that he could read the souls of other men with extraordinary sureness and ease.

The many-sided genius of Newman and the multifarious shapes in which it sought expression make his total achievement difficult to follow. It may be well to begin with what seems to have been his chief concern—a problem that has stirred the modern world

to its depths, even as it shook the old. The existence
of God has been universally accepted as a fact by all
peoples to account for the Source of all good and the
end of all aspirations of the human soul. For Newman these reasons for believing in a Creator were
strengthened by his absolute trust in the voice of conscience, a voice that speaks unmistakably to the moral
nature of man of a Moral Lawgiver. On the other
hand, he realized unflinchingly that there is evil in
the world, evil of such magnitude that it can never be
compassed. Now as the reason of man was steadily
trained upon this monstrous fact, as it came to learn
more of the processes of nature and the constitution
of the cosmos, there was grave danger that the material
order of things would be considered a sufficient explana-
tion of all existence, and that the idea of the Personality of God and the reality of His Providence would
be thought chimerical. Men would say, had said, that
there was no tangible evidence for the action of God
in the world, while on the other hand proof of the
total indifference of natural laws and natural forces
was overwhelming. Why, then, set up the idea of
Absolute Good and serve it, instead of taking the universe as it is, a blind entity of mingled good and evil,
governed by immutably rigid "legislation" and only
vaguely capable of betterment? Newman understood
this point of view very fully; in fact, skeptics from
Huxley to Paul E. More have felt that he himself
was at least half an unbeliever.

The mystery of evil is always somewhere in the background of Newman's sermons, but is, perhaps, best
stated in that celebrated passage of the "Apologia"
which reads:

"To consider the world in its length and breadth, its various history, the many races of man, their starts, their fortunes, their mutual alienations, their conflicts; and then their ways, habits, governments, forms of worship; their enterprises, their aimless courses, their random achievements and acquirements, the impotent conclusion of long-standing facts, 'the tokens, so faint and broken, of a superintending design, the blind evolution of what turn out to be great powers or truths, the progress of things, as if from unreasoning elements, not toward final causes, the greatness and littleness of man, his far-reaching aims, his short duration, the curtain hung over his futurity, the disappointments of life, the defeat of good, the success of evil, physical pain, mental anguish, the prevalence and intensity of sin, the pervading idolatries, the corruptions, the dreary hopeless irreligion, that condition of the whole race, so fearfully yet exactly described in the apostle's words, 'having no hope and without God in the world';—all this is a vision to dizzy and appal; and inflicts upon the mind the sense of a profound mystery, which is absolutely beyond human solution."

This, he felt, was the real state of affairs, but human reason *would* busy itself with a solution; having discarded the authority of a teaching Church, it would pride itself more and more upon its discovery of hidden natural forces and their practical applications; it would erect the dogma of science on the one hand, and, acting as the "universal solvent" on the other, would decry every idea of the super-physical, and make of the moral law revealed by God a mythological caprice, a delusion that could not endure the test to which other hypotheses are subjected. Newman realized the fascination of the skeptical mood, and in fact stated the "creed" of the agnostic very brilliantly before even the term had been invented.

"The teacher then, whom I speak of," he says, "will discourse thus in his secret heart . . . without denying that in the matter of religion some things are true and some things are false, still we certainly are not in a position to determine the one or the other. And, as it would be absurd to dogmatize about the weather, and say that 1860 will be a wet season or a dry season, a time of peace or war, so it is absurd for men in our present state to teach anything positive about the next world, that there is a heaven, or a hell, or a last judgment, or that the soul is immortal, or that there is a God. It is not that you have not a right to your own opinion, as you have a right to place implicit trust in your own banker, or in your own physician, but undeniably such persuasions are not knowledge, they are not scientific, they cannot become public property, they are consistent with the allowing of your friend to entertain the opposite opinion; and if you are tempted to be violent in the defense of your own view of the case in this matter of religion, then it is well to lay seriously to heart whether sensitiveness on the subject of your banker or your doctor, when he is handled skeptically by another would not be taken to argue a secret misgiving in your mind about him, in spite of your confident profession, an absence of clear unruffled certainty in his honesty or in his skill."

From experience he knew that the Christian view of the world seems ascetic and that its mandates of sacrifice demand an effort of the will acting on motives of a very unmaterial complexion. Men living in the here and now must bridge the chasm to eternity before they can commune with the Creator; and the crossing is difficult to make. Epicures like Omar prefer cash to credit; Positivists, nobly Stoical though they be, prefer paradise on earth to heaven beyond. There is, sometimes even in religious minds, the desire that the Just Judge might be eliminated from the field of human action. Why not, then, follow the obvious choice of modern reason and substitute pantheism or naturalism for the Christian scheme?

In this manner—though the statement we have given is bare to the utmost—did Newman visualize the protest of scientific reason to Faith, long before it became the strong commonplace that it is today. In a very remarkable way he anticipated the future, divining even some of the general positions which skeptical philosophy would take up—Evolution, for instance, and the realm of the subconscious. Nevertheless, he did vastly more than state the case of the opposition: unaided, opposed even by his own friends, he indicated the broad formations which Christian apologetics must assume in the combat with the world. The old evidences, nicely arranged in mathematical tableaux, were good but ineffective; they had never convinced many, nor did they confront the spirit of the times on the ground where it lay entrenched. For the eager apostle they were baggage, scarcely more. Newman did not succeed, as did St. Thomas, in stating a synthesis in which the prevailing philosophic doctrines were brought into harmony with the faith. His incomplete success was in some ways the direct result of his genius; he forestalled his opponents by attacking their arguments before they had been drawn up; he did not have the benefit of the full, free, coöperative discussion of the Middle Ages, but was hampered by narrow theological interference from men whose understanding of the issues at stake was childish, and besides he was, like all other moderns, too individual to work harmoniously with his neighbors.

It remains for us to consider some of the solutions Newman offered for the difficulties created by a skeptical view of life. In the first place, if one wishes to show that Faith is just as sensible as demonstration, that the mind can believe, it is necessary to present a correct sketch of the mind, or, in more technical language, to provide an adequate theory of knowledge. This, however, is difficult, for as Newman said: "The human mind is unequal to its own powers of apprehension; it embraces more than it can master." It is all very well to talk of logic and demonstration, but these are useful only in limited fields, just as the spade is efficient in a garden-plot, but scarcely practical for turning the sod of a vast plantation. In proceeding, then, to explain the processes by which the mind can arrive at a justifiable conclusion, Newman became exceedingly broad and subtle; while insisting on the concrete and supplying a wealth of striking illustrations, he was dealing with a subject which is almost incapable of definition and which assuredly requires acute attention. Again, while the "Grammar of Assent" is his most exhaustive treatment of the problem, it had been considered already in the "University Sermons" and to a lesser extent in the "Dublin Lectures."

First, he set out resolutely to attack the exorbitant claims of logic. Relying on a remarkably shrewd psychological insight, he showed that the assents

treated of in this science are only notional, or in a
way abstract, while the mind in practice requires real,
or concrete, assent. Logic does not reach to the first
principles upon which inferential thinking is based, or
take up those hidden but very effective working processes of the soul which arrive at conclusions accurately,
but which underlie consciousness so completely that if
a man is asked how he came to hold this or that belief
he is unable to explain his way step by step, although
he knows its entire safety. There is no such thing
in real life as a detailed enumeration of the reasons
why a certain conclusion has been arrived at and acted
upon.

Again, logic is the refuge of the non-original mind,
which cannot employ the inexplicable gift of intuition,
by means of which genius reaches its goal with the
sudden directness of a ray of light. For these reasons and more, it is not entitled to the elaborate claims
that have been made for it. One must bear in mind
that Newman does not cast the science of demonstration overboard; on the contrary, he places a high estimate on it wherever it proves useful, as this passage
from the "Apologia" will suffice to indicate: "There
was a contrariety of claims between the Roman and
Anglican religions, and the history of my conversion
is simply the process of working it out to a solution."
There is involved in this part of the great Oratorian's
theory, many think, a distinct anticipation of and
application to apologetics of the modern theory of
subliminal consciousness.

Man, however, is not merely a machine that ratioci-
nates; he is primarily a person who acts. Conse-
quently, his conclusions will surely be modified by

motives, conscious or otherwise, and he will have difficulty in arriving at the Truth. Can he attain to it?

"Shall we say," Newman asks, "that there is no such thing as truth and error, but that anything is truth to a man which he troweth? And not rather, as the solution of a great mystery, that truth there is, and attainable it is, but that its rays stream in upon us through the medium of our moral as well as our intellectual being; and that in consequence that perception of its first principles which is so natural to us is enfeebled, obstructed, perverted, by the allurements of sense and the supremacy of self, and, on the other hand, quickened by aspiration after the supernatural; so that at length two characters of mind are brought out into shape, and two standards and systems of thought—each logical, yet contradictory of each other, and only not antagonistic because they have no common ground on which they can conflict."

If, then, the Unseen Things in which a man has faith are not manifested directly by the science of reason and may be modified by the inclinations of the moral or conative nature, how shall we know that the conception of those Unseen Things which is formed in our minds is in consonance with reality? How shall we be saved from superstition on the one hand and from unbelief on the other? Newman argues that faith is based on slight evidence but on overwhelming antecedent probabilities existing in close union. Thus, a miracle is evidence to a religious mind of the truths of Revelation; whereas to Hume, the atheist, it is an illusion because miracles are *ipso facto* impossible. In both cases the mind acts upon presumptions which are dictated by what Newman later termed the "illative sense"—that is, the living mind's power to weigh probable causes, analogies, and desirable effects which cannot be arranged in logical order. Although the individual who believes cannot state the reasons for his faith in perfect order, his mind has satisfied itself on the validity of those reasons. So much for faith; but "Right faith is the faith of a right mind; right faith is an intellectual act done in a certain moral disposition. . . . As far as and wherever Love is wanting, so far and there, Faith runs into excess or is perverted."

This recognition of the important part which the will plays in the determinations of the mind is one of the most striking parts of Newman's subtle apologetics; it is virtually the anticipation of a line of thought which, pushed farther, would be called Pragmatism. The lectures of William James on the Pragmatic System set out to show that every truth must be essentially verifiable, which means that our experiences must find it coincident with themselves. Thus we conclude that truth is what is useful, the word being taken in no mere Hedonistic or Utilitarian sense, but as synonymous with being capable of satisfying ethically the observer and the thinker. Stripped of vagueness and strengthened by a firm reliance upon the objectivity of intellectual and moral standards, this becomes Newman's doctrine of "antecedent probability" and "the right mind."

In still another way did Newman show his reliance on the practical, conative side of human nature: in his statement of the reasons for believing in the existence of God. Here he seems to reduce, in accordance with the spirit of his age, the intellectual evidence to a minimum. For physical arguments, particularly the one from design, he seems to care very little; nor does he regard as probable any direct communication with the Unseen since the days of Revelation, thus modifying the testimony of mystic saints and the theology to which they have contributed. Miracles even appear to him rather ineffective arguments against the unbeliever, although they are most important to the Christian and deserve his humble credence. The apostle in Newman had decided correctly; for the agnostic like Zola, when confronted with evidence which he cannot controvert, will distort the facts willfully in order to save his negative first principles. That which makes the existence of God absolutely certain for Newman is the voice of conscience, speaking within the soul of man and imposing its "ought" with the sanction of Eternal Authority. Here is the root of action and the root of belief; here is the *point d'appui* for the spirit lost in the din of a moving world. Religion's "large and deep foundation is the sense of sin and guilt, and without this sense there is for man, as he is, no genuine religion." Conscience insists upon the good, teaches the God of Judgment and Justice; for, by its emotional character, "it always involves the recognition of a living object towards which it is directed." It is an "instinct" for the Supernatural and Divine; though it may be perverted, it will not die without anguish; but if it is heeded it "has a living hold on truths which are really to be found in the world, though they are not on the surface," it reads the scroll of the world by its own steady light and is able to assume that the laws of nature "are consistent with a particular Providence." It is, therefore, "a connecting principle between the creature and the

Creator"; and thus we have the ontological argument of St. Anselm concretized, made real and practical, and brought out of the mists of a faulty idealism within the range of every honest man. We cannot hope to review here any adequate treatment of this most vital section of Newman's philosophy; what has been said may suffice, however, to give an idea of the general trend of his thinking.

From this deep and subtle recognition of "facts as they are" Newman was driven to admit that, despite the tremendous questions involved, personal interest and right disposition are prerequisite to successful theological investigation. While the ordinary man will receive truths and the inferences drawn from then on "testimony," the especially gifted individual alone can assure progress in the science of theology or venture to study the ultimates of religious consciousness. Nevertheless, just as the pragmatist would verify his findings by the compass of normal beliefs, or "common sense," so the personal element in Newman's theistic inquiry is guided by the coördination of the single mind with other living minds. "Truth," he says, "is wrought out by many minds working freely together," and he, therefore, had great sympathy with the open discussion which prevailed during the Middle Ages— something like which the Oxford Movement had been. Moreover, since conscience and the right frame of mind are so essential and so beset with temptation, since Revelation, once given, is the bulwark of all times, he naturally sought out the one divinely appointed Power which can successfully resist the attacks of reason and the seductiveness of the world; this, he saw, is the Catholic Church. Obviously, this part of his theory, when isolated, gives critics the opportunity to say that Newman submitted to Rome in order to save his belief in the supernatural; however, the statement falls to the ground when this item is carefully correlated with the rest of his thought. Repeatedly he emphasized the fact that' faith can exist "without creed or dogma"; but understanding human nature as it is, taking the *facts in the case*, he saw clearly that such faith was little likely to endure in the teeth of a hostile world, and that besides being the guardian of Revelation the Church is the medium of the sacramental graces that make for supernatural life.

At this point Newman came face to face with a new objection and met it in a way that is truly remarkable. Reason must follow and study the revealed truths in the Christian dispensation, and in history reason has done so. "At the very beginning," says Newman, "St. Paul, the learned Pharisee, was the first fruits of that gifted company, in whom the pride of conscience is seen prostrate before the foolishness of preaching." The successive victories of the Fathers over heresy, the devotion of the saints, the energy of monastic orders, and the decrees of Popes and Councils, have surrounded the simple precepts of revealed religion with a dense array of dogmas. Is not, then, the greater part of the Church's teaching today the work of human minds whose conclusions do not warrant any more adherence than that given to systems of philosophy? Or is it all Divine? By a striking anticipation of the evolutionary hypothesis, Newman answered these questions with his idea of the development of Christian doctrine. In his essay on the subject he maintains that what seem at first sight to be mere extraneous additions to the teaching of the Saviour are in fact outgrowths of a living, active power, inhabiting that teaching and developing it in consonance with the needs of the time. By a careful analysis of the history of dogma, he shows that the Scriptures are capable of diverse interpretations and have, in fact, received them; but, far from countenancing any change, the Church has kept the same viewpoint from the beginning, having merely expounded and clearly stated its belief when occasion demanded. Theology, then, becomes not a repository for dead corollaries and rigid syllogisms, but an organic body, every member of which is infused with life from the center. As a matter of fact, this theory of Newman is considered by many as his ablest contribution to the thought of the world; it is at the very least a satisfactory test of the originality of his mind.

Thus stated, Newman's system will be found to possess coherence and ample breadth of view. It has already been suggested, however, that he differed largely from the representative philosopher in the use which he made of his thought. Essentially speculative, he proved the worth of speculation by combining with his critique of reason a rich imagination and a burning will. His thought is never divorced from the actual, from the here and now. Although his avowed respect for Aristotle, St. Thomas, and Bacon was most sincere, still it may be doubted whether he possessed an erudite knowledge of any of the three. What Newman understood perfectly was the mind of his neighbor; he divined with surprising correctness not only the deficiencies, the cravings, and the difficulties of the individual soul, but also what was most likely to have a salutary effect on that soul. In his longer treatises he met the general spirit of modern times on the very field it had chosen for the combat; in thousands of personal letters he replied to the difficulties with which those who looked to him for guidance were beset. Newman realized fully the influence of personality in teaching; where argument proved too subtle, or dissertation too callous, he did not hesitate to invoke the romantic mood in the souls of his hearers, and thus to carry them along by the impetuosity of his feeling. This was the alembic in which his reasoning was combined with his mission and moulded into a unity that is as round and full as the world of great poetry, and yet as candid and recondite as the doctrines of Emmanuel Kant.

This outline does not aspire to the presumption of proving that Newman was a great philosopher; it wishes merely to state what his philosophy was and how it came into being at all. When, in the "Dublin Lectures" Newman made a synthesis of the worthwhile aims of education in our day, he insisted on the liberty of literature and science as well as upon the freedom and dignity of theological inquiry. Reading clearly the spirit of the era in which he lived, he believed that its convictions could easily be harmonized with traditional Christianity, but that the practical acceptance of the Christian system would entail difficulty, that, in fact, the struggle with the skeptic mood would be intense and bitter. Newman fought with the weapons of genius an antagonist that was as yet stirring in the future's womb, forestalling the great offensive strategy of the evolutionist, the pragmatist, and the agnostic in metaphysics. Never has Christian apologetics wagered so much, dared to risk all with the confidence of absolute faith. Newman was not a skeptic hiding in the robes of the Church; he was an apostle rifling the wardrobe of the unbeliever. The great warrant for such an undertaking is the warrant which genius always demands—success. If his system has answered difficulties, cleared away any doubts, stirred religious feelings, and won souls, then it has been genuinely useful, whatever its departures from traditional method.

However small may be the influence of heredity on the mind it is strange that Newman should have been utterly Hebraic in his devotion to the one God, and quite French in the nature of his philosophic thought. Canon Barry has outlined a parallel between Newman and Renan, which is interesting indeed: the imaginative Breton with his horror of systems and syllogisms, his desire to weld the ends of the world together in the crucible of his thought, his passage from Christian faith to the ironic skepticism of a totally disillusioned man, and Newman equally poetic, equally concrete, equally conscious of the multitude of deeps upon deeps on which the world has been built, but secure in the quiet citadel of his faith, obedient Christian to the end. Again, there is striking similarity between the faith of Newman and the faith of Pascal: they have the same distrust of reason, the same reliance on intuition, the same sense of the overwhelming power of evil. But, though Renan dreamed of conquering the world by his intellect, and Pascal had won it over by the greatness of his contempt for its follies, there lived in neither the flaming eagerness of the apostle which made of Newman an *ignis ardens* that fed on the saving of souls.

Those to whom this means nothing, or who think it

of small importance, will never succeed in taking Newman at his true worth. One may admire his lucid statement of a proposition, the brilliancy of his illustration, and the subtlety of his intellect, and rightly so; but these are qualities which the great Oratorian would have despised for their own sakes. Only when they served as means by which to present the message of the Redeemer, only when they hovered like ministering angels over desperate souls, did he value them at all. Newman belongs to the history of religion first, and then to literature. Behind him lay the past of Christendom with the splendour of its schools, the beauty of its sanctuaries, and its concern with the multitude of souls; before him loomed the future of a world for which the Saviour had come, and from which He seemed about to be cast. And, finally, there existed nothing which could come between him and his Creator; for he had gone, *ex umbris et imaginibus in veritatem.*

CHAPTER FIVE

"Heart speaketh to heart."

NEWMAN'S work is literature, of course, because he was an artist. And here the difficulty is not that he has been underrated, but that this side of his genius has been distorted, to the discredit of his ability as a thinker and a man. "One can never get too much of Newman," says Augustin Birrell; Professor Gates has shown the remarkable suitableness of his style for university study, and Canon Barry has much to say of lights and shadows, of the "English of the center" and the eloquence which runs through Newman's every page. Nevertheless, there are people for whom this supreme ability detracts from the worth of his prose; who see in it the note of insincerity as of siren melody woven with honest battle-song: and thus the "Cambridge History" finds that the author of the "Apologia" was "always, subconsciously perhaps, an artist." As if the weather-beaten theologian whose gaze was resolutely fixed on the everlasting verities was some kind of scented æsthete, fashioning phrases for their comeliness! He tells us, indeed, of the stern fatigue which the work of writing cast upon him; of times when he was ready to sink exhausted beside his table; of the similitude between the labour of getting

73

out a book and the anguish of child-birth. He believed that the secret of style lies in an "incommunicable simplicity" which arises from the fact that an author has a single purpose and a single vision, and that through all his possible amplifications he adheres to it sternly. Newman's literary polish is something like rubbing a mirror to make the image stand forth clearly and realistically.

No. In order to understand Newman's artistic ability, one must know what Art meant to him. It was not Beauty only, or its reflection, but Beauty rendered useful: Beauty not as a spinster, a maiden, or a harlot, but Beauty wedded to Truth. To the end of his life he was Platonic in his love for symbols and in his reading of nature as a screen; hence the famous identification of music and angel-song, and his trust with Wordsworth in the religious instincts of children. The artist is always a man who sees things, realities, in pictures, who has shattered the daylight into a rainbow; but unless he is a modern or perverted artist, he does not turn the spectroscope upon his individual candle. Newman saw the splendour of God through the windows of the world and refused to close his eyes; for his concern was not with abstractions but with men, images of a Creator. In consequence he was an artist who in following with abandon the light of his mission, turned the faded pathways of teaching and polemics to streets of glory.

What is most interesting in Newman's controversial work is the poise of his personality. One feels sure that he has looked the ground over, calculated the chances of the engagement carefully, and provided against any emergency. There will be no impetuous

charge on an unimportant position, no reckless fan-
flare, or waste of energy. He will engage the enemy
all along the line, meeting him with reënforcements
where they are needed, but will never forget the essential thing, which is to advance. Not that he keeps
forces in ambush; he seems rather to deploy all his
troops upon the field in open sight of the enemy and
then to beat him none the less vigorously. These elements in Newman's construction are matched by the
spirit of his style. He is now restrained, keeping his
natural impetuosity sternly in rein, then vigorous in
pressing the attack, and finally exuberant, eloquent,
copious in the triumphant din of the victory march.
This close correspondence is found also, in a remarkable way, in the steady mutual development of Newman's mind and expression. As his religious convictions deepen, his writing hand grows more elastic and
he is not so sparing of emotion. There is one kind
of inner life behind the "Oxford Sermons" and another
behind the "Dublin Lectures"; the man who wrote
"Lead, Kindly Light" could not have composed "The
Dream of Gerontius"; and Wilfrid Ward is right when
he says, "An eventful personal history and experience
is the main cause of all that is recognized as beautiful
in his style."

The materials out of which Newman fashioned his
prose were all of the best. Early in life he had felt
the sonorous rhythm of Gibbon's somewhat archaic but
stately sentences, and a mind that fed on Locke and
Whately could not have been indifferent to the sense
of a word. Besides the classics, among whom the
Cicero who "writes Roman" was his favourite, he loved
the older poets, particularly Crabbe and Southey

(strange association!) and the novels of Scott and Thackeray. Above all, however, he owed a debt to the English Bible, whose simple and fascinating diction has benefited so many authors. Newman never played the "sedulous ape," but found the pen a weapon which he gradually and laboriously came to understand. There are times when he speaks with actual contempt of the "literary essay," and he considered his poems trifles devoid of intellectual significance. In short, for all his attachment to meditation and prayer, he was a plain, blunt man whose writing was part of his business and who strove to make of it, accordingly, an efficient instrument. To speak of Newman as an "artist," then, is to employ the word in a sense which Oscar Wilde would scarcely have understood; for a counterpart to it one must go back to the ages of Christian art, when monks painted the walls of their churches in order to gain souls; when the workman was a sculptor because he had an idea to express and a prayer to say in his daily toil; when music sang the *Miserere* and the *Gloria* in the shadow of the Cross. Of course there were times when Newman succumbed to the temptation of a phrase. But the lapse is far less frequent with him than it was with the great churchman who most resembles him—St. Augustine.

Among the numerous forms which Newman's writing assumed there was, apparently, none in which his genius exercised itself so spontaneously as in the sermon. Here he was most closely in touch with his ministry, and here his words seemed most certain of their effect. Moreover, as in the case of Emerson, much speaking gave him an accomplished ear for the effective sentence and provided scope for the test of his insight into other souls. At first Newman felt insecure; it was only too true that the ideas he laid down in the homilies preached at Oxford led to other ideas which as yet he had not explored. Deeply conscious of a voyage upon which he was being led, he was often forced to grope where he should have seen. After his conversion this difficulty vanished, and to the day of his death he spoke as a man confident, calm, seeing things as they are. What could be more striking than the contrast between the style of the Oxford sermon on "Faith and Reason," and that on "The Second Spring"? Note an unusually eloquent sentence from the former: "He that fails nine times and succeeds the tenth, is a more honorable man than he who hides his talent in a napkin: and so, even though the feelings which prompt us to see God in all things, and to recognize supernatural works in matters of the world, mislead us at times, though they make us trust in evidence which we ought not to admit, and partially incur with justice the imputation of credulity, yet a Faith which generously apprehends Eternal Truth, though at times it degenerates into superstition, is far better than that cold, skeptical, critical tone of mind, which has no inward sense of an overruling, ever-present Providence, no desire to approach its God, but sits at home waiting for the fearful clearness of His visible coming, whom it might seek and find in due measure amid the twilight of the world." How evidently is the spirit here held in leash!

Place beside this a sentence chosen at random from that pæan of religious victory which Newman has called "The Second Spring": "And in that day of trial and desolation for England, when hearts were pierced

through and through with Mary's woe, at the Crucifixion of Thy Body mystical, was not every tear that
flowed, and every drop of blood that was shed, the seeds
of a future harvest, when they who sowed in sorrow
would reap in joy?" The difference in inspiration here
is quite evident. But from the clean sanctity of the
rhythm in his later sermons Newman went apparently
at will to the ornate eloquence of the lectures at Dublin
University. In this case, too, his heart was wholly in
his work, but that work trembled in the balance of Irish
opinion. And the passage in which he treats of the
amicable relations that had existed between England
and the Sister Isle during the ages of faith will compare,
for powerful appeal to an audience, with the best
pages of Bossuet. Newman's rhetoric was the product
of the successful and subtle blending of his own spirit
with the views of his hearers. This it is that makes
of oratory an art; and when the subjects upon which
it dwells are perennially latent in the human breast,
then it is immortal art.

It is in the "Sermons" that the lover of Newman will
continue to find his most profound reproductions of the
image of this world and the next. None the less, his
thought would scarcely have become complete, or his
style have reached its full strength, had it not been
for the treatises. "The Development of Christian
Doctrine" considered merely as literature provides an
interesting study; it was written during a period of
tumultuous transition, and the supreme inner struggle
of a giant mind is reflected in the sentences which
sometimes clench like fists and then open and are extended in conciliation. The idea of the book itself is
original, daringly so; and the difficulties to be en-

countered hedge it in like a circle of spears; but Newman disposes of them, *en passant*, it would seem, were it not for his candour and earnestness, and moves steadily ahead with the force of his intuition. There are illuminative sketches, given by the way; brilliant illustrations wherever these are needed; and the whole is welded into a goodly vessel by indefatigable devotion and religious zeal. The epilogue is worth noticing, for it is really a dedication placed at the end. The author, torn by parting with his Anglican friends, leaves them his work for guidance, and goes into the future with his eyes shining but cast down with the weight of tears. To many these lines have seemed Newman's greatest prose.

The careful study and calm, clear analysis of historical situations borne out in the essay on "Development" are present also in the "History of the Arians," the "Via Media," and the "Essays," but these works rarely show Newman at his best. In them the student is more at work than the apostle or the seer, and after all these are the more interesting. The "Grammar of Assent," however, is not only Newman's most subtle book, but, perhaps, after the "Apologia" his most brilliant in the matter of style. There are a few pages at the beginning unworthy of him—schoolmaster pages, justifiable only because the subject matter is too formal for inspired treatment. But what marvelous passages one meets with farther on, vivid with analogy and concrete presentation, glowing with the breath of a great cause! Chapters on the awakening of religious ideas, on the nature of intuition, and on the operation of conscience, have the slow, sure march of conviction moving about in the labyrinth of the human mind with perfect tranquillity. Or again, the treatment of natural and revealed religion walks the surface of the sea with ideal Christian faith, and the waters are calm; only the heart of the pilgrim beats with the melody of mingled humility and joy. The "Grammar of Assent" is not an easy book to exhaust; if one feels sufficiently interested in philosophy one can return often and discover new beauties, unnoticed before. It is an epic of the human soul, a subject perpetually interesting because of the darkness of its mystery.

Careful handling of a philosophic theme is what might reasonably be expected of a man so deeply religious as Newman, but the artistic alchemy with which he was gifted changed his thought into a variety of appealing forms. Ordinarily reserved with a quite Victorian dignity, he sometimes, when occasion demanded, indulged in laughter that was Gallic in its incisiveness. There are only a few traces of it in his earlier works, but when he set himself to the task of defending the rights and reputation of Catholics, his ability proved startling. What an amusing and yet effective exposé is his picture of the Russian who had discovered the iniquities of Blackstone and set his countrymen right! "Loss and Gain," too, intersperses the story of a convert with witty portraits, of which that of the bore is the most famous. Still, he was urbane here even if very serious; the same quality later appeared to advantage in the "Idea of a University," where his description of a gentleman gives one of the most delicately ironical interpretations of insincerity to be met with anywhere. These things, he knew, would appeal to his hearers much more strongly than anything he could say directly.

Occasionally, however, this note of laughter turned acrid and struck its man down.   Thus, in his attack on Achilli the ex-priest Newman minced no words, and though the blow he delivered cost him the humiliation of an unfair legal trial, it silenced Achilli forever.   Who can forget, if he has read them, the mordant paragraphs of the reply to Kingsley, with their terrible arraignment of the latter's method in controversy? Kingsley was overwhelmed, and when Newman finally concluded and bade his devil's advocate "fly into space," there was precious little of him remaining to take the advice.   In these pages words seem to burn, not with the morbid light of Byron's verse, but with the full radiance of indignation aroused to the defense of a holy cause. But this gift, which would have sufficed a Junius, was, as in Pascal, severely curbed. It was the same with Newman's other strictly literary powers.   In "Callista" he wrote a novel which lacks, indeed, the broad life of Dickens or Scott, but which is as finely wrought as anything by George Eliot.   In this study of the soul of a pagan girl who awakened to the appeal of Christianity and finally suffered in its defense, Newman read the spirit of a bygone age, the third century, as well as anyone had read it.   There are delightful, fascinating descriptive passages, of Juba's madness, for instance, and dramatic scenes like that of Callista's martyrdom, which are not to be found in everybody's novels.   Of course, there is no perfect technique and not enough human interest to satisfy the inebriate fiction-reader; Newman did not write for him.   Nevertheless it seems safe to affirm that if he had elected to transfer his powers to the art of story-telling, he could have equaled the other great Victorians in the baking of what Thackeray called "sweet-meats."

There is, however, one book which in its own time and ours has been accepted as the highest indication of Newman's literary genius. The "Apologia pro Vita Sua" not only gained a complete controversial victory over hostile public opinion, but has been confidently placed by great critics beside the "Confessions" of Saint Augustine. It captivates by the absolute candour of its mood and impresses by the vigor of its conviction. Written at white heat, out of the experiences of a life singularly devoted to a noble cause, the sentences lose everything that is not elemental and tumble after one another like jets of crystal water. There is in the book no trace of flippancy or insufficiency, but the impetus of a full philosophy, an intimate religion, looking upon life with eyes that have seen. It is Newman's genuine novel, the tale of a soul that has hitherto shrouded itself in reticence, and now dares to show the purity of its nakedness. The traces of pain which it cost the author to make the revelation are evident; but he does not end until he has found the note of love and paid a gentle lyric tribute to the friendship that had shadowed his loneliness—that of Father Ambrose St. John.

Nevertheless, though the book is a personal record, it is remarkable to note how little Newman really says of himself; Jean Jacques would have narrated more private business in one chapter. What he is discussing are his personal beliefs, which he felt were objective realities that in some marvelous way had been vouch-safed him. Newman is frequently lost in the midst of Keble, Froude, Pusey, and others, but what is always kept in the foreground is the Faith. That alone mat-

tered, and unless the reader understands this fact,
Newman's clearest book is likely to remain the most obscure. He narrated the process of his conversion, the
long duration of his doubts, his desperate effort to per-
severe in the face of strengthening conviction; and
while he was quite individualistic in all these matters,
what he was defending was the ministry of the Truth
from the insinuation of dishonesty. That Truth would
brook no taint, it would countenance no moral heckling; and to save it he took the last recourse of the
apostle and became a witness, a martyr. In the Latin
title there is the final, completing link with the original
testimony to the Faith.

Newman's prose is at its best in the "Apologia,"
but it is good everywhere. He could and did write badly,
but the bulk of his work is amazingly well done. Into
almost all of it he threw the whole of his conviction and,
having thought out a purpose, carried it resolutely
through to the end. A master of the high art of refutation, which not only defeats existing objections but
visualizes and meets others before they are aware of
existence, makes his work bristle with barricades over
which he sweeps with enthusiasm to the goal ahead.
Newman felt the rhythm of speech as not even Ruskin
perceived it, and his English is the language of melody
that winds its coils about a theme as do Bach's notes
in a fugue. He attuned the medium of sound not only
to his own ear but to that of his auditor, and finally
enunciated what seems the declaration of a great style:

"And since the thoughts and reasonings of an author
have, as I have said, personal character, no wonder
that his style is not only the image of his subject but

of his mind. That pomp of language, that full and tuneful diction, that felicitousness in the choice and exquisiteness in the collocation of words, which to prosaic writers seem artificial, is nothing else but the mere habit and way of a lofty intellect . . . the elocution of a great intellect is great. His language expresses, not only his great thoughts, but also his great self. Certainly he might use fewer words than he uses; but he fertilizes his simplest ideas, and germinates into a multitude of details, and prolongs the march of his sentences, and sweeps round to the full diapason of his harmony as if rejoicing in his own vigor and richness of resource."

It remains necessary to say a word for the poetry which Newman created out of the leisure of his genius. Perfectly spontaneous, it has none of the artful diction, the compressed sensism, of modern' verse. The lyrics of his earlier life, among which "Lead, Kindly Light" is the most popular, if not the best, are very simple expressions of simple moods, and in neither the thought nor the expression is there any of that haunting musical paradox which is the life of Francis Thompson. They either sing their way to the heart or fail utterly. "The Dream of Gerontius," however, is different, for there underlies this poem a powerfully dramatic conception. As the dying soul quits the earth and passes from judgment to the waters of purgatory, it is surrounded by the final life of eternity—by the rapture of the angels and their Maker, by the malice of the demons and the damned.

"It floods me like the deep and solemn sound
Of many waters,"

cries the soul of its guardian, at the same time describing the quality of this poem. The songs of the Angelicals, severe in their classic restraint and yet realistically fervent, are equal to any of the choral odes in Sophocles. "The Dream of Gerontius" is the only modern poem that could have been sung in its entirety under the chaste, aspiring arches of mediæval Bourges.

Much might be said of other special qualities in Newman's genius: of his remarkable method of argumentation, for instance, which hemmed in an opponent on all sides with almost the cruel science of a German general at Sedan, left no avenue of escape, and then fell upon him and beat him flat to the ground. Again, Newman the letter-writer is an interesting figure, not only in the public epistles to the Duke of Norfolk, to Pusey, or to Bishop Ullathorne, but in that vast private correspondence which he conducted with infinite care, especially after his conversion and during the long years of his Catholic repudiation, for the solace of souls, for the conversion of friends, or merely out of the goodness of his heart. The private letters reveal Newman's character as no other documents do: they show his reticence, his melancholy, his purity, his joy, his pain at the criticism and alienation of friends. Here he was intensely human and most lovable; the service which Wilfrid Ward rendered English literature by publishing them without reserve is one that can never be too highly appreciated. All of these matters, however, are subjects for special study and will appeal to those who are fascinated by the manifold genius of a great Christian.

Newman's art is, then, a large and varied gift which he lent unstintingly to the demands of an apostolic life. Intensely personal, allied to the romantics by his trust in instinct and emotion rather than in mere caustic ratiocination, he is a modern whose soul is in tune with the soul of mediæval aspiration. There was, however, nothing unbalanced in him, nothing simply picturesque and quite untrue; he had the center of the Great Tradition as well as its trappings. Examining life as it appeared in the arena of a large and cautious mind, he avoided sacrificing harmony to exuberance, without losing the vitality that alone makes art to endure as long as the human soul. Despite the fact that Newman was something of a Hamlet, one is struck by the absence of the static within his composition, by the ease with which he handled his numerous weapons and brought them into the service of his cause. Visualizing Christianity as a living institution which had grown into a great tree as the parable of the mustard seed had foretold, he studied the future in the light of the past, and drew from both the subtle strains of his art. The Christian Ages were for him not dark but splendid, and he listened to the mingled strains of the "Dies Irae" and the "Tantum Ergo" coming from the temples where saints and kings and people worshipped, until his tongue had learned the rhythm of the solacing music that sings the love and fear of God while it muses bravely on the eternal mystery of Man.

BOOK NOTE

The works of Newman are published in a uniform edition by Longmans, Green and Company. There are special editions of some, particularly the "Apologia" and "The Dream of Gerontius." The best single work covering the entire period of Newman's activities is still "La Renaissance Catholique en Angleterre," by

Paul Thureau-Dangin (3 vols.) of which there is now an English translation in two volumes. "The Life of Newman," by Wilfrid Ward, is the best and most complete biography and should be supplemented by a reading of the same author's "Last Lectures." Other biographies are by R. H. Hutton, W. Meynell, William Barry, and S. J. Fletcher. A good French view may be obtained from the various treatises by Henri Bremond—"The Mystery of Newman"; "Newman. Le Développement du Dogme Chrétien"; "Newman. La Vie Chrétienne." See also "The Oxford Movement," by Dean Church; "The Anglican Career of Cardinal Newman," by Abbott; "Letters and Correspondence of Cardinal Newman during His Life in the English Church," edited by Anne Mozley (2 vols.); "A Memoir of Hurrell Froude," by L. I. Guiney; "The Life of Cardinal Manning," by Shane Leslie; "Memoirs," by Mark Pattison; "Studies in Poetry and Philosophy," by J. C. Shairp; "Phases of Thought and Criticism," by Brother Azarias; "The Drift of Romanticism," by Paul E. More; "Obiter Dicta," by A. Birrell; and "Four Studies in Literature," by Prof. Gates. The periodical literature on Newman is vast. One may note with profit, "J. H. Newman and Renan," by William Barry (*Living Age,* vol. 214:347); "Newman," by T. J. Gerard (*Catholic World,* vol. 95:61); and "Recollections of Newman," by Aubrey De Vere (*19th Century,* vol. 40:395). See in a general way the Catholic Encyclopedia, the "Cambridge History of English Literature," and Chesterton's "Victorian Age."

CHAPTER SIX

LEADERS AT OXFORD AND CAPTAINS OF THE CHURCH

"Either the Catholic religion is verily the coming of the unseen world into this, or there is nothing positive, nothing dogmatic, nothing real in any of our notions as to whence we come and whither we go." NEWMAN.

THE Oxford Movement and the vigorous Catholic revival that surrounded it produced many strong, interesting men who challenged the attention of England with a success that often made the stolid, conservative citizen gasp. Most of them had groped their way to Rome from the outposts of Anglicanism, and bore not a few scars as memorials to that difficult pilgrimage. Some were bluff and hale; as intellectual leaders they lived in the din of controversy, and their writings do not as a rule possess the spirit of reflectiveness, the poise of imagination, which alone make art. Certain of their books are good literature, but most of them are simply good theology. In considering their lives from the literary point of view, as we must here, it should be remembered that they wrote from the battle-ground where their achievements were stirring and fruitful; that another kind of history chronicles the nobility of their sacrifices and the worth of their campaigning. Anyhow, they were soldiers for a Cause, with a brusque distrust for laudation that concerned them personally.

In the university circle that was drawn round Newman there moved a number of gifted men who either
influenced him or were developed by his teaching. Some
of these felt to the fullest extent the beauty of Catholic
tradition, which divides the world like a sword but heals
the wound with the loving touch of Christ; others were
hard, thoughtful, farsighted men who saw, as their
great leader did, the intellectual difficulties with which
men around them were beset, and who humbly gave their
lives to the solution of a great mystery. But the
Church was larger than Oxford; and when the rift in
English public opinion had grown wide enough to permit the action of a Catholic hierarchy, it must have
been providential that so many enthusiastic, powerful
leaders were ready to move towards a position where
the Church could breathe the air of freedom, and direct
the manifold enterprises of her apostolic mission. That
such men were concerned with literature is a fact;
it remains to view the result and to see what part they
contributed to the enormous summary in which are written all the fancies, aspirations, moods, and vistas of
man.

With the exception of Hurrell Froude, that zealous
though hesitant student of the Christian past, whose
"Remains" represent him inadequately in literature,
no one influenced so strongly the development of Newman and his friends as John Keble. Born four years
before Napoleon the First, and dying four years previous to the fall of Napoleon the last, Keble's private
life seemed to possess all the serenity which his environment lacked. Although a fellow of Oriel College, and
at one time professor of poetry at Oxford, he was
consistently the country vicar of mid-Victorian times.

A book of poems entitled "The Christian Year," which he published in 1827, made Keble as famous as he remained humble. These simple songs, half-ballad, half-hymn, delighted a large English public with their sincere, fresh, religious mood, the intensity of their attachment to the quiet country home, and their rich, fervent meditativeness. Keble felt Christianity as life, when so many about him thought it merely convention; and the delicate reserve with which he read the divine symbolism of nature was at once simple and intangible. He would have been the last to claim for his verses classic form or romantic passion; he wrote always with a kindly friend in mind:

> "No fading frail memorial give
>   To soothe his soul when thou art gone,
>   But wreaths of hope for aye to live
>   And thoughts of good together done."

Despite the blemishes in the book—false analogies, commonplaceness of thought and expression—the poetry was genuine and made of its author a spiritual leader whose power and sincerity were recognized by Newman. Gifted with a beauty of character that made unforgettable friendships, he lacked the stern spirit of the logician; and with the possible exception of a few lectures on poetry, nothing he wrote after "The Christian Year" has made a lasting impression. Keble began the Oxford Movement by preaching the sermon on "National Apostasy," but he was too conservative to follow in the steps of Newman. Though religion meant everything to him, he was quite content with its sentiment and could never grasp the vital significance

of dogma. To the end he remained steadfast in his allegiance to those beliefs which had cast about his youth
the radiance of joy, and which may have breathed
into his poetic spirit something of immortality.

Of Keble's lifelong associate in religious endeavor,
Edward Pusey (1800-1882), it must be predicted that
little will eventually remain of all his learned preaching and exhaustive polemics excepting the name which
a wittier person gave to his system of theology—
Puseyism. A sincerely spiritual man, no one ever felt
more strongly the pressure of English tradition: it
seemed to him most deplorable that the Anglican communion should not be considered a perfectly respectable descendant of the Apostolic Church. As a protest
against the secularizing of the Establishment, he joined
the Oxford Movement at the hour when his aid was
most needed, and had a share in the writing of the
"Tracts for the Times." Later, when Newman had
gone over to Rome, Pusey spent his efforts trying to
effect a compromise with the Holy See. The first
"Eirenicon" was written to emphasize certain matters
of dogma which its author did not see his way clear to
accept; this was followed by others when he began to
despair of success in his dealings with Rome, and Newman finally replied in the tender though firm "Letter to
Pusey." The liberal elements in Anglicanism also regarded Pusey with disfavor, and his whole life may be
construed as a fruitless attempt to fortify a religious
position that was untenable. Nevertheless, he was a
man whose religious enthusiasms never waned, and
whose extravagant conservatism was saved from folly
by its boundless charity.

Although Keble and Pusey stood fast in their re-

sistance to Rome, other notable Oxford men went with
Newman along the stony road of conversion. One of
the most interesting of these is the ebullient William
George Ward. Born in 1812, he remained mentally
belligerent to the day of his death in 1882. At Oxford
Ward came under the spell of Newman, but, being
somewhat hastier in drawing conclusions than was his
illustrious master, succeeded in being publicly condemned by the University Convocation, and in joining
the Church on August 13, 1845. Later he taught
theology at St. Edmund's with great success, although
the fact that he was a layman proved an eyesore to
many older churchmen. Cardinal Wiseman, always
his benefactor, finally induced him to assume the editorship of the *Dublin Review*.

Ward had in him many great qualities both of heart
and mind: the master of an almost grotesque sense of
humour, he lived in the realm of metaphysical and theological speculation with a totality and partisanship
rarely matched. While wielding a strong personal influence that relied for effectiveness on candour and
depth of thought, an influence felt and acknowledged
by Mill and Newman alike, the written word seemed to
rob him of his individuality. "The Ideal of a Christian
Church," "The Philosophy of Theism," and his other
books have little in them that is attractive for us now.
But the man who shook Newman before his break with
the Anglicans, who directed the *Dublin Review* so ably
and so long, who undertook a rigorous defense of the
Papacy in the face of English thought, and who
brought the masters of the "Experience" philosophy
to recede from more than one position, is a memorable
and picturesque figure. Essentially he was a man of

warm character and powerful logic, who was entirely
redeemed from commonplaceness by the exuberance of
his interest in religion and the heartiness of his laughter.   In a good many ways he was the Doctor Johnson of the Catholic revival—a man of burly form,
brusque language, fixity of conviction, and fundamental
melancholy.   To his last day he was a fighter, though
he loved best the charity of peace; and from the first
he was a friend, no matter how strenuous the controversy or how definite the disagreement.

As Ward threw all his fervent energy into the examination of the metaphysical aspects of religion, so a
beloved priest and friend of Newman, Father Frederick
William Faber, gave his strength to the creation of
devotional literature.   The beauty of Catholic practice
had led him to scrutinize his early religious beliefs,
and of that beauty he never grew tired of writing.
Born in 1814, Faber entered Balliol College in due
time, and having taken orders became rector at Elton.
The spell of Newman drew him irresistibly to the
Church, however, and his conversion took place in
1845.   After a short stay in Birmingham he established
the Brompton Oratory in London, proved indefatigable in the performance of his religious duties, and
gained great fame as a devotional writer.   He died in
1863.   Father Faber's temperament was naturally ardent, but his lovable disposition is best testified to, perhaps, by the response of his Anglican congregation at
Elton to his announcement of dissatisfaction with the
doctrine he was preaching.   They begged him to preach
any doctrine he pleased, but to remain with them.

Faber has scarce an equal in English as a writer of
devotional books.   Such volumes as "At the Foot of

the Cross" combine some of the fervour of St. Teresa
with the sweetness of St. Francis. Veuillot described
their power by saying, "He has strange tweezers for
getting at the finest and most hidden fibers under the
skin which he removes so dexterously." Of his poeti-
cal writings, influenced so deeply by an intimate understanding of the beautiful natural surroundings in
which he had been reared, it is enough to say that some
are like Wordsworth at his best, others like Wordsworth at his worst, but all of them like Wordsworth.
How well the following stanza presents the enchantment of a winter night at Oxford:

"The winter night, when, as a welcome boon,
Down the giant stems the stealthy beams may glide,
And stray sheep lie sleeping in the moon
With their own fairy shadows at their side;
While through the frosty night air every tower
In Abingdon and Oxford tolls the hour."

The current of Catholicism at Oxford was swollen
by the addition of many other men, whose learning, in-
tegrity, and piety have influenced the soul of England
more than we can tell, but whose literary talents were
comparatively small. The flood of writing which
swirls round this fountain of vigorous spiritual energy
contains much that is valuable temporarily, much that
slakes the quest about it, but which dries up as the
years move and soil is drenched and new genius finds
new sources of inspiration. Still, it cannot be out of
place to recall in passing the name of T. W. Allies, tireless journalist and controversalist, whose "Life's Decision" is still a readable book; Father Dalgairns, the

intimate friend of Newman; Lady Herbert, a graceful
and intimate writer; and of others not so closely associated with Oxford, though their spirits followed its
message, Kegan Paul, for instance, and Father Martineau, whose sermons moved the hearts of numerous
people who had grown indifferent to preaching and are,
in printed form, rarely beautiful testimonials to a
natural eloquence. Nor does the lover of this revival
forget those toilers whose names and books are forgotten, who will soon have fallen into the general oblivion with the people they served, but who are stalwart,
surely, in the sight of Him they loved.

II

Among the captains of the Church in modern England, especially among those who had gifts for letters
and used them, the plain though enigmatic figure of
Henry Edward, Cardinal Manning is probably the
most arresting. For years he watched over the religious life of London with resolute and far-seeing eyes;
his way into the Church seems somehow more acrid or
worldly than Newman's; and no modern Englishman
has stood so close to the Papal throne or been so intimately associated with sweeping ecclesiastical reforms. But, though he moved constantly among men,
preaching, organizing, attending philosophic discussions, and even settling strikes, no one in his age lived
more absolutely alone: as Francis Thompson puts it so
effectively:

> "Anchorite, who didst dwell
> With all the world for cell. . . ."

The shadow cast over the memory of Manning by the malicious biography of Purcell has already been lifted somewhat, and now that the Life by Shane Leslie has appeared, it will undoubtedly be entirely dispelled. He was born in 1808, the son of an influential financier, entered Oxford in due time, and later accepted a position in the Colonial Office. The call to the sacred ministry proved insistent, however, and upon his election to a fellowship in Merton College Manning took orders, married, and accepted a curacy. When his wife died, he was appointed archdeacon of Chicester, where he remained until his conversion in 1851. Ordained almost immediately, he studied in Rome for a time, and then returned to London, where he established the Congregation of the Oblates of St. Charles. A vigorous zeal for missionary organization brought ecclesiastical recognition; and upon the death of Wiseman, Manning became the Archbishop of Westminster; later, in 1875, he was made cardinal. At his death in 1892, there was an expression of grief rarely equalled for universality; the funeral was attended by people of all classes, for, while his relations with the leaders of Britain had been close, the Cardinal's heart bled for the poor.

His was the character of the reformer, martial, dominant, at times overbearing. If Newman was too sensitive, Manning was almost brutal. There was something in him of that stern quality of Alphonsus Ligouri, which made the great Redemptorist saint command a transgressing cleric to step on a crucifix, "for he had already done so in spirit." England was a field that needed plowing badly, and Manning chafed at everything that resembled cautious restraint, was for getting to work on the hour. The saving fact is that

he actually mastered the appalling: reorganization of
the clergy, rescue work among the poor, revivified
Catholic education, and outspoken public action were
successfully undertaken. As the "Workingmen's
Cardinal" he directed public attention to industrial
evils, and was Leo XIII's chief adviser for the famous
encyclical, "On the Condition of Labour." It must be
admitted, however, that his enthusiasm was often im-
prudent; the attitude he took on Infallibility and on
the Temporal Power, his unfriendly relations with religious orders, were assuredly not wise. Manning was
no intellectual Napoleon, though he might well have
congratulated himself occasionally on playing the Iron
Duke.

Some of this rigorous quality of efficiency, this reformer's mood, is always to be found in his writing and
despoils it of that candour of thought and expression,
that chaste whiteness of style, which great books must
have. Certain of his treatises, "The Eternal Priesthood," and "The Temporal Mission of the Holy
Ghost," for instance, may continue to interest theologians, but the aridity of their inspiration will grow
more apparent as time advances. If Manning is known
to the future as a writer, it will surely be for his private journals. They are the records of a searching
and powerful self-analysis, and the following extract
may serve to indicate their character and, also, to give
some insight into the soul of Manning:

"When I look down upon London from this garden
and know that there are before me nearly 3,000,000 of
men of whom 200,000 are nominally in the Faith and
Grace of the Church, that 1,500,000 never set foot in

any place of even fragmentary Christian worship, that hundreds of thousands are living and dying without baptism, in all the sins of the flesh and spirit, in all that Nineveh and the Cities of the Plain and Imperial Rome ever committed, that it is the Capital of the most anti-Christian Power of the nominally Christian world, and the head of its anti-Christian spirit . . . I confess I feel that we are walking on the waters and that nothing but the word and presence of Jesus makes this great calm. I feel sure that the mission for London is to preach the Love of God and the Love of Jesus, and that in the spirit and the voice of love. They will listen to no denunciations and no controversy. They will only stone us before they understand us." [1]

The lovable, influential Cardinal who preceded Manning is still remembered and revered for the fine *humanness* of his character. In thinking of Wiseman one feels the keen truth of Chesterton's epigram: "The two persons that a healthy man hates most between heaven and hell are a man who is dignified and a woman who is not." The secret of his amazing success in the rebuilding of the Catholic Church in England, was perhaps, his ability to show that a bishop might be a man. The time was crowded with stirring religious events: the conversion of the Oxford leaders, the restoration of Catholic hierarchy, the appearance, after many years of repression, of the Catholic man in public life. Wiseman, going everywhere, discussing the most diverse questions, gained the ears of a public which had hitherto regarded "Papists" as preposterous wretches ostracizing themselves for an absurd delusion. The many-sidedness and the cosmopolitan background of

[1] *Dublin Review*, Jan., 1920. Vol. 166.

his personality were exactly what was needed for the work in hand. Born in 1802 of an English family residing in Seville, and having spent his early years in Ireland, Wiseman was educated in England and in Rome, became rector of the English College in the Papal city, acquired fame for linguistic ability, and made friends of Popes and all the noteworthy personages of Europe. His tact was as astonishing as his energy, and his Cardinalate was something like a reign. Though infirm in his old age and accordingly unable to cope with the nuances of ecclesiastical policy, he was universally venerated until his death in 1865.

Wiseman's eloquence, though it served the cause well on numerous occasions, lacked the searching analysis of eternal truths and the delicately attuned expression that made of Newman the immortal preacher. Nor do the treatises he wrote on important questions seem vital enough to hold their own in the maze of books. "Recollections of the Last Four Popes," however, is charmingly written reminiscence, and supplies an English view of the Vatican during some historic and stormy years. Still, it is as the author of "Fabiola" that Wiseman will live, if at all, in letters. Catholics generally have loved the exquisite piety and charming characterization of this tale of the catacombs, and may be pardoned for having overlooked its somewhat slipshod construction and the tinge of sentimentalism that spoils its art. After all, no one has done a better book on the earlier Christian story, and probably no one ever will.

Though there.are other Cardinals who, like Herbert Vaughan, did good work for English letters, we shall pass them by and make a brief mention of a most in-

teresting man, Archbishop Ullathorne (1806-1889).
This sturdy assistant of Wiseman and defender of Newman has told the story of his life better than any one
else could. In addition to being a member of the hierarchy, he was a Benedictine and championed his order
bravely. As the author of "The Endowments of Man"
Ullathorne deserves some attention as a writer in philosophy, and his letters reveal a mastery of that difficult form of composition. His "Autobiography," however, is his masterpiece and a genuinely original and
fascinating book. It is one of the delightful few among
life-stories which are personal without being egotistical;
it has also the advantage of incident. The Archbishop
had led a roaming, lusty life, that took him first to sea
and later to the saving of souls. One doubts that Defoe could have told the story of Ullathorne's missionary
experiences among the convicts in Australia with more
gusto or better disposition of detail. Shane Leslie declares that he has always preferred the Autobiography
to "Robinson Crusoe," and the comparison is not at all
bold. Whereas it is the glory of Defoe to have given
fiction the appearance of sober fact, the Archbishop
may be said to have clothed reality with the graces of
entrancing narrative. He was very decidedly English, loving the sea, his plain fellowmen, and a round
tale as every good man ought to love such things. The
religious background of his life is, of course, duly
stressed, but the apostolic character of the writer involved none of the contemplativeness, the inner intellectual struggle, of such a genius as Newman. Instead,
the saving of souls is attempted with ardour on board
French whalers, in Chili, New South Wales, England,
Ireland, and France, in prison and on the episcopal

throne.   Quite evidently, the noble Archbishop, who
was as kind-hearted as he was zealous, took great pleasure in the writing, although the book was not intended
for publication, but merely for the satisfaction of a
few friends.   What frank courage, what keen relish
for a spiritualized democracy it reveals!   Here is a
tonic for tired souls.

In general, when one thinks of the genius, the energy,
and the fervour which the leaders of England's new-
born Catholicism brought to the performance of their
extremely difficult tasks, when one remembers the temper of that Britain whose deep-rooted contempt for
Rome was suddenly confronted with Rome's accredited
representatives, one cannot help believing humbly that
the Spirit of God was active in them as it was in the
first Apostles.   It is not strange that so much of their
writing was mediocre; the wonder is that they found
time to write at all.   Art is necessarily self-centered,
comparatively uninterested in the struggle of surrounding souls.   And yet the journals of the ubiquitous Manning, the life-story of Ullathorne, who was as active in
missionary labours as a Jesuit martyr, and the "Fabiola" of Wiseman, written almost while waiting for
trains, are books that have given to English literature
new points of view, and to Catholics a record of glory
which they can never cherish too deeply.   While these
great men laid safe and solid foundations of ecclesiastical polity, they did not forget one of the oldest and
loveliest concerns of the Church, devotion to art.

The most noteworthy effect produced by the movements which we have tried to chronicle as succinctly as
possible was to bring the Catholic Spirit forward into
the English world.   That light which had taken refuge

in chapels, in the houses of brave men who suffered bitterly for their fidelity, and in a few stray, poverty-stricken religious houses, stood over the market place again in the sign of a flaming cross. Peter was no longer rockbound, and the men who had thought him imprisoned discovered his officers on inexplicable parole, gaining victories where defeat seemed foredoomed, smiling where tears were in the nature of things. The literary achievements of the Church's representatives conformed with the total unexpectedness of their careers. Who would have thought it possible that an Archbishop could write like a gifted journalist, or that a learned Hebrew scholar should take time to compose the moving story of the catacombs? Or, to return for a moment to the converts of Oxford, would any prophet, taking his stand at the opening of the nineteenth century, have been rash enough to predict that within seventy-five years the placid Horatian University should have come earnestly to stand for its ancient motto, and to send forth its most gifted scholars to preach the buried beliefs of Catholicism to a listening world?

Catholics do not always realize the splendour of the revolution. We find it easier to understand the elusive soul of Newman, writing itself down in matchless prose, and gazing enraptured into star-dim distances, the rhythm of whose shadowy going he seems to have heard. It is simpler to follow the backward gaze of Kenelm Digby, lost on the routes of Christian chivalry, forgetful of everything but the silent spires of a broken cathedral. After all these men seem more Catholic, as they assuredly are more literary; but the men who ventured into the streets wore manly armour, and their song was a valiant marching hymn.

BOOK NOTE

Those who wish to study the men treated of in this chapter should begin with the works mentioned, although certain others like Manning's "Religio Viatoris" and Pusey's translation of St. Augustine's "Confessions" may in the end prove more interesting. Consult the following biographies: of Manning, those by Shane Leslie, E. S. Purcell, Dom Gasquet, Wilfrid Meynell, and John Oldcastle; of Wiseman, those by Wilfrid Ward and Lord Houghton ("Monographs"); of William G. Ward, that by Wilfrid Ward; of Faber, that by J. E. Bowden; of Keble, that by Mr. Justice Coleridge; of Pusey, that by Liddon; of Father Martineau, that by Maisie Ward. Valuable works that treat of the entire period are "La Renaissance Catholique en Angleterre," by Paul Thureau-Dangin; "Fifty Years," by Percy Fitzgerald; and "The Oxford Movement," by Dean Church. See also, "Letters of Archbishop Ullathorne," edited by A. T. Drane; "Mid-Victorians," by Lytton Strachey; "Pusey," by G. W. E. Russell; "Father Faber," by W. Hall-Patch; "Gladstone," by John Morley; "Studies in Contemporary Biography," by James Bryce; "Memories," by Kegan Paul; "Studies in Poetry and Philosophy," by Shairp. Of interest are the various articles in the Encyclopædia Britannica, the Catholic Encyclopedia. and the "Cambridge History of English Literature."

CHAPTER SEVEN

"The best poetry is quite close to us."

NOVALIS.

FOR all the chattering of the anthologist and the improved sale of recent verse, poetry is clearly not popular. It is no longer common property; there are no troubadours in our village streets and no drinking songs in our empty taverns. Democracy's persistent attitude towards poetry is that of refusal to look at the stars without a telescope; it has concluded that the bards are seeing things which do not exist, that they are loving the moon for a goddess when she is only a corpse. Free verse cannot be said to have helped matters much. The value of such experiments is not here denied, but their recent modishness was probably due to the fact that nobody except the illuminati mistook them for poetry. Democratic literary judgment may in this instance have been right, although its general attitude towards lyric expression has been hopelessly wrong. There is more than a difference in form between Shakespeare and Sassoon; there is a gulf between their ways of looking at the world. It is because the older poets were near enough to things to be neighbors that they wrote kindly, in rhythms that marched and sang. Their measure of earth, in so far as they used one, was

104

genially variant; they judged by the homely but living standard of the soul's desire. A modern man measures things by what they are worth, and therefore by a rigidly conventional standard, the principles and limits of which have been fixed by society. It may be that the modern versifier is free because he, too, is mathematical; that he no longer obeys metrical law because he has adopted the metric system. Perhaps, unwilling to be bound by cadences whose origins are mysteriously prehistoric, he has sworn allegiance to lines.

All this is not facetious but symbolic; the new intellectual poet has learned too many statistics ever to be taken for a fool even by a king. He has called so many things illusions that he has forgotten even the spirit of the *Ludus*. It is not altogether his fault. The people who to-day scorn all mention of the poets are descended from a people who in past ages filled the streets with song; the people who scoff at poetry as "beyond" them are really beyond the poets. They have locked their heavy doors to the sun; with a sudden taste for exclusiveness, they have shut out the skylark and the sky. Poetry, the simplest, most natural of things, is the vision-heritage of the simple. A girl whispering to a doll is a poet because she has given reality to an image of the real; a boy whose wooden sword is the blade of Robert Lee has made, with a tremendous gesture, a drama of life and death. In later life this creative impulse weakens, as Wordsworth once took the trouble to suggest. An elderly gentleman cannot by any supreme magic transmute a fellow mortal into Robin Hood; the best he can do is to reverse the process. It is the opinion of every lover that an angel has deigned to be worshipped by him; and the aging Dante, on his part, made an angel of her whom he had adored. This means very simply that the grown poet, the master of words, must have rhyme and reason. But there will be in his work, if he is uncramped by an industrial education, some of the old natural movements of the human body: his song will march or leap, it will dance or stumble.

The bard achieved his towering renown in the past not because he was a freak of nature but because he was popular. He merely did the plain, necessary task of song a little better than other people. Then as now poets were born and their enemies were unmade, but there is a blight on our time. Now as ever the man who derides verse is an ungrateful child: he scorns his first parents in paradise because he is doomed to wear clothes; he ignores the moon because he is a slave to her image in his pocket. And the difference between what a man can put into his pocket and what he can put into his head is always the difference between beauty and material value; that is, between what will supply a merely external need and what, without ceasing its work in the world, will become part of the soul. For there exists an ancient and recently endorsed theory that man has a soul, that he is not merely the child of an ape, but verily the child of God. And the wildest hypothesis of the scientific intellect cannot conceive of God's being pleased with stocks and bonds or piles of metal that were the ashes of His morning fire; but the simplest mind will be content with thinking Him happy in the lovely faces of His sons.

The theme of this sketch, however, is not verse in general but Catholic verse in particular. Admittedly nobody could be more indifferent to poetry than the

average English-speaking Catholic; but from what has
been said it may reasonably be inferred that the Catholic poet has an advantage in being truly a child. He
has behind him the ancestry of image-makers, and a
radiant Mother whose care it has been to make of nature a divine plaything. She has fed the soul with
Bread and Wine; she has made a mystic comedy of the
bitter tragedy of the Cross. Having begun with seven
sacraments, each of them a towering symbol, she ends
with illuminating all things, living and dead, with
grace. With a great and abiding faith she has written
the baffling difficulties of her creed into the simplest
of flowers: the rose is mystical and the clover which
grows by the wayside is a picture of One whom none
can bear to see. If sometimes her images are fantastic, it is because her adventure, for high and unut-
terable stakes, is real enough to be infinitely more
strange than fiction. Not satisfied with humanizing
nature, she has mothered it. The poet who is a child
of Christendom must first of all, then, be a child.
He must make believe in the awful future; he must
realize that he is still held in arms. Not always a
hymn-writer, he knows that there is nothing on earth,
even among things which had better be forgotten,
whose image cannot be found in a cathedral. But he
knows that Satan belongs in hell and not in a palace;
he avows that the villain must not be defended with a
sword. Remember, there is in his soul the bliss of
obedience; you will find him in the "nurseries of
heaven."

It was natural, then, that the revival of the Catholic
spirit in England should have borne goodly fruit in
verse, although the break in tradition could not easily

be healed. Something has already been suggested concerning the writers who made occasional poems—men like Newman and Faber for whom verse was only an aside, like a dream to a soldier. Now we shall greet those for whom poetry was the business of life. There are many, but at first there come three men whose art is not supreme, but who were none the less markedly children and children of the Church. Aubrey de Vere, constant and calm, found his reflective song in well-trimmed gardens; Gerard Hopkins, strangely solitary, was driven by fear to shut out the world from his eyes, but when he opened them he beheld earth shimmering with lucent rainbows; and Coventry Patmore, greatest among them, perhaps, went from the love that is a sacrament to the Love that is beyond vision. But in their separate ways they were brothers.

At first sight it would seem absurd to say that the simplicity of nature had any noteworthy relation to Coventry Patmore, for he was a quite amazing egoist. None of the other Victorians, not even Carlyle, was so frankly a cosmos unto himself. Still, when "The Angel in the House" appeared in 1858, the world greeted a poem which treated the most banal of subjects in the most commonplace of meters. That subject was domestic happiness, and that meter the rhymed octosyllabic quatrain. Anthony Trollope, or Archibald Marshall in our day, might have used the incidents in the story; a widower, with three goodly and pious daughters, beholds a young poet fall in love with all of them at first and finally with one; there is a pretty wedding and a subsequent serene family life. Patmore never completed the poem, but what was done sinks gently back into the languid posture of a decorous age.

The immense popularity of the work, similar to that which attended Keble's "Christian Year," was, however, the result of the high and novel light with which the poet illuminated his theme.

Patmore had boldly made himself the poet of love. In his understanding of the influence exerted by a pure passion he is extraordinarily discriminating; the subtlety with which he analyzes, step by step, the attraction which two young people come to have for each other is matched only in the ancient mediæval romances. But in addition to these matters of psychology, he possessed the key to the religion of sex. In the consecration of virginity to its fellow and in the alternating assertion and surrender of each ego, he saw the liturgy of a sacrament. Virtue blending with virtue in a kind of ethereal sacrifice gains steadily in loftiness; and love which began in the garden achieves, by its mystical crucifixion, a resurrection unto the stars. Do the modern poets say of marriage that it is the ice into which passion finally freezes, the congealing of ecstasy into something which a humdrum bourgeois can keep in his kitchen? It is because they have made of love a convention, says Patmore, and conventions sit fast, but the high and constant purity of matrimony is vivified by the splendid variety of the soul. And thus the imagination of the poet, visioning the things that are hidden in the nature of man, defends the noblest and oldest of human institutions with ultimate originality.

This idea, which is Patmore's distinct contribution to literature, developed naturally with his character. Born in 1846 of an eccentric father, he took a youthful interest in science which he seems to have pursued for a while with the intensity of a boyish Edison. During this time he prided himself upon being an agnostic; but strong instincts, which in Patmore's case always overtopped the slower methods of reason, led him safely to religion and to love. In his mind the two were closely interwoven, and when he came to feel that he could write, poetry made the third among his trinity of guiding stars. His was an ardent, impetuous temperament, expressing itself only when the uniform glow with which it was suffused sought, spontaneously, a discharge in words. Landor, Tennyson, and Rossetti, who befriended his early years, saw Patmore's genius but were quite incapable of forming it. "The Angel in the House" was the criterion of its author's career: he would stand in the midst of men, but he would know how to be alone.

Gradually his insight deepened. Just as he had gone swiftly from science to faith, so now he advanced to the science of faith. During many years his mystical sympathy with Catholic doctrine had drawn him towards the Church, but the quiet creed of his first wife held him in restraint. Some time after her death Patmore journeyed to Rome and engaged in meditative study of religious life. For a while he found it impossible to make a submission, but suddenly, in the middle of the night, certainty flooded his soul, and with characteristic impetuosity he hastened at once to a Jesuit house and craved admission to the Church. From that day on, not the slightest shadow of religious doubt fell across his mind. The engrossing subject of the identity of love and religion was taken up with even greater conviction as he found that Catholic mystics had long proclaimed his doctrine. In the end he became the seer, beholding the mystery of God's nature and His love in the analogy of human marriage and in the never-ending interlacing of force and matter which constitutes the world. Treading these high realms of vision, he was serenely conscious of the value of his mission, and though he was buried in the habit of St. Francis, he cannot conceivably be imagined to have welcomed "Brother Ass."

Indeed, the stalwart egoism with which Patmore proclaimed his intuitions was the natural complement of his thought. Thoroughly honest in his enraptured idealism, he viewed with some disgust the lowlier philosophies about him; when aroused he attacked with bitter anger and his paradoxes were staggering. There is in his statement of opinion a great deal of emotional exaggeration which developed from his extreme love of liberty. In politics, to which he devoted much prose and even several odes, Patmore was a violent opponent of popular government in all its works and pomps; very particularly obnoxious to him were such mandates as prohibition, with which democracy threatened to bind the individual. Nevertheless, the man who could thus work himself almost literally into a towering rage was otherwise the most tender of men. Life with his first wife, Emily Andrews, was beautiful in its perfect concord; and the second woman of his choice, Marianne Byles, was the object of an affection scarcely less deep. There lay in his soul the tenderness of tears, and his most enduring work is that in which this very human and very ordinary quality dares to enter the sanctuary of vision. No one in his age quite resembled him, for modern society is complex and he was utterly simple, with the strong moods and strange ecstasies of a hermit during the broken ages of Rome.

Unless one bears the character of Patmore constantly in mind, no study of his achievements as a Catholic poet will prove satisfactory. The great work of his later years is that now generally grouped under the title, "The Unknown Eros." In these odes he sang of the august analogy between Divine and human love, adapting the Pindaric form to the requirements of his straightforward emotion and stripping it almost bare of poetic language. God, "The Husband of the Heavens," is the deathless Lover of the Soul, and reverently the poet feels

> "This subject loyalty which longs
> For chains and thongs
> Woven of gossamer and adamant,
> To bind me to my unguessed want,
> And so to lie
> Between those quivering plumes that **thro'** fine
> ether pant
> For hopeless, sweet eternity."

Its direct analogy is human love, composed of two well-suited parts:

> "Your might, Love, makes me weak,
> Your might it is that makes my weakness sweet."

The surrounding mysteries, those of pain and defeat and unrequited longing, are the subjects of Patmore's most appealing poems, "A Farewell," "Tristitia," and the exquisite "Departure." Love holds the universe firmly to its heart:

> "But for compulsion of strong grace,
> The pebble in the road

Would straight explode
And fill the ghastly boundlessness of space."

And love will in the end make certain that hunger is
appeased and the heartbreak healed. Browning was
right when he glorified the fighter for, as Patmore
saw,

> "The man who, though his fights be all defeats,
> Still fights,
> Enters at last
> The heavenly Jerusalem's rejoicing streets
> With glory more, and more triumphant rites
> Than always-conquering Joshua's when his blast
> The frighted walls of Jericho down cast."

This is, of course, the poetry of the prophet, even if
of a very human one. Truths were made known to him
by meditation achieving insight, and their effectiveness
depends upon a recognition of their honesty. His are
moods to which not everyone will obediently succumb;
but Patmore would have been the last to maintain that
all should scale the mountain peaks to which he had
ascended. The "Odes" fail, then, to attain to that
universality of appeal which the great Catholic lyrics,
those of the liturgy, so securely possess; they fail
again in being too predominately intellectual and vio-
lating thereby the inspired mandate of charity. There
will, however, always be some to whom Patmore's odes
will speak the very words of Beauty, for whom his
sublime idealization of love will be the key to life. In
thus carrying the ideal of "The Angel in the House"
aloft with his vision, the poet lost somewhat of his
subtle ability to interpret the lowliest of human ex-

periences in words of light. In "Amelia," however, he developed a commonplace theme—the feelings of a girl who is about to take the place of a dead wife—with a deftness, a splendid and perfect sympathy, and a grace of fine poetry that are scarcely matched even by the masters. The delicate restraint with which the nature of a beautiful woman is presented with all its virginal purity and power of passion, preserves the morning tint of poetry; it is a memory of Paradise.

The poet's unsteady strength and increasing attraction to direct speech left many things to be said in prose. There are keen readers who prefer the slender epigrammatic volumes—"Religio Poetæ"; "Principle in Art"; "Rod, Root, and Flower"—to any of Patmore's verse. It may be granted that his mystical philosophy is very succinctly set forth in these brilliant essays; the oracle speaks plainly, if violently, in them. No one can ever boil down Patmore's utterances, for he gave only the bare quintessence of his thought. In general his essays deal with the same themes as those which underlie the poems, but undraped as they are of poetic symbolism they will strike the average reader as outrageous. The humble Christian, staring incredulously at unfathomable paradoxes, is likely to mark his copy of "Rod, Root, and Flower" with irate question marks. Such cryptic utterances as "Heaven becomes very intelligible and attractive when it is discerned to be—Woman," need setting forth in the raiment which the poet alone can supply. In prose Coventry Patmore the seer becomes a figure as alien from these matter-of-fact days as his beloved St. John of the Cross.

His death in 1896 was preceded like that of another

master of hard sayings, Huysmans, by much physical suffering borne with sublime fortitude. In numerous other ways the two men, so different in their attitude toward the native question of sex, were alike. Both saw in Woman the central figure, but one beheld her as the fount of evil, while for the other she was the image of all Good. Together they testify to the power of the Church to quench the thirst of intensely original minds, to grant that intellectual freedom without which the egoist, product of our age, must die. Patmore's memory will rest secure on his individuality. It would be easy to show that Huysmans' influence on modern literature has been very vast, and later on we shall attempt to make clear that the doctrine for which Patmore lived has also been fruitful in disciples. For all his hardness of speech and his limitations as a poet, he has proved himself, as Mrs. Meynell says, "the master —that is, the owner—of words that, owned by him, are unprofaned, are as though they had never been profaned; the capturer of an art so quick and close that it is the voice less of a poet than of the very Muse."[1]

II

Of Gerard Manley Hopkins, poetically tongue-tied and chosen for suffering, the world has heard but little and that is strangely perverse. The one poet friend who appreciated him sufficiently to edit his work failed utterly to understand his religious life; and so Robert Bridges' memoir has left the impression of a man hopelessly entangled in fatal asceticism, guilty of an absurd

[1] "Rhythm of Life," p. 96.

devotion to Mary, and altogether quite despondent. From the most famous anecdote concerning him one learns that he advised Coventry Patmore to burn the manuscript of "Sponsa Dei," thus depriving literature of a remarkable essay and Patmore of a crown. Recently this story, grossly annotated with theological "learning," has been repeated in the reminiscences of an educator-person whose sole titles to fame are a second-rate decoration from the French government (which has made other mistakes) and Patmore's occasional unwariness in selecting acquaintances. It ought not to be necessary to state that Father Hopkins' sole remark was, "That's telling secrets," probably a mere reënforcement of the author's own conclusion. But these matters are curious examples of what life meant for Gerard Hopkins—a lovable individual whose only possible love was silently religious; a poet who could only lisp in numbers, and a child whom nobody could understand.

The man is too elusive ever to be caught in a portrait. A delicate, brooding youth, alive as few men are to the seductive glow of the world, came to Oxford and fell in love with Greece. This was his natural habitat, coloured with those fiery, unreal skies which enraptured Keats and later Rupert Brooke. Hopkins' religious intuition, however, shrank quickly from the temptress, and following his prayer he was received into the Church by Newman. Even so he felt unsafe against the teasing stars and made the poet's final renunciation by joining the Jesuits. There is nothing to show that he was misunderstood, but the reward of his election was an unremitting pursuit by the demon of ugliness. Never was a man more delicately sensitive, more keenly responsive to the subtle nuances of form; and upon this instrument the world smote with the hand of the Cyclops.   He went from preaching to the classroom at Stonyhurst; thence to the slums of Liverpool, and finally to Ireland where, as an examiner in the Catholic University, he withered in an atmosphere which was, for him, deadly.   Father Gerard Hopkins made his religious sacrifice with the stolidity of a soldier; but it was torture as real as the martyrdom of Lallement.   This brief record of pain is all that can be given for a life that began at Stratford, near London, in 1844, and ended on June 8, 1889.

His poetry, like his character, is cryptic.   Could anything be more nobly simple than this youthful song of renunciation, come so straight from the heart:

> "Shape nothing, lips; be lovely dumb.
>   It is the shut, the curfew sent
>   From there where all surrenders come
>   Which only makes you eloquent.
>
> "Be shelled, eyes, with double dark
>   And find the uncreated light:
>   This ruck and reel which you remark
>   Coils, keeps, and teases simple sight."

But that repression in the end precluded expression; having bound himself hand and foot against nature, he threw his body amid the thorns of Greek prosody. When his penance had been done, he could not extricate his art from the coils of a theory which is interesting but impossible.   In the midst of dicta about running rhythm, sprung rhythm, rocking rhythm, and counterpoint, he stood, a futurist poet before the shrine of

Mary. Eschewing all the familiar grammatical transitions, his verse became a sort of verbal pantomime, gesture on gesture, ecstatic and arresting very frequently, but seldom graceful. This method was associated with even further oddities such as perplexing dialect words and strange Æschylian combinations, and a radical departure from the rhythm to which the English ear has been attuned.

Of course there is power in it, as of flashes. Such a line as, "Kiss my hand to the dappled-with-damson west" brings with it a glimpse of the true evening sky, and one knows not what image of the wild seacoast. Motion—which was one of Father Hopkins' fascinations—is most vividly reproduced in such lines as these:

> "Into the snows she sweeps,
> Hurling the haven behind."

But all these advantages gained from a nearly scientific exactness in registering impressions are offset by utter failures, when the picture is lost in the formula and nothing remains but an array of abstruse symbols. He is most truly poetic when the emotions which control his life govern for a time his response to the display of the world. The poem, "The Blessed Virgin Compared to the Air We Breathe," is one of those truly powerful and fervent Marian hymns in which modern literature rivals the old. The sonnets of his last days, too, are most poignant outcries of a soul shrouded in mystic darkness, bowed and bloody under the lash. There are not many more moving lines than this: "I wake and feel the feel of dark, not day." The greater portion of his slender volume is, however, intellectual

verse which is sometimes gifted with power but generally lies beyond the boundaries of song. The sonnet
to "Duns Scotus' Oxford" is probably the best among
this group, but even it is for the very patient reader.
It was natural, also, that Father Hopkins, whose life
was a crucifixion and at whom kindly human things
generally looked from behind strangers' windows,
should have aspired to be the poet of pain. In "The
Loss of the *Eurydice*" and "The Wreck of the *Deutsch-
land*" he came very near the sublimity of his favorite
Greek tragedian, and sang of God the Controller of
men's wills as no other English poet has done. It is
interesting to note that his manner here is very much
like that of a modern German Catholic poet, Annette
von Droste-Hülshoff.

Immediate reaction to the verve of nature and the
resolution to set *that* down in words, regardless of environment and continuity, are the characteristics of
Father Hopkins' verse. He was a child enchanted with
a sunbeam and oblivious of the light which floods the
world; he was a master of the phrase but a mere tinker
at composition. Now these same qualities are so
strongly manifest in his prose that one cannot refrain
from setting down an entry from his diary:

"Sept. 24. First saw the Northern Lights. My
eye was caught with the beams of light and dark very
like the crown of horny rays the sun makes behind a
cloud. At first I thought of silvery cloud until I saw
these were more luminous and did not dim the clearness
of the stars in the Bear. They rose slightly radiating
thrown out from the line of the earth. Then I saw
soft pulses of light; one after another rose and passed
upwards arched in shape, but waveringly and with the

arch broken. They seemed to float, not following the warp of the sphere as falling stars look to do, but free and concentrical with it. This busy working of nature wholly independent of the earth and seeming to go in a strain of time not reckoned by our reckoning of days and years, but simply as if correcting the preoccupation of the world by being preoccupied with and appealing to and being dated to the Day of Judgment, was like a new witness to God and filled with delightful fear." (*Dublin Review.*)

That is prose which almost seizes the intangible by itself becoming intangible. It is a break, perhaps not altogether happy, from the conventions of the literary craft; for a counterpart one must visit the strabismic art displays of modern painters.

Are there many who care, or will learn to care, for the poetry of Gerard Hopkins? Probably not. It seems impossible that poetry should ever follow the direction of his teaching, no matter how different its form may come to be. He was the elf-child playing with the fringe of the sober modern sea, and such children are rare and even unpopular. Certainly he can have no place except as the priest-artist who, resolute in his search for "Uncreated Light," paused for an occasional song before the shrine of the Virgin. As a Marian poet, seeking refuge in the arms of the Mother from the torment of life, he makes a distinct appeal, although the delicate odour of his incense will be lost on the crowd of worshippers. As a man he shall go down with the mystics and victims of song, with Campion and Blake, into the keeping of those who love the memory of the luckless dead. He had much to say that was left unspoken, but which comes eloquently, none the

less, from the sad eyes of the priest who loved the soul
above all else in the world—his own and his neighbour's
equally.   And what he had lived for was surely not in
vain.

III

In contrast with the bold vision and tense mystical
language of Gerard Hopkins and Coventry Patmore,
the school of poetry established by Wordsworth read
nature tranquilly, gravely, in search of "the breath
and finer spirit of knowledge."   Reason, living simply
beside the stream that washed the roots of aged trees,
could observe the spiritual background of nature as
Plato had envisaged it.   Poetry was content to walk
meditatively under the stars and to be transported
occasionally by the distant horn of Triton.   Chief
among the Wordsworthians was Aubrey de Vere, a
writer of exquisite mental poise and word-control.   He
tempered the landscape of England with Christian
moods as no other poet except Keble has tempered it;
but it was the ordered landscape of rural England,
charming in the twilight of memory but safe from the
storms that raged on England's sea.   If he saw anything else it was Ireland, but he could not have formed
an idea of an independent Celtic nation.

This staid Victorianism would have made of Aubrey
de Vere a mediocre poet had it not been for the one important break which he did venture—his conversion
to the Church.   Profoundly moved by the thought of
Newman, he went with the help of Coleridge and Manning to Rome and discovered the divine continuity of
Christendom.   De Vere was now able to invest his gar-

den with the religious aura of the past; he read back
into the life of the society which had borne so much
that was beautiful in saint and virgin. In short,
though he did not equal Wordsworth in wresting from
nature the sublime intuition of immortality or the vigorous protest against industrialism which are inherent
in her, he did surpass him in the sanctification of the
common shrine. He gave to earth not only personality
but also personages; and perhaps it would be well to
turn aside for a moment to De Vere's own individuality.
Born in Ireland, January 10, 1814, he was educated
at Trinity College and at Oxford; in youth he became
a disciple of Wordsworth and remained faithful to the
last by making an annual pilgrimage to the master's
grave. A gentleman of the rarest personal charm,
De Vere held the friendship of notable men like Gladstone, was the center of a brilliant society, and the
idolized poet of people like Kegan Paul. His religious
fervour had the sweetness as well as the rigour of sincerity, and his influence on other souls was remarkable. A long and hard-working literary career came
to a close with his death in 1902.

Being a poet whose literary power lay rather in
tranquil thought than in any kind of emotion, De Vere
was not bound to a particular verse form, but used
them all at will with dignified success. In the epic he was
least successful, in the sonnet perhaps most genuinely
at home. If his essays are largely forgotten now, many
of them have suffered an unkind fate: their veracity and
geniality should appeal to the lover of human things,
and the skill with which the themes are set forth is not
so usual in recent prose. There is power in them, even

if that power is sternly reposeful, and a simple grandeur of diction that one must match with something earlier than modern romanticism. The classic art, sure of itself and guided by philosophic restraint, speaks in many fine passages; to such calm poise of feeling the modern mind is not addicted, but literature may come back to it from erotic exhaustion.

The various books of lyrics and ballads do not sound the peculiar present-day song note. They contain verse of much charm, carefully groomed and exact as Horace, and of a rare sweetness of religious feeling which critics like Professor Saintsbury can only call "pretty." Nevertheless they are actually in touch with Nature and her soul, for De Vere boldly attempted a vision of the two in harmonious union. "Minds repelled by the thought of a God who stands afar off," he said, "and created the universe but to abandon it to general laws, fling themselves at the feet of a God made man." And though he may have been too weak to bring the world to its knees, there can be no doubt that Aubrey de Vere himself was kneeling in adoration. He felt certain that

> "Some presence veiled, in fields and groves
>   That mingles rapture with remorse;
> Some buried joy beside us moves,
>   And thrills the soul with such discourse
> As they, perchance, that wondering pair
>   Who to Emmaus bent their way
> Hearing, heard not. Like them our prayer
>   We make: 'The night is near us. . . . Stay!'"

Platitudes often have the advantage of being sensible: it must still be proved that great art is usually insane.

But his reflective description of natural scenery is not always devoid of ecstacy, for there are occasional flashes of gold and red, and the tranquil vista may shimmer with "lucidities of sun-pierced limes." De Vere's historical poetry lacks all the fire of an apostolate, is merely reminiscent, Thackerayesque. He found that the saints were beautiful in the legendary twilight, and drew from them a consolation not hinted at in the gorgeous pageantry of Hugo and Scott. As one of the first to put the Celtic sagas into English verse, De Vere may be regarded, also, as one of the forerunners of a most important literary movement, even though he succeeded no better than had Pope with Homer.

In "St. Peter's Chains" he wrote what may be termed a sequence of historical sonnets. Of this verse form he was truly a master, but the sonnets referred to are vastly inferior to the group included in the "Search after Proserpine." Here, as in all other good sequences, the poet's philosophy of life is presented in a series of carefully wrought miniatures. Of course, they are not Shakesperian nor does their art match the chiseled perfection of Heredia; but they are gentle vesper lamps, lighted with splendid sympathy for all things and thoughts, touched with spiritual refinement. "Sorrow," the best perhaps, is only a little inferior to "Our Human Life," and the rest are strikingly even. Aubrey de Vere was not a master of vision and it may be wrong to say that he possessed a single one of what are called "great" ideas, with which the modern egoist is so bountifully supplied. But he felt sincerely and courted honourably, "Great thoughts, grave thoughts, thoughts lasting to the end." "In everything that he has written," says Coventry Patmore, "his aim has been grave and high. He has never been sectarian even when Catholic."

Yet Catholic he was in a fine way that did his brethren honour. Throughout life he haunted the shrines where God had manifested Himself, and studied reverently the images of His majesty. He had none of the abnormally sensitive responsiveness of Father Hopkins, and Patmore's robust and paradoxical statement of the highest truth was alien to him. May it not be said, however, that in many ways he was (and is) a better everyday companion, more constant in his fervour and less rigorously disdainful of the humble things? For all his thorough culture, De Vere was the most charitable of men, one of the most self-sacrificing of the poets. Those petty jealousies which so often disrupt the Muses' coterie touched him not at all; free and firm to the end, he came to earn the title of chevalier of song. Whether his poetry is ever to be more popular, whether we shall learn to overlook the absence of *élan* which flattens it so much, are questions no one can answer; but of the man it may be said, simply, that he was nearly a saint.

BOOK NOTE

The complete works of Patmore and De Vere include poems and essays. The only edition of Gerard Hopkins' verse is that issued with a memoir by Robert Bridges. Note the following biographies: of Patmore, by Basil Champneys and Edmund Gosse; of De Vere, by Wilfrid Ward. The manifest incompleteness of Bridges' estimate of Hopkins is corrected to some extent by a series of short essays in the *Dublin Review,* 1920. The Diary is in the possession of Father Keating, S. J. See also, "Idea of Coventry Patmore," by Osbert Burdett; "Essays," by Alice Meynell; "Collected Works," vol. 3, by Joyce Kilmer; "The Poet's

Chantry," by Katherine Brégy. Paul Claudel's French translation of Patmore is interesting. For an enthusiastic estimate of De Vere's poetry see "Memories," by Kegan Paul, and the *Quarterly Review* for 1896. Magazine articles on Patmore and De Vere are, of course, numerous.

CHAPTER EIGHT

"Look for me in the nurseries of heaven."

*M*ERRY ENGLAND, a magazine that bore the
interesting device, "We shall try to revive in
our own hearts and in the hearts of others,
the enthusiasm of the Christian Faith," was edited by
a genial and remarkable man. Wilfred Meynell had,
no doubt, a temperate and gracefully romantic soul,
but he was fundamentally what he claimed to be, a re-
vivalist concerned with the nineteenth century and the
problem of spiritual restoration which Catholics
thought so intimate a part of it. The excuse for beginning an essay on Francis Thompson with the name
of Meynell is simply that without the latter's influence
there would have been no poet of the "Sister Songs."
Thompson, it is true, accepted the friendly editor's
largesse with diffidence and repaid a hundred fold; for
when on April 18, 1888, the derelict author who had
been responsible for "Paganism Old and New" tiptoed
warily into the office of *Merry England*, that journal
assumed immortality, though it has long since ceased
publication. This wretch whose bodily destitution
could scarcely have been more complete, this wanderer
of the streets who reeked of laudanum and whose face

was already set for the death-mask, had indeed inherited the "enthusiasm of the Christian Faith," and
would do as much to revive it as any other man.

Mr. Meynell anticipated very little of Thompson's
story, something of which is now known everywhere.
Born at Preston, Lancashire, on December 16, 1859,
Francis was the son of a benevolent doctor whose medicine had a kindly habit of getting into the hands of
people who could not pay for it. He and his family
were sincerely religious converts. It is to be doubted
whether either father or mother understood at all their
strange, solitary child. Ought one to expect of earnest,
workaday parents that they shall immediately divine
genius in a boy who reads Shakespeare and Scott in
solitude when not busy at make-believe with his sisters;
whose indolence is quite extraordinary; who, when sent
to Ushaw (1870) manages somehow to keep himself
unspotted from the rougher world of boydom, suffering meanwhile indescribable agony from affronts to
which a normal lad would respond with a grimace; who
is finally counseled to quell his aspirations to the priesthood because of his "absent-mindedness"?

The fact is that Francis Thompson was already a
contemplative, an initiate into the small band of those
whose intellect bids them sit with Mary, whether the
final object of their intent be truly God or merely
nature. But Francis was the disciple of saints, not of
Walter Pater. It is interesting, though useless, to
speculate on what would have become of him had the
spiritual directors of Ushaw, too much concerned with
the vineyard, guided him to some mystic commuity
that would have received him with joy. Might not the
poet have turned saint and have written glowing vol-

umes, which would trace for a world so little accustomed to them the adventures of the lover's pilgrimage? Doubtless the Providence which led him had prepared the poet's darker night of pain, at the end of which would come the poet's ecstacy and the coveted release.

Surely there can be nothing more surprising in fiction than Francis Thompson's rather indifferent acquiescence in his father's plans for making a physician of him. A man less fitted for wielding the pestle never lived. In 1877, however, he entered Owens College, Manchester, and began that study of death which, had he not already been somewhat aloof from the world, must have crushed him. There were, it happens, several doors to freedom: literature, music, and cricket, all from the spectator's point of view. During the six years spent in Manchester he learned the speech of Coleridge and tasted laudanum. Thompson must then have fancied himself at the bottom of life, but the downward movement had only begun. After definitely abandoning the study of medicine and all other practical schemes which a patient father could think of, he went off alone to London and began on the cobblestones that existence of comatose misery which has seemed to most persons either terribly romantic or romantically terrible. It was, of course, neither. The simple fact is that Thompson, through no personal fault, had missed the vocation after which his nature yearned. This dreary waiting for a sign in London, this hunger and cold and opium-muddled dreaming, were merely the humdrum daily business of one who was an outcast from the regal enterprise that had no room for him. These things, especially the laudanum, left scars which never healed; but deep battle-wounds seldom do anything else.

At length the hand which had led Thompson so strangely astray, and as near the abyss as even Saint Teresa was allowed to venture, drew him from the seething streets to the one place for which he was now suited. "Enthusiasm for the Christian Faith"! What had this waif who had

> "Suffered the trampling hoof of every hour
> In night's slow-wheelèd car"

to do with such a venture? Everything. No more stalwart crusader, not Richard or Godfrey, had ever ridden for the Christian cause than this vagrant troubadour whose body seemed scarcely less material than his soul. That at least was firmly knit, had served its long campaign. The strength which leaped within him, the voice fresh and resonant in an age well used to voices, came from seclusion encrusted with the wealth of the past: the imagery of the Elizabethan poets, the Catholic outlook, the ritual of the Church, and the age-long aspect of the firmament and its God. The singer was eager for the song, and there came marvelous days when melodies formed in the dark opened to the morning; when praise seemed void to those who understood the music and empty to those who did not. What, indeed, was a lover of his time to make of these verses which flaunted it, which spoke a language that only forgotten poets understood ? There was disaparagement enough, excessive neglect.

Gradually, however, the note of praise increased and was sustained. Many a young poet, like Walter de la

Mare or Richard le Gallienne, walked the streets oblivious of everything except the haunting stanzas of
"The Hound of Heaven." Even the doubting critics
came to see the genius in their midst and believed,
though they were sorely tried. Today there is no
Francis Thompson controversy for the lover of poetry.
He is "comparable only to Shakespeare," "the greatest
product of English Catholicism during the nineteenth
century"—an enthusiastic remark surely—a master
more adored than Browning or Shelley, and raised to
a dizzy pinnacle from which only his real emninence
can prevent a disastrous fall. "Sister Songs" are in
everybody's hands; there is even a staid American
scientist who has taken to reading the breviary because
of certain rhythms in "Sight and Insight."

It is inevitable that shadows should fall on the picture. The poetic heat, repressed so long, could not
outlive the poet's fragile fire. Thompson stalwartly
refused to write mediocre poems when his powers were
inadequate for great ones, and so the bulk of his verse
is small. There remained, however, many things to
say, and these he put with great care into prose which,
less regal than his poetry, remained a faithful companion until the end. Generally it served the kindly
office of criticism, and, with the exception of the "Shelley" has scarcely been recognized for what it is worth.
The Shelley essay is, of course, a poet's prose at its
supreme best; but are not the Olympian papers on
Coleridge, Crashaw, and Landor also among the original, certain literary productions of their kind? Again,
Thompson put his entire personality into a life of Saint
Ignatius Loyola. Surely no one has done, or is likely
to do, this task with so much understanding and rev-

erently fervent art; nevertheless, it is not very easy to get a copy of the book. In short, the fame of the poet has made men forget the writer of prose. Thompson's genius, so remarkably intuitive and so daringly individual, cannot, however, be understood unless one remembers that he began with an essay—"Paganism, Old and New"—and ended with a biography—"St. Ignatius Loyola." Since his death no one has doubted the inspiration of his poetry; there is no reason either for refusing homage to his prose.

Extensive critical appreciation of Francis Thompson's poetry has made quite clear its divergent excellencies. The impassioned melody following with surprising ease the curves of a rigidly conceived structure (like a group of colored sails on the strong sea); the vividness of the imagery, intricate and satisfying as a ritual; the vitality of the imagination which shapes the poet's idea: all of these good qualities have been emphasized. We have learned to accept the most formidable of his Latinisms with some relish, and traces of the older poets—Shakespeare, Spenser, Donne, Crashaw—in his verse have been duly pointed out and forgiven. The ode structure of the great poems is considered a sign of artistic mastery as baffling as is Shakespeare's in the triumphant Elizabethan blank verse. Interesting studies have been made of the method and motive of individual poems—studies which are useful, too, because Thompson believed that poetry ought to be popular. Neither does anyone doubt the authenticity of his vision, although there is often considerable vagueness about the actual import of that

vision. Men are made humble in his presence, and
Spenser has a rival as the poets' teacher.

Now such analysis of Thompson's verse as will be attempted here must necessarily be confined to the general
attitudes which it assumes. Do the poems permit of
grouping by reason of some object common to all? It
would seem very evident that the most striking characteristic of Thompson's work is its curiously Gothic
nature—the verve with which it sweeps to airy pinnacles in the dizzy blue of the sky; the involute and ex-
haustless imagery, as of crowded friezes, in which its
dream finds expression; the vital concreteness of the
execution; and the firm mastery of outline which impresses this otherwise inchoate symbolism into the service of a religious idea. But Thompson was not the
servant of the past. There was surprisingly little in
him of the backward glance toward the pageant of
mediæval life which fascinated men like Scott or Digby.
He even took the trouble to state that "the spirit of
such poems as 'The Making of Viola' and the 'Judge-
ment in Heaven' is no mere mediæval imitation, but the
natural temper of my training in a simple provincial
home." The fondness he felt for Elizabethan poetry
was indeed very great; yet this does not signify an intense visualization of the spirit of Shakespeare's time.
By comparison, Thompson's interests lay wholly with
the present and the future. Nevertheless, the Gothic
spirit was there in all vigour and fulness, and it may be
said without willfulness that while he did not imitate
the mediæval artist, he *was* that artist, spontaneous
and individual, reborn in verse.

There underlies all of Thompson's poetry the intuition that the beauty of earth is in some way the reflection of the beauty of heaven; earth's beauty fragile and soon decayed, material for the constant synthesis of birth and death. The Cross is dissolution's presage of the Resurrection hope. Thus, in the "Ode to the Setting Sun," the poet says:

"Thou art of Him a type memorial.
Like Him thou hang'st in dreadful pomp of blood
Upon the Western rood,"

and Christian mysticism advances far beyond the idealism of Plato. The "Hound of Heaven," gazing from behind His tumultuous windows, knows that the man who is temporarily appeased with the mere reflections of His countenance will never remain satisfied, and slowly, steadfastly draws him in. Again, the comparison drawn in the "Orient Ode" between day and the Benediction service, is a poet's attempt to grasp, with nature's help, the mystery of the Incarnation:

"O Salutaris Hostia
Quae coeli pandis ostium,
Through breached ramparts, a
Divine assaulter, art thou come"—

manifests a daring application of exalted liturgy to an interpretation of nature. These few examples deal with cardinal points; but the Christian mystic's understanding of the world is upheld everywhere in Thompson's poetry.

Now this was exactly the method of the mediæval artist. By means of a highly intricate coördination the builder of the Gothic cathedral brought all nature

round the table of Divine sacrifice. The mighty pillars
of the nave, with their clamorous commingling of arches
and the leaf-like forms of their delicate galleries—
what were these but the forest rendered mute and im-
mobile for the sheltering of the Host? Flaming windows, crowded with figures, reproduced all the colours
of the sky and ocean illumined by the sun, as these
saints had been inspired by their Sun. Outside, marvelous groups of statuary gathered virgins and heroes,
children and labourers, flowers and fruits, and the
pageants of all seasons under the protecting shadows
of majestic spires, themselves encrusted with symbolic
forms. Under all, in the midst of all, there lay the
Cross, and upon it the Corporal Presence for whose
sake this monument had been fashioned: real and living, lending all things a new and startling beauty by
the terrible joy of His marriage of life and death.

But Francis Thompson was a master of mediæval
art as well as of mediæval doctrine, and his work takes
on an added beauty when considered in this manner.
"Sister Songs" are radiant, charming façades, miracles of spring—with here and there a touch of autumn—driving up graceful pinnacles into the sky, but,
though reaching far, never quite attempting the audacity of a spire. Does not the poet himself say:

> "I faint, I sicken, darkens all my sight,
>   As, poised upon this unprevisioned height,
>   I lift into its place
>   The upmost aery traceried pinnacle.
> So: it is builded, the high tenement,
>   —God grant!—to mine intent:
> Most like a palace of the Occident,
>   Upthrusting, toppling maze on maze,

> Its mounded blaze,
> And washed by the sunset's rosy waves,
> Whose sea drinks rarer hue from those rare
> walls it laves."

There is grave, sweet seriousness in his handiwork, though occasionally it grows flamboyant, as in the riotous "Corymbus for Autumn." Here he is master of a maze of imagery that crowds into every available place, turning the somber stone of diction into lace whose counterpart one must seek at Lincoln or Saint Maclou. But the stern outline of the cathedral itself has long been drawn and its interior made ready. All that stands without, even the "giant arches of the years" and the "labyrinthine ways," are not the Beauty upon whose service the artist is bent. And kneeling in humble prayer before the tabernacle of the "Hound of Heaven" he hears the words,

> "Whom wilt thou find to love ignoble thee,
> Save Me, save only Me?"

These are the selfsame words which inspired the master of Gothic stone, who brought together all things that make earth goodly as a sign of his relinquishment of them to Him.

Such was the edifice into which Thompson set windows and placed statues, tender at times, like the "Little Jesus;" again, terrible in aspect, like "The Veteran of Heaven," and human finally in the tearful image of her of whom he sang in "The House of Sorrows." He celebrated the coming of music and light into the temple he had reared, by the "Ode to the Set-

ting Sun"; and at the mortuary Mass read there for
the "Dead Cardinal," he did not forget his own, the
artist's "Dies Iræ":

> "Good friend,
>   I pray thee send
>   Some high gold embassage
>   To teach my unripe age.
>   Tell
>   Lest my feet walk hell."

Thompson is also the brother of the mediæval artist
by reason of his use of imagery. Here there is question not so much of untrammeled imaginative power
as of the transfiguration of the commonplace. Long
ago Alice Meynell pointed out one of the secrets of
Thompson's power—the likening of great things to
small ones—which the attentive reader will soon discover for himself. For example in the "Mistress of
Vision" we are told:

> "The sun which lit that garden wholly,
>   Low and vibrant visible,
>   Tempered glory woke;
>   And it seemèd solely
>   Like a silver thurible
>   Solemnly swung, slowly,
>   Fuming clouds of golden fire, for a cloud of
>   incense smoke."

Again, in a simpler poem, "New Year's Chimes," it is
written:

> "And a world with unapparent strings
>   Knits the simulant world of things."

Mr. Meynell, in the "Life of Francis Thompson," comments thus upon certain of the poet's analogies: "The whole scale of comparisons is unexpected in the case of one who goes to the eating-house not only for his meals, but for his images; who finds nothing outrageous in naming the Milky Way a beaten yolk of stars; who takes the setting sun for a bee that stings the west to angry red." [1] Numberless additional examples might be given, some of them equally fantastic, others, like "the flaming brazen bowl of the burnished sun" suggestive of the modern impressionist.

The sole artistic medium able and audacious enough to use such imagery unsparingly has been the ritual (and architecture) of the Church. In this alone one finds the highest and lowliest in that intimate conjunction which has been, from the human point of view, the motive force in Christendom. The Incarnation tells of nothing else, nor does the life and mission of the Saviour: it is written in the *Magnificat*, it is the fulfilment of the *Domine, non sum dignus*. Christ, in the parables, lent dignity to infinitesimal things like mustard seed. And just as the ritualist who first conceived the idea of representing Jesus by means of the wax candle, or the sculptor who in the dim regions of the catacombs modeled Him as a Fish carrying a basket of Bread through the waters, did so with all reverence and love, so our derelict poet fashioned for himself a comforting vision of heaven from the things he trod under his feet. With a surprising buoyancy of spirit he loved the dreams he drew, and if sometimes they closed in pain he knew that the artist must suffer,

[1] Chap. X, page 207.

like St. Jerome or St. Monica, in expiation for the
ugliness of the world.

The house of worship built, Thompson follows the
guidance of Coventry Patmore, his friend, and is
wrapped in mystical contemplation before the throne
of God: the shadows thicken and the One Light burns
in the midst of that universe of images; there descends
upon the meditative worshipper "Sight and Insight,"
the end, the *desideratum*, the goal of mediæval art.
In this immaterial raiment the soul might best sever
itself from the body, throw aside the train of the beauty
of Earth. It is not pretended, of course, that Thompson consciously made any such disposition of his poetic
faculties as has been suggested here; that it *was* made,
however, in a marvelously complete way, that he did
become the counterpart of the builder in the Ages of
Faith, seems both evident and remarkable. He was
the Gothic artist in verse, and two things are thereby
made clear: that God did not disdain the services of
one who was naturally a priest and a contemplative,
but gave him the boon of an exalted mission as "the
poet of the return to God," and that, in the ordinary
sense, he had not sinned against the Light, but kept
his soul bright as it had been in boyhood.

It is not easy, when one has reviewed the excellencies
of Francis Thompson's poetry, to have patience for an
examination of his short-comings. That his work was
not free from faults is a platitude; but as Mr. John
Macy, a critic quite different in temperament from his
poet, suggests, they are always the sins of a Meister-
singer. Elizabethan conceits are not always charming,
and those in several poems, especially "Manus Animam

Pinxit," show clearly a lack of inspiration. In certain stanzas of even the best poems the thought is spun out almost into thin air, grammatical constructions are mismanaged, and words too exclusively poetic usurp, for the mere sake of melody, the rightful places of homelier terms. It requires no master of the art to detect the flaw in such lines as these:

> "The burning rhetoric, quenchless oratory,
> Of the magniloquent and all-suasive sky,"

when Thompson writes them; but they might serve lesser poets well. On the whole he proved a very conscientious workman, and the mystery of his rhythmic patterns will baffle all imitation not deeply erudite. The eager pilfering which Thompson graciously confessed was, of course, Shakespeare's privilege; but the suspicion that "the great earthquaking sunrise clanging past Cathay" is derived from Mr. Kipling, or that the Edinburgh reviewer of 1895 was right in finding traces of Cowley in "Sister Songs" does prove somewhat disconcerting. These blemishes and all others that may be cited do not, however, mar the supreme originality, the regal beauty, and the spiritual ecstasy of Francis Thompson's verse. He was the master-builder of song; among all the poets of later years, he is the one who guarded best the citadel of the soul.

The poet that Francis Thompson so magnificently proved himself to be left plenty of room for the humbler writer of prose. When the temple of his song had been built, during one brief, intensely creative period of power, the master grew weary and could no longer venture on the spires, among the bells. Dreams

remained kind, but gradually became elusive guests.
With prose Thompson felt at home always; the critic's
hand is somehow firmer than the poet's, though it need
not lack almost equal delicacy and strength. "Paganism, Old and New," which rescued him from the darkness, is Thompson's measure both as a writer and as
an individual. It is quaint, semi-poetic, and despite
its oddities, oddly powerful; but it bears the imprint
of a strangely simple man. His mind was made up:
he knew the story of the continuity of Christendom,
and understood how fully it had drawn from the older
Paganism which is dead forever. "Aurora may rise
over our cities, but she has forgotten how to blush":
the derelict who wrote thus had already come into his
kingdom, and all that earth could give was the wreath
for the brow of Her he craved. In later years his
mysticism grew stronger, and he sharpened his wits
on the golden sands of love. Essays and book reviews
caught something of his thought, which disregarded
occasionally the paths in which it strayed. At the
end there came the "St. Ignatius Loyola," surely a
noble tribute in which there is as much of the real
Francis Thompson as one can find in "The Hound of
Heaven."

His greatest achievement as a prose-writer is, of
course, the "Shelley." It is not only an apology for
that wayward poet, but also a defense of song. Thompson, pausing for a moment at the white heat of his
own creative energy, rides to the rescue of a younger
brother, gorgeous in the armour of regal imagery.
Was insight in its highest intuitive form ever so thoroughly alive under jeweled garments of state? It is
Shelley who keeps the tryst by the eternal proxy of

genius; Shelley the audacious, the absurd, the spoiled poet, but after all, Shelley the boy. Or has Thompson made a tomb of prose in which the singer shall live—a tomb of filigree marble rising from a floor of rich encaustic tile, delicately wrought, vibrant in every detail, surely the despair of the pedant?

"Coming to Shelley's poetry," says Thompson, "we peep over the wild mask of revolutionary metaphysics, and we see the winsome face of the child. Perhaps none of his poems is more purely and typically Shelleian than 'The Cloud,' and it is interesting to note how essentially it springs from the faculty of make-believe. The same thing is conspicuous, throughout his singing; it is the child's faculty of make believe raised to the nth power. He is still at play, save only that his play-things are those which the gods give their children. The universe is his box of toys. He dabbles his fingers in the day-fall. He is gold dusty with tumblings amidst the stars. He makes bright mischief with the moon. The meteors muzzle their noses in his hand. He teases into growling the kenneled thunder, and laughs at the shaking of its fiery chain. He dances in and out of the gates of heaven: its floor is littered with his broken fancies. He runs wild over the fields of ether. He chases the rolling world. He gets between the feet of the horses of the sun. He stands in the lap of patient Nature and twines her loosened tresses after a hundred wilful fashions, to see how she will look nicest in his song." [1]

Some reasonable objection might be made to the metrical strain of this prose; but the most noteworthy quality in Thompson's criticism is not the rhymthic verve of the language or its pell-mell imagery, but its

[1] Pp. 39-41.

shrewd knowledge of mechanics and no less uncanny divination of artistic motives. The critic's sight becomes a divining-rod poised over depths unsuspected before. Thompson was not always able to find the vein of gold, nor was his assaying infallible. But there is little poetic criticism in nineteenth century English literature to equal his. If one takes, for example, the temperately written "Crashaw," wherein admiration for the master is curbed by the disciple's inspection of his workmanship, one feels that here a mason is busy studying the mortar of a sturdy old wall. Crashaw had spoken, for instance, of the "curved" snowflakes; Thompson was perhaps the only modern to note the actual "curve" which had fascinated the older poet. Coleridge, so much of genius bound and gagged, is thus summed up: "the poet submerged and feebly struggling in opium-darkened oceans of German philosophy, amid which he finally floundered, striving to the last to fish up gigantic projects from the bottom of a half-daily pint of laudanum." What most readers have sensed in reading Milton, but few have known how to express is thus succinctly stated by Thompson: "Milton lacked, perhaps . . . a little poetic poverty of soul, a little detachment from his artistic richness. He could not forget, nor can we forget, that he was Milton." This is the consistent tenor of his criticism, which is always journalistic but never feeble or flitting; it is "creative" criticism, if you will, though not impressionistic in manner. For Thompson knows and obeys the canons of taste; his outlook upon literature is Elizabethan, and therefore warmly classical, while the windows of his judgment are face to face with nature gorgeous in spring. At the bottom of his driven mind lies the pearl of humour, beyond price. "This is commendable neither in poet nor errand-boy," says the "Shelley" with a twinkle not of this age, but gracious as Beaumont.

Most important among Thompson's qualities, however, was the seer's hearkening to the heart-beat of Truth, the mystic's reading of a manifold script written to spell out the Word. He knew when to shut his eyes. As Patmore says in "Aurea Dicta," "Lovers put out the candles and draw the curtains, when they wish to see the goddess; and in the high Communion, the night of thought is the light of perception." The ordinary reasoning process counts for little in Thompson's mental operations; instead there is the flash of understanding traversing the distance between the outer world and its Core with a stately ease that must be purchased with pain. He served the two queens, Beauty and Truth, with his life. Of prose and poetry he made a continuous *homage aux dames*. This was a privilege inherited from the saints who, in paying tribute to God, have loved His vesture. From time immemorial, indeed, the idea that nature is a veil has been the inspiration of both poetry and thought. For Thompson, Coleridge had spoken truly: "Absolute nature lives not in our life, nor yet is lifeless, but lives in the life of God; and in so far, and so far merely, as man himself lives in that life, does he come into sympathy with Nature; and Nature with him. She is God's daughter who stretches her hand only to her father's friends." Later there came from Patmore the teaching of the universal sacrament of union, the sublime harmony of the Trinity envisaging itself in all the world's diversified conjugation, especially in

matrimony.   It was not given to Thompson to become
so rapturously certain of this doctrine as his master
was, nor had he any deep knowledge of woman.   The
whole of this exalted, unearthly teaching is controlled
by a reverent observation of the *disciplina arcani;* this
Thompson realized, and though it was part of his
inspiration he would not have cared, perhaps, to have
it publicly insisted on.

What shall we make in the end of this man who knew
so little of the world's ways and yet understood it so
well?   His character was fascinatingly simple and
though crowded with pain escaped moroseness.   In
reality one thinks of it as pervaded with penitential
peace; his life is like a procession through bitter and
suffering streets, dark with things that one sees in
laudanum dreams, to the house of laughter.   Thompson had wedded Poverty when she was no longer a lady,
but the child was most beautiful song.   Who can
analyze a soul so patient, so reverent, so governed by
the best instincts of childhood; a soul which lacked
utterly the complexities which arise in a nature disturbed by the grapple of evil with good; a soul proudly
conscious of its powers and lineage even in the throes
of despair?   The man who had not been vouchsafed
the earlier priesthood, fulfilled the later ministry with
quiet pomp.   During the time of his visits at Panta-
saph, where the Franciscans received him amiably, he
indulged to the full that longing for monastic retreat
with which he had been marked at birth; if in other
surroundings he gratified the more ordinary desire for
companionship, it was because kindness would repay
charity.   The laudanum which seems to stain his fin-

gers, if not his soul, was after all the terrible key with which he could enter solitude when all other doors were closed.

There is no room here for mention of his personal peculiarities, which are all to be had for the asking from his biographer. The portrait which Lytton drew shortly before Thompson's death on November 13, 1907, is that of a prophet, visualizing "the dread future without dread"; so that after all he had nothing to regret in the manner of his life. As for his poetry, that is *ære perennius*.

BOOK NOTE

The Standard (Scribner) Edition of Francis Thompson's poetry and prose in three volumes is the desirable one. The Modern Library (Boni and Liveright) contains the "Poems" in convenient form. "The Life of Francis Thompson,'' by Everard Meynell, is the authoritative biography. See in addition, "Francis Thompson," by G. E. Beacock; "The Spirit of Francis Thompson," by a Sister of Notre Dame; "The Hound of Heaven," by F. P. LeBuffe, S. J.; and the "Shelbourne Essays," 7th Series, by P. E. More. A study of Thompson's prose has been prepared by Charles L. O'Donnell. The following essays in the *Dublin Review* are of interest: by A. C. Cock, vol. 149; by Alice Meynell, vol. 153; by William Barry, vol. 147. See also, Joyce Kilmer, "Works," vol. 3.

CHAPTER NINE

"Pinguescent speciosa deserti."
                                    Psalm 64.

POETRY is not only natural but also as universal
as nature. While every truly poetic era listens
to masters, it welcomes minstrels as well—wandering minstrels who sing in chorus and are often
forgotten before the applause has died away, but who
bring something quite like sunshine into the streets
through which they pass. Of course, there is really
no such being as a minor poet; one might speak as intelligently of minor sunsets or major mornings. Not
all, however, are ample and gorgeous, mastering the
heavens and the earth, and some are even the children
of an hour, dispensing swiftly the beauty which is their
secret treasure, and disappearing for evermore into
the mute and obscure poverty which rewards their giving. The fact to be noted is that the priceless things
in literature are not always signed with resounding
names. There are lyrics by humbler poets from Catullus to Donne and Dobell that are as fragrant as any
rose in Shakespeare's garden; we should rather have
the "Dies Iræ" than "Paradise Lost." And among
the matchless psalms of David there is none to equal
the *Magnificat.*

147

It is very much the same, of course, with the other arts. The little town of Thann, in Alsace, has a church which, when everything has been said, is rather simple. But adorning the façade, on the slenderest of columns, stands a statue of the Madonna, the work of some utterly forgotten fourteenth century artist. There is in this representation of the Mother and Son that ultimate originality which endows the dream of the artist with the vision and vitality of the people to whom he belongs. Here is a Virgin whom everybody instinctively recognizes for a Mother, and a Child whose loveliness seems too real, too blissful, for stone. And perhaps it would be better to make a pilgrimage to Thann, of which the world knows little, than to visit the towers of Cologne or even St. Paul's in London, for all its Renaissance majesty.

To return to poetry, let us give thanks that the Catholic Spirit has been enshrined in songs beyond number. There are many poets with whom this narrative cannot deal, although it is true that neither Browning nor Meredith, Tennyson nor Arnold, were uninfluenced by the revival of Christendom; in multitudinous and separate ways they bore testimony to the beauty which is the garment of God. But the glory of these men is to have reflected the spirit of the modern age, to have caught its optimism or its quandary, its aspiration or its despair. The Catholic poet, although alive to the rhythm of the surrounding time, is necessarily a mediævalist at heart, for the moderns believe in God and also in If, but the Middle Ages were conscious of Him, simply, as a fact. Herein lies all the difference in the world, but chiefly it is the difference between deference to the tables of science and to the tables of the Law. "Every artist," says Ernest Hello, "should live in austere conformity to Order," and certainly this is a golden rule. But the Church has not been a principle, but a mother, and has marshalled men not as soldiers but as future citizens; she has said to man and poet, "Go your own way, but remember the household into which you are born." Nothing is more remarkable in the writers whom we shall consider than the diversity of their temperaments and their likeness in the consciousness of their heritage.

Alice Meynell, the first of these poets, belongs unquestionably among the number of the immortals. She was, moreover, the earliest literary woman to take an active part in the revival of the Catholic Spirit. The feminine mind, from the days of Sappho, has brought to letters qualities of gold—intimacy, restraint, delicacy of emotion—and immortal women, Mme. de Sévigné, Jane Austen, St. Teresa, have written with something akin to the virtue of silence. The defense of the shrine of womanhood lies, it is evident, in the poise of reserve, in the attitude which stands half way between repulsion and embrace. Mrs. Meynell, understanding this principle well, has written with a magnificent tranquillity that might have been the mood of Venus de Milo were it not for a subtler shadowing of the flesh, a more resolute devotion to spirit in its pure form. She wrote, like Emerson, prose and poetry remarkably similar in character, each distinguished by fine humorous intelligence and the chaste rhythm of secluded feeling. How it is that in this modern age woman should keep best that high Stoicism of character, that classic frigidity of expression, which belonged to Sophocles and Joubert, we shall not attempt to explain.

The first slender volume of poems, "Preludes," has been followed by other collections just as fragile and spare. There is scarcely a line that lacks the ultimate touch, that Mrs. Meynell might conceivably have done better. All the poems are ideas, visions, and prayers; but none of them could conceivably be quoted either in Parliament or in church. And here is at once the secret of Alice Meynell's power and of her limitation; she goes infallibly to the reason of things, but seldom, if ever, to the heart of things. There is no Rachael mourning for her children and no Magdalen drying the Saviour's feet with strands of golden hair. In her verse you meet always the marble figure with the heart-beat in the eyes alone, the poignant cry that is never uttered except in a gaze. "Renouncement" is such a poem, "Maternity" another:

> "Ten years ago was born in pain,
> A child, not now forlorn.
> But, oh, ten years ago, in vain,
> A mother, a mother was born."

But it is thus that the ideal woman of the ages, not La Giaconda but Mary of the Stabat Mater, has spoken to the hearts of men. And if Mrs. Meynell's emotions are thus carefully repressed for the show they must make in words, her prayer is no less closely shrouded. Sometimes the comparatively simple vision is put with utter simplicity:

"For no divine
  Intelligence or art, or fire, or wine
  Is high-delirious as that rising lark—
  The child's soul and its daybreak in the dark."

Again, the insight into remoter things is clouded with
its own remoteness, though the naked lines speak everything that can be said. Such a poem as "A General
Communion" is pure idea kindled by an almost incommunicable spiritual ecstasy:

"I saw the people as a field of flowers,
  Each grown at such a price
  The sum of unimaginable powers
  Did no more than suffice."

This poetry can be the product only of a mind both
remarkably original and remarkably disciplined. By
necessity Mrs. Meynell was driven to have her say on
life, and while this declaration is very forcefully made
in poems like "The Fugitive," it is really the business
of her prose. In three surprisingly even series of
essays, "The Rhythm of Life," "The Colour of Life,"
and "Hearts of Controversy," she manages to suggest
her own firmly balanced intellectual position while
piercing to the rotten core of everything that smacks
of decivilization. Her ideal is self control and decidedly not the modern business of self expression. A
good deal of subtly restrained opinion is devoted, naturally, to a consideration of art, for Mrs. Meynell is
always primarily the artist. She has made of the short
prose essay a medium as perfect in form, as responsive
to the intimacies of sensibility, as the Epistles of

Horace. It is to be expected that such treatment of life will sometimes taste bitter in the mouth, or seem *trop raffiné pour ce monde*. Neither the prose nor the poetry of Alice Meynell has been written for the multitude; she has courageously elected to say a word to the teachers and to characterize the gaudiness of contemporary romantic philosophy with the withering adjectives it invites. But in her own way she has also been the oracle of consummate womanhood, of mothers whose maternity has only made them graver children of the divine. It is, of course, unsafe to venture an estimate of Mrs. Meynell's ultimate literary position; but there is no other contemporary English writer whose work seems so safe from time.

No poet could offer a greater contrast to the refined sexlessness—feminine insight manfully controlled—of Alice Meynell than the rugged, masculine verse of Wilfrid Scawen Blunt. This man of genius, whose career has been so varied and so impetuous, is perhaps the only modern whom Richard of the Lion Heart would have welcomed for a brother. Both have been men of action with a turn for song; they might have ridden out together to the ends of the earth, championing the oppressed almost singlehanded, and come out of the desert shoulder to shoulder, knowing the Moslem. Both, in short, have made a knight's homage to the dreams that pulse through the heart of the world. Wilfrid Blunt, at eighteen, was a member of the diplomatic corps; at twenty-nine he married and began with his wife a series of exhilarating though dangerous journeys across Spain—then the scene of a Carlist revolt— Algiers, Egypt, and Asia Minor. Some of his adventures gained the attention of Britain and upon returning home Blunt wrote a series of essays on England's policy of outrage in Egypt and India. Not content with this anti-imperialistic mission, he warmly espoused the cause of Ireland and in 1887 was cast into prison for having taken part in a prohibited meeting at Woodford, Galway. "Whoever writes the lining of English history," says Shane Leslie, "must consult the little-known monographs of Wilfrid Blunt criticising England's rule in Ireland, Egypt, and India."

If all this is not of itself very poetic, it will suggest very clearly the kind of verse to which Wilfrid Scawen Blunt affixed his name. Most of his best work is to be found in "Love Sonnets of Proteus" and "Seven Golden Odes of Arabia," a series of translations done with the assistance of his wife. They are songs distinctive of the man of action, impatient of cloying colour, conventions of form, and subtlety, but they are instead direct, genuine, and surprisingly virile. The individuality of the man is further shown by his quixotic choice of the sonnet form, which he employs, however, with more than Shakesperian modifications; but that is after all the man's way, and it is the sentimentalist like Walt Whitman who betrays his weakness by running wildly over the page. Here is a sextet from a love-sonnet, "St. Valentine's Day," to show the vigorous chafing of his muse:

"I knew the spring was come. I knew it even
Better than all by this, that through my chase
In bush and stone and hill and sea and heaven
I seem'd to see and follow still your face.
Your face my quarry was. For it I rode,
My horse a thing of wings, myself a god."

That Wilfrid Blunt is a genuine Englishman, despite his political opinions, the fine sonnet on "Gibraltar" will suffice to show: but he is the Englishman of an age now almost forgotten—the age before industry, when man was free as the hills he roamed, and when chivalry was constant in its service of the star. In many ways he has been a Stevenson whose craving has been appeased, whose hunger for the wild paths around the world has sought its fill in more substantial things than sonorous sentences. Blunt's poetry is too much the expression of his independent character to become popular in these days of æsthetic rhythms and carefully groomed ideas. His definite intellectual position is, of course, not due to his breaking of the conventions, nor did he utter paragraphs of nonsense from the philosophy of Rousseau. He has not been a radical but a spectre—something that in the older days was more plentiful and deserves in these the almost obsolete title of "man."

From the rugged manliness of Wilfrid Blunt one goes, with a sense of fitness, to the delicately feminine charm of Louise Imogen Guiney. Although she was the poet of a few in days when no poetry addressed itself to many, she has been remembered since her death with an affectionate admiration to which only the finest, most genial spirits have a right. Her verses were flowers and she, perhaps, was fairer than any of them—a woman of the morning, with a taste for the beautiful ages. Born in Massachusetts and educated nearby, Miss Guiney came to feel "the love of man which calleth overseas, and from towers afar off." The later years of her life were spent with modest

grace at Oxford, where as "a mere mole of the enchanted Bodleian" she stained her fingers with the lore
of Christendom. Memories of the Catholic past grew
real under her eyes, and she whom the beauty of life
had stirred to song knew also the silent beauty of
death. She was of straight American descent, of
course; but we have placed her among the English
poets because that seems to have been her election.

The bulk of Miss Guiney's work was done in prose
of a vibrant, intimate texture that rivals the earlier
mastery of Mme. de Sévigné. Perhaps it was her Irish
blood, or perhaps it was destiny, that made her write
so well in the best manner of the French. Her prose
is not so perfect as Mrs. Meynell's, but it is more
responsive, less didactic, more tenderly human. There
are passages to which the heart answers directly, and
the refinement of them is like a subtle natural perfume.
"Patrins," a book of crisp personal essays, is probably
the most familiar, but it seems that if any work of hers
is worthy of immortality it is "Monsieur Henri." This
"Foot-note to French History" is the gay and poignant story of Rochejaquelin. His was a character to
which Miss Guiney's nature called out in answer: his
chivalry, gentleness, and *bravoure* were her own. One
feels that the book, small and exquisite though it may
be, is full of regulated virility. The words move with
the symmetry of noble speech and sparkle with the
gladness of youth. "Stress must be laid," says the
author, "upon heroes; they are the universal premise":
and her emphasis is unforgettable. Beside the fine
grace of this book, Ruskin is ponderous and Howells a
mere bludgeoner; it is not given to men to write thus.

Yet, though this is her best work, there is art for the most critical in "Goosequill Papers," in the Memoir of Hurrell Froude, in everything she did.

As a poet Louise Imogen Guiney wrote what her heart dictated and no more. It is to be regretted that she could not leave a half-dozen portly volumes rather than one slight book; but that is a sheaf heavy with grain and gold. The cheerful audacity with which she faced life was characteristic to the end, but appears brightest, perhaps, in the ballads:

> "Let cowards and laggards fall back! but alert to
>   the saddle,
>   Straight, grim, and abreast, go the weather-worn,
>   galloping legion,
>   With a stirrup-cup each to the lily of women that
>   loves him."

Yet, though the smile was bright, tears stood close by with something of the sweet Celtic melancholy in them,

> "The cabin door looks down a furze-lighted hill,
>   And far as Leighlin Cross the fields are green and still.
>   But once I hear the blackbird in Leighlin hedges call,
>   The foolishness is on me, and the wild tears fall!"

Then, best of all there was the loyalty to Faith that warmed her inner life, expressing itself with veiled reticence and yet appealingly. No woman could have been less an Amazon, and still her religious verse throbs with pain met and overborne, with the victorious peace of prayer. Knowing when to bow her head, she met life sternly though in tears, mindful of the beauty which is hidden by the thorny hedge. Perhaps she said all these things best in that perfect poem, "Beati Mortui," written for those

"Who out of wrong
  Run forth with laughter and a broken thong;
  Who win from pain their strange and flawless grant
  Of peace anticipant;
  Who cerements lately wore of sin, but now,
  Unbound from foot to brow,
  Gleam in and out of cities, beautiful
  As sun-born colours of a forest pool
  Where autumn sees
  The splash of walnuts from her thinning trees."

From Miss Guiney's virginal presence one goes gladly and with a sense of fitness to a boy whose short life was busy with stealthy verses made in homage to the loveliness of God. Digby Dolben, dead at nineteen, was already a poet, leaving verse that is remarkably mature. Handsome of body and soul, carefully educated and blessed with a radiant disposition, his soul consecrated itself to religion with a kind of abandon. Unaided he entertained a vision of the Church which alone possesses the Reality, and sought to grope his way. Death overtook him before he had entered the gate, chiefly because family opposition had made delay necessary. Dolben's poetry is a series of tributes to the things of faith, together with examinations of conscience before the Lord whom he dared not confess. There is pure melody in his lyrics and wide knowledge of the invisible world: is it a boy, one asks, who writes the "Shrine" or "Sister Death"? But wonder increases to the point of amazement with the reading of "Dum Agonizatur Anima," a poignant confession of

religious irresolution, of weakness, and of hope, done
in the manner of Newman's "Gerontius."

"And we who follow in His martyr train
Have access only through the courts of pain,
Yet on the *Via Dolorosa* He
Precedes us with His sweet Humanity."

Two months after laying aside this impressive but
unfinished revelation, Digby Dolben fainted while swimming and all that he might have been ceased to be.
But there had come into his story a kindly fulness from
the mothering shadow of the Church.

Let us go back for a moment to the memory of Adelaide Proctor, the eldest daughter of "Barry Cornwall."
Her verse lacks the artistry, the inner glow, of great
poetry, but strikes a simple chord to which the humbler
mind instinctively responds. "Legends and Lyrics,"
the best of Miss Proctor's work, has shared the great
popularity of Longfellow; and such poems as "A Lost
Chord," "Thankfulness," and "A Legend of Provence"
were known to a whole generation of the poor. It is
easy to scoff at the fluent rhythm, the commonplace
ideas and the general didacticism of such verse, but it
is impossible to deny that it sprang sincerely from the
sincerest of lives. Adelaide Proctor found her way
into the Church without any desperate effort. "She
was," said her admirer, Charles Dickens, "a finely sympathetic woman with a great accordant heart and a
sterling noble nature." Having given her life wholly
to the service of the unfortunate, she died from the
strain of devoted overwork. Certainly she understood
the songs of the modern poor, for whom

"The Past and the Future are nothing
In the face of the stern today,"

better than any mere intellectual can hope to. If this
be the only reason for keeping her memory green, it is,
at least, a reason.

One passes naturally from a life so austerely given
to charity to the blasted careers of those poets who
came out of the darkness of decadence into the Church
for the warding off of final despair. She who for two
thousand years has busied herself with the sins of men
did not disdain to aid these at the last, although they
could give Her no service in return. There is a shred
of Catholic tradition in the work of Oscar Wilde, but
it is a soiled shred, polluted with that touch of moral
leprosy which the brilliant debauchee left an imprint
of on everything that came into his life. Even "De
Profundis," probably a sincere effort to write sincerely
of the soul, has somehow the odour of medicaments.
The career of Ernest Dowson, who retarded his conversion until a life of indulgence had sentenced him
irretrievably to an early death, did write poetry which
is touching as a recognition of the mercy of God.
"Extreme Unction" is a Catholic poem, but its inspiration is the grave. Like Aubrey Beardsley and so many
of the French decadents, these geniuses, unbalanced by
the sickly caste of modern matter-worship, came at last
to the foot of the Scarlet Hill. It is something that
the Catholic Spirit, which could not save their lives,
did heal their souls. The entry into the Church of
Lord Alfred Douglas, at one time intimately associated
with Wilde, did not altogether calm the spirit of this
recklessly impetuous man. A journalist virulent in

his defense of conservative government, Douglas is a master of the sonnet. His poems, while not so abstract in inspiration, have the finish and verbal brilliancy of Santayana.

With an ancestry so varied and in general so distinctly regal, the future of the Catholic poetry in England cannot fail to be beautiful. It is natural, however, that this new age should bring changes in attitude and method—this age so restless in spirit, so raucous in its expression of discontent, and so fiercely wounded, too, in its martyrdom. The cry is for facts in the midst of delirious laughter; for dogma (covertly) in the clutches of despair. It is not true that the Victorians despised truth (shades of Newman and Carlyle!) but that what they knew of it was still considered effective. The modern man clamours for the naked truth and expects to see it shivering and impotent; and so, what he really admires is the half-truth, dark, ugly, and animal. To this no genuine poet can consent, but the singer of to-day, like his predecessor of yesteryear, must make the commonplace extraordinary, and this he cannot do if his tunes have worn out with the times. No one need be surprised, therefore, if the rhythm and imagery of the Victorians are to be somewhat summarily dealt with; if there is to be woven into the fiber of verse a wealth of elemental things, of images taken from the streets, of words gathered from the market place, and of strange, barbaric colour and music—tom-toms and indigo.

The struggle for the mastery of verse is being fought out to-day between an ideal that is older than the Renaissance and an ultra-modern principle which never

has been, and probably never will be, put into successful practice. In reality it is a contest between the
poet born of nature and the poet begotten of modern
thought; it involves more than *vers libre* and the sonnet, it is assuredly not narrower than the distance
between a pibroch and a klaxon. No one can foretell
what is going to happen; but it is comparatively easy
to point out the relation that exists between the new
Catholic poet and the older masters, who lived closer to
nature than men have come during the past century.
One is quite warranted in saying that Patmore's protest
against the diction of Wordsworth has been accepted:
"The best poet is not he whose verses are the most
easily scanned, and whose phraseology is the commonest
in its materials, and the most direct in its arrangement: but rather he whose language combines the greatest imaginative accuracy with the most elaborate and
sensible metrical organization, and who, in his verse,
preserves everywhere the living sense of meter." But
just as the pre-Raphaelites sought to follow nature
instead of convention, the mellifluent word-artistry of
Tennyson has been abandoned by the poets for something more homely and homelike. The Chaucer revival,
carried so far by John Masefield, the earthiness of
"The Shropshire Lad," and particularly the nature
poetry of Yeats, Russell, Ledwidge, and other masters
of the Celtic revival, to some extent govern the direction of modern English poetry where it has not grown
bizarre in its revolt and followed the amazing intellectual antics of Ezra Pound.

From this movement Catholic poetry cannot fail to
gain, for Catholic art in its best, most vital forms
antedates the Renaissance. May we not cast out our

semi-Methodist English hymns for something more substantially like the songs of Fortunatus? Francis
Thompson was fearless enough to borrow rhythms from
the breviary; Patmore went to St. John of the Cross,
and Hopkins to the old Greek hymnody. Catholic
verse to-day is not less resolute in its choice of melody.
The poetry of Chesterton and Belloc, tuneful, martial,
close to earth, will be considered later. For the moment we shall content ourselves with Mr. Theodore
Maynard, a poet of the things which Mr. Chesterton
prizes most highly: laughter, religion, freedom, and
wine.

> "And the little grey imp of laughter
>   Laughs in the soul of me,"

he sings, with just a bit of futility. Somehow one cannot imagine Mr. Maynard's soul thus taken possession
of. "Cecidit, Cecidit, Babylonia Magna" expresses a
manly contempt for inhumanity; "The World's Miser"
is a reverently mystic hymn, and the later poem to "St.
George," quiet, sad, not at all imbued with laughter,
is almost great verse written out of a mood of defeat.
Mr. Maynard is a good poet, though perhaps essentially
a poetic Boswell. Almost every idea to which the masterful G. K. C. has given expression is chronicled somewhere in Mr. Maynard's songs. He is an admirable
reflector, too; confident of his inspiration he forges
the tune with fervour, and confident in himself he hums
his drinking songs in the face of a boresome world. Of
course, Mr. Maynard is not personally a boisterous
man, but instead an admirable, human, rather reticent
one; a man whose humour, delicately keen, makes the

stoutly defended dogmas of his religion seem a handsome soldier's code of honour. If he is not very original, he has at least caught originality from one of the
few places on earth where there is still danger of con-
tagion.

And in all, it seems that the most significant work
being done by any of the contemporary English Catholic poets is that of Helen Parry Eden. This sturdy
and altogether admirable convert to the Church is the
author, as everyone ought to know, of two distinctive
volumes of verse, "Bread and Circuses" and "Coal and
Candlelight." These are songs of a woman with a
home and children, songs that seem so obvious a part of
daily life that their realism is one of the most brightly
optimistic facts in modern letters. A number of the
poems are written to children or about children, a
matter which Patmore and Thompson also considered
of some importance. The rest is soul verse, not theosophic banality, but remarkably sane, workable, and
yet intensely spiritual poetry. One cannot help thinking that if Saint Jerome had met, during the course of
his spiritual labours, with a feminine poet who said,

> "Sweet Sorrow, play a grateful part,
> Break me the marble of my heart
> And of its fragments pave a street
> Where, to my bliss, myself may meet
> One hastening with pierced feet"

he could not have kept back an expression of intense
satisfaction. How admirably close to the real a sacrament may be brought is shown by "A Purpose of
Amendment":

"So when the absolution's said
Behind the grille, and I may go,
And all the flowers of sin are dead,
And all the stems of sin laid low,
And I am come to Mary's shrine
To lay my hopes within her hand—
Ah, in how fair and green a line
The seedling resolutions stand."

Whether Mrs. Eden is writing "To Betsy-Jane, on Her Desiring to Go Incontinently to Heaven," or to "Thomas Black, Cat to the Sloane Museum," she never fails to take delight in the epistle and to say something quite as delightful. "Coal and Candlelight" is a better domestic poem than Wordsworth managed to write, and "Trees" succeeds, where others have failed, in really saying a word about trees. If the good humour and the spontaneous piety of these verses are noteworthy, the element of satire has a scarcely less prominent place; the poet has profited by the teaching of Jane Austen. Dean Swift would have chuckled over Mrs. Eden's rebuke to a time-suffering journalist who had complimented a noble lord on his nobleness— in hard cash:

"Here is a rule to save the like mistakes
And sift the patriots from the money-makers,
These take an interest in their country's aches
And those an interest in their country's acres."

Mrs. Eden has written altogether too little; it is unfortunate that this is not an age for "Canterbury Tales." If one may venture an opinion based on her later poems, the war has borne heavily upon her soul; and *that* is after all the fount of song.

If Catholic poetry can move forward with the spontaneity, rich candour, and genuine fervour which it has manifested thus far, its position in English letters will be free and great.   Asserting as it does the stability of the universe, it can hold its own while the earth rocks.   Is it not true that the freedom of the human race is measured by its bondage to song, that its buoyancy will always seek an outlet in make-believe?   Let it be repeated: the poet is a child and the Catholic poet is a normal and obedient child.   And in more ways than one are the words fulfilled: only the children shall enter into the kingdom.

BOOK NOTE

The best work of Alice Meynell has been issued in three volumes: "Poems," "Essays," "Mary, the Mother of God."   Now that W. S. Blunt's "My Diaries" have been republished, information about him may be sought with great profit there.   Louise I. Guiney's own selection of her poems is entitled, "Happy Ending."   A large part of her prose has not been collected; "Monsieur Henri" is out of print.   The only edition of Digby Dolben's verse is that issued, with a memoir, by Robert Bridges.   "Louise Imogen Guiney" by Alice Brown, is an inspiring memoir.   An interesting sketch of Miss Guiney's personality is that by Jessie B. Rittenhouse, *Bookman*, vol. 52.   Dolben is presented sympathetically in an essay by B. W Cornish, *Dublin Review,* vol. 151.   In connection with Adelaide Proctor, see the introduction by Charles Dickens to the volume of her poems.   G. K. Chesterton supplies a sparkling introduction to the first volume of Maynard's collected verse.   For information about the decadents, see "Oscar Wilde," by Frank Harris; "Oscar Wilde and Myself" by Alfred Douglas; "The Letters of Aubrey Beardsley"; and "Palms of Papyrus," by M. Monahan.   For details of a more general or a biographical character, see "The End of a Chapter," by Shane Leslie; "The Catholic Encyclopedia"; and "The Catholic Who's Who."

CHAPTER TEN

RUSKIN, PATER, AND THE PRE-RAPHAELITES

"Domine, dilexi decorem domus tuæ; et locum habitationis gloriæ tuæ."

Psalm 25.

"EVERYTHING that is Romanish," wrote the liberal and sincere Bishop Wilberforce, "is a stench in my nostrils." He was a worthy man and, it need scarcely be added, given to straightforward diction; wherefore one hopes charitably that he did not altogether realize the inroads which Catholicism had made into the English thought of his time. When Darwinism and Bishop Colenso began to disturb the complacency of the British spirit with their negations, the Church was already abroad with scarcely less revolutionary affirmations. She did not always carry the day completely, and there were many who loved her garments well without ever being able to persuade themselves that she was altogether respectable. Some idea of the half-way house reached by Pusey, Keble, and others has been given; it remains to suggest the influence of the Catholic idea on one of the most influential literary movements of the nineteenth century, the movement which is sometimes called æsthetic and which at any rate began its consideration of life with a study of art. Seeing how things were in fiction, it demanded

166

that they be thus in fact also; its chief proponents were almost Malebranches of the museum.

In a good many ways such thinking seems like putting the cart before the horse; but its great and unforgettable merit is that it really puts something before, that is, believes that the cumulative experiences and intuitions of humanity have their value. Once a man is inclined to adopt such a view of things he cannot neglect the Catholic Spirit, which is the past of Europe. Nor did the English movement we are about to examine fail to make this discovery. It may be said to have begun with John Ruskin, a very original, stormy, and sensitive man, whose career scarcely needs to be outlined here. Reared in strict Evangelism, his poetic nature was fired first by Walter Scott, then by art, and finally by the great memorials of Christian art. Perhaps it is not too much to say that Kenelm Digby was in the end Ruskin's chief teacher except in the matter of style, wherein the pupil proved *magister magistrum*. His doctrine, despite all errors of detail and judgment, gained everlasting effectiveness by insisting that half of life at least is beauty and that the better half. Having made it possible to speak aloud of art, he preached it vigorously to society.

Civilization, he declared, had turned aside from its ancient highway into ugly and degenerate paths. Ruskin saw clearly that there had been a break in England's history, and for him it was something like the smashing of beautiful glass. "I simply cannot paint," he writes, "nor read, nor look at minerals, nor do anything else that I like, and the very light of the morning sky, when there is any—which is seldom nowadays, near London—has become hateful to me, because of the misery that I know of, and see signs of, where I know it not, which no imagination can interpret too bitterly." And the aging Ruskin abandoned the examination of pictures to become the antagonist of political economy. For this he has never been forgiven by temperamental amateurs, but it was a great discovery: Ruskin understood that there had once been a connection between beauty and society, between the artist and the artisan, and that unless this were restored the crafts would remain crushing and mechanical. His practical schemes, like all such isolated expedients, made little progress; the Guild of St. George was merely an honourable undertaking. The doctrine he preached was the important matter, for its roots lay firm in human memory: it was a gospel to which the commonest man would turn by atavistic instinct and to which Christendom had been dedicated.

Farther than this Ruskin never went. Looking upon nature as everyone's heritage, his egoism became social; looking upon the past, his knowledge begat collective power. He was not really a philosopher but a poet, and although poets make mistakes, their intuitions are generally correct. And while the æsthetic movement in England was not altogether dependent upon Ruskin, he remains its first parent. Perhaps that is why the younger æsthetes will have nothing to do with him. The older ones, however, who were not so far advanced, took dictation from him rather obediently. Of no one is this more true than of Walter Pater, the subdued, twilight-loving acolyte of beauty whose carefully written sayings are now strangely sought after. His voice is stronger than even Arnold's in present-day criticism, for his outlook seems more modern. If there is one thing which distinguishes Pater's mind from that of his age it is, besides his concern with beauty simply as beauty, the fact that his intellect was centripetal while others were centrifugal: that is, while his neighbors like Carlyle, Arnold, and even Newman began with a fixed idea and followed it, like some philosophic North Star, as near the confines of knowledge as they could come, Pater traveled vaga-bondishly through the realms of Beauty and finally reached a destination as closely resembling Truth as his mind was probably capable of dwelling in.

Being a man who has been extravagantly praised and severely satirized, and concerning whom even his two chief biographers disagree vehemently, Walter Horatio Pater's very reticent simplicity of life baffles insight into his personality. He was born on August 4, 1839, into a family whose Dutch ancestry seems to have been held in high regard and whose male members had, until the defection of Pater's grandfather, been reared as Catholics. The lad was always keenly responsive to the beautiful in his surroundings and often played at Mass, being decked out for the purpose in a set of miniature vestments. Education meant for him very largely the classics and the influence of Keble, whom he came to know at Oxford. His hard literary work, however, led him to abandon any predominant religious inclination for the cult of humanism; he studied the great French stylists, Sainte-Beuve and Flaubert, and came to sympathize earnestly with the pre-Raphaelites. Gradually his purpose in life became the writing of a few essays annually and he finally resigned even the Fellowship in Brasenose College.

Pater's long residence in a few small rooms at Oxford

and later at St. Giles made him a traditional university
figure, although he cannot be said ever to have been
an academic enthusiast. He took a friendly interest
in those young men who came to him for advice, corrected their essays carefully, lectured rather loftily
on philosophy, and loved the games and by-play
wherein youth is always freshest and most comely.
Occasionally he went to the Continent for a visit to
the shrines of loveliness—Amiens, Azay-le-Rideau, the
whole of France—and then retreated to Oxford, where
he laboriously brought together his random notes for
their fusion into another essay. Kindly, almost ascetic,
he loved the beautiful in life only after it had been
exorcised, as it were, by the tranquil intellect. Naturally such a mode of living, which after all was contemplative without any robustness of vision, made for
isolation, for misunderstanding, for nonsensical imitation even. Pater's only luxuries were a bowl of dried
roses, a jaunty tie, and a beautiful style; his disciples
had numerous others. It was not that men could not
rise to the master's level; they mistook it for a hill
and leaped over. "I wish they wouldn't call me a
'hedonist'," he once remarked a little sadly to Mr.
Gosse. "It produces such a bad effect on the minds
of people who don't know Greek." Pater was, in fact,
the anchorite of truth, striving to "burn with a hard,
gem-like flame" and like the Suttee, also to do his duty.
That it brought happiness he would have been the last
to assert, and would probably have declared with
Musset: *"Je sais d'immortelles qui sont de purs sang-
lots."*

It must not be forgotten for a moment that Pater's
chief business was style, and that he succeeded in merit-

ing Bourget's adjective, "perfect." Writing was attended for him with something like a ritual, to which he lent all the pomp denied himself in other ways. What his theory was may be gathered easily from the famous essay on style. He tried not only to rear the straight and symmetrical bell tower, but also to put into it the bell, whose melody was never brazen or triumphant but approached that *perfume* of sound which the mediæval ringers are supposed to have drawn from their chimes. The method was most toilsome, being the merging of many separate thoughts into the whole, accomplished by a steady, careful meditativeness that was redeemed from servility by the artistic pleasure it gave. Somewhat humorous instances of Pater's meticulous industry are numerous; thus, upon being asked by a puzzled friend the meaning of a sentence, he studied it anxiously and then replied, "Ah, I see the printer has omitted a dash." His style, in the end, achieves both music and architecture and is charming chiefly by reason of this complexity, this interweaving of purpose, while it lacks the vibrancy, the ready healthfulness, in which English prose from Scott to Newman has been the counterpart of Attic composition. If there be any truth in the statement that the writer has the best style who seems to have none, by so much truth does Pater miss the mastery of words.

Now any consideration of Pater's ideas will necessarily involve a consideration of his development. In early youth the seductive appeal of outward form had been modified for him by a deep religious instinct which rendered the beauty of nature something like a sacrament. Later the religious side of his nature weakened under the application to metaphysics and

left him the devotee of a paganism which did not dull
the one leading urge of his life, intellectual contemplation. With the essay on Winckelmann Pater's thought
assumed form. "Religions," he says, "as they grow
by natural laws out of man's life are modified by whatever modifies his life. They brighten under a bright
sky, they become liberal as the social range widens,
they grow intense and shrill in the clefts of human life,
where the spirit is narrow and confined, and the stars
are visible at noonday; and a fine analysis of these
differences is one of the gravest functions of religious
criticism." Here he confesses, despite the liquefaction
of dogma assumed, to two things: his perception of the
continuity of the religious instinct and his great attraction to mediæval life, which interested him most to
the end. He wanted to prove that Christianity was
nothing more than the natural outcropping of a
vegetarian pagan sentiment in order to make it earthy
and enjoyable rather than supernatural and trouble-
some.

This pragmatism of beauty is at its height again
in the essay "Leonardo da Vinci," with its famous
interpretation of La Giaconda, "the woman who, as
Leda was the mother of Helen of Troy, and, as Saint
Anne, the mother of Mary"; in the later essay, "The
School of Giorgine" where it is asserted that "all art
constantly aspires towards the condition of music";
in fact, throughout both "Greek Studies" and "The
Renaissance." Pater understood full well that the
mirth of the Attic day had been lost and one need not
believe that he was really much concerned with getting
it back. After all, he dealt with modern complexity,
"that strange perpetual weaving and unweaving of our-

selves," rather than with the blithe simplicity of Homer. His avowed purpose was "to define beauty not in the abstract, but in the most concrete terms possible, to find not a universal formula for it, but the formula which expresses most adequately this or that manifestation of it." Indeed, for the contemplative without the vision of God, this is the only possible position; and Pater therefore promulgated the atomic theory of art and insight which he dignified with the title of Cyrenaicism.

A slightly different position is taken up in that most remarkable of all Pater's books, "Marius the Epicurean." The young philosopher moving from the beautiful seclusion of his ancestral estate to the center of pagan society, comes armed with an idealized form of Epicureanism and determined to find a philosophy which will quiet the restlessness of his thought. He meets the best minds that Rome can boast of—Apuleius, Marcus Aurelius, Lucian—but in each instance is confronted with a system that breaks down at the point of tension. Marius' reaction to the meditations of Aurelius is especially interesting; he unfolds the bands of thought in which the great Stoic is enshrouded and finds the man shivering underneath his skillful optimism, bent with the burden of inexplicable evil. Then, at last, there is Cornelius the Christian and the house of Cecelia where the mysteries of the Faith are celebrated and whence the odour of defeat seems to have been banished by mystic and eternal roses. Marius bows to the hope vouchsafed here, and more sincerely to the beauty of the ritual. Taken captive during a raid upon the Christians, he contrives the escape of Cornelius, is abandoned in a small town to die, and is attended by other Christians who, considering him one of their own, administer the last rites. With happy resignation and a temperate curiosity in the journey which he is about to undertake, Marius dies.

It is, of course, a very personal book in which Pater patiently reflected the moods of his own spirit and let it be known how near his pagan wanderings had brought him to the Christian bourne. Closer than this hopeful interest he did not come, for as is shown in his review of "Robert Elsmere" and in the final essay on Pascal, religious belief was based for him upon the assumption of a consoling probability and not upon what are termed facts. Newman might have written the "Grammar of Assent" with Pater in mind. The conclusion to be drawn from "Marius the Epicurean" is that while its hero did not accept Catholicism as truth, he accepted it, in preference to paganism, as beauty. He saw that every form of naturalistic philosophy is insufficient in the face of evil and is, therefore, too simple; that the Christian view, if one can accept it, cures the inner malady of nature with a supernatural remedy.

Any criticism of Pater must begin with a frank statement of his position. Throughout life, it was the sensuous, the physically graceful, which fascinated him most, however much he might intellectualize it. He was almost naturally a pagan, and if there is anything that distinguishes paganism from Christianity it is this: paganism is stationary and statuesque, while Christianity is mobile, adaptive. It is the difference between the Parthenon and Bourges, between the Hercules and the Moses of Michael Angelo. Now this fact is paradoxically matched with another: whereas paganism with its multitudinous contours is fluid, Christianity is straight and solid. Parmenides the static and Hereclitus the kinetic are the types of heathen thought and, in a sense, are complementary; Christendom is different because it has dogma. Now the upshot of this is that Pater's conception of art and thought was that they resembled the musk-sweet waters of music, but that they were waters which did not move, which were forceless. This, too, is what formed his style, so admirably adapted to eliminate the gulf between Helen and Mary the Maid. What spoiled the apprehension of Christianity for him was that he beheld the Mass as a tableau instead of as a drama. Marius was a marble hero, goodly to look upon but useless in battle.

This pale immobility he never escaped; in fact, the still waters were to prove themselves stagnant. In "Denys l'Auxerrois" and indeed throughout the "Imaginary Portraits," we are face to face with the unrestrained morbidity which will later mark the decadents. These are stories which demand dramatic manipulation, which cry out for a solution from angel or devil. It is rather appalling to find them treated with refined Epicureanism. Still, if he had gone a little farther, Pater might have discovered the Demon as did Villiers de l'Isle Adam. Both were egoists, but the French novelist's individualism was a sincere concern with himself in conflict with the age. Of Pater it is even possible to assert that his egoism was the result of not thinking enough about himself. A serious grasp of his own acting personality would have saved him from a too exclusive concern with his thoughts. He sat entranced beside the beautiful waters of his own mind, and nothing could have induced him to disturb their shimmering perfection by taking a swim.

In the end one says of Pater that he was a contemplative whose meditation eliminated the element of personality. With his innate nobility of character and his devotion to the beautiful, he would have become a mystic of the highest rank had he been able to feel certain of the reality of God. The reasons for his failure to do so are inscrutable. Still, his discovery of the Christian tradition as the one sufficiently beautiful idea, as the one release from the darkness that haunts the brighest places in nature, is truly remarkable. As the explorer of the outlying, resplendently purple mists of thought he had hunted one refuge for a heart whose quest was beauty. That he asked for nothing more is not his fault, but his manner. Believing that art should have "the soul of humanity in it," he tried honestly to be an artist.

Although many men have felt the influence of Pater, no disciple of his makes the same nobility of appeal as Lionel Johnson (1867-1902). Slender, graceful, impeccably neat, and earnestly recollected, this young poet was a man whose blood was that of a soldier race but whose soul was given to the priesthood of art. Admitted into the Church during his Oxford career, he caught from Pater a hunger for the stateliness of those ages which bred and saved our culture, and this he never appeased. What the master stood for in Johnson's life may be seen from an essay on the "Work of Walter Pater" and better still from the beautiful elegy:

"Gracious God, keep him; and God grant to me
By miracle to see

That unforgettably most gracious friend
In the never-ending end."

Johnson's own work falls very naturally into two
parts: "The Art of Thomas Hardy" together with
shorter essays, and his poetry. The great criticism of
the Wessex novelist is noteworthy for many reasons;
its fairness of judgment (though the author was only
twenty-seven when the book appeared), its thorough
grasp of the classic spirit, and its unflagging beauty of
style which, not so ornate or intricate as Pater's, has
greater virility. If the volume was dedicated to a consideration of Mr. Hardy, its author was by no means
averse to expressing his views on literature in general
and on the work of his own time in particular.

"Great art," he declares, "is never out of date, nor
obsolete: like the moral law of Sophocles, 'God is great
in it and grows not old'; like the moral law of Kant,
it is of equal awe and splendour with the stars. . . .
In our day, many men of admirable powers love to
think of themselves as alone in the world, homeless in
the universe; without fathers, without mothers; heirs
to no inheritance, to no tradition; bound by no law,
and worshippers at no shrine; without meditation,
without reverence, without patience, they utter, and
would have us hear, their hasty and uncertain fancies.
. . . It is the office of art to disengage from the conflict and the turmoil of life the interior virtue, the
informing truth, which compose the fine spirit of its
age; and to do this, with no pettiness of parochial
pride in the fashions and the achievements of its own
age rather with an orderly power to connect what is,
with what has been, looking out prophetically to what
will be."

For Lionel Johnson, then, the inspiration of Pater had led to the idea of embracing culture as a transcendent inheritance which was common as well as invaluable. He conceived of art as the living residue of a succession of immortal minds.

This view is, no doubt, that of a poet and Lionel Johnson was a master of song. But he had a straightforward, clean, unprejudiced mind that found the beauty of life largely in the moral law. No one will object to this except when it hampers the emotional glow which is poetry's priceless treasure. Johnson is always, at first, a trifle too stately and ponderously reflective for his mission as a troubadour; still, once the melody has been struck, he becomes free as any jovial singer. Such lyrics as "Our Lady of the Snows," "De Profundis," and "Our Lady of the May," are most delicate and fragrant, but best among these lyrics is, perhaps, that stirring defiance of evil, "The Dark Angel."

> "Do what thou wilt, thou shalt not so,
> Dark Angel! triumph over me:
> Lonely unto the lone I go;
> Divine, to the Divinity."

Religious in feeling as all of Johnson's work is, he found a mighty source of inspiration in the martyrdom of a neighboring people to whom "Ireland and Other Poems" is dedicated. The title poem is a magnificent expression of sympathy, a worthy companion to Mangan's imperishable lament, "Dark Rosaleen." Johnson devoted himself to the Celtic cause with the ardent energy of Byron, but with a greater pity and

love. His heart bled for Ireland because he could not
help it; sympathy was the natural expression of his
manhood and its motive force. "With all his deference," says Miss Guiney, "his dominant compassion,
his grasp of the spiritual and the unseen, his feet
stood foursquare upon rock. He was a tower of wholesomeness in the decadence which his short life spanned.
. . . He suffered indeed, but he won manifold golden
comfort from the mercies of God, from human excel-
lence, the arts and the stretches of meadow, sky,
and sea." After all, it was a tragically short life,
broken at the end by disease and loneliness, and crushed
finally by an accident in the streets of London. Nevertheless it was a sweet, full life, too, into which nothing
entered that was mean or vile, which was fired by a
noble understanding of the synthesis of the ages, and
beautified and rendered secure by the consecration of
the Church. That which Pater had sought in vain
came to his disciple as a fresh and easy gift; but his
possession of it found him meek even though he was a
soldier.

While Lionel Johnson made the step forward which
Pater could not learn, other disciples of beauty pushed
the cult of paganism to a lower level and coveted the
disease from which their master had shrunk. There
came into English letters the voice of feverish Paris;
intoxicated by the fetor of life mingled with religion's
incense, hopelessly degraded because it was not altogether hopeless. Something has been said already of
the enigmatic and jaundiced figure of Oscar Wilde,
who in writing "whatever is realized is right" made at
once a horrible epigram and a horrible lie; of Dowson
and Beardsley, victims of the modern educational de-

nial of the will. These were not so much followers of
Pater as interpreters of one aspect of that humanism
which he had been the first to revive in England.

Such, in brief, is the story of the men who sought a
refuge in the past from the complacent industrial ugliness of England. None of them succeeded fully, and in
the eyes of the world all proved themselves Quixotic.
None the less, it was something to have discovered the
great tradition of Beauty which the modern philistine
hates worse than hell; it was even better, surely, to
have felt that this tradition had been sanctified, that its
roots lay in the religious spirit which Christendom had
trained to the lovely service of the Cross. But in the
end they were all outsiders who wrested the key to the
citadel of culture as men do who realize that it has not
been born into the family. In a different way there
came into our nineteenth century literature a force
from a land where the past was still in the soil—Italy.
With the appearance of the Rossettis, Dante Gabriel
and Christina, the Dantean groves for which England
so mysteriously yearned sent ambassadors to the North.

Their influence, which has been large, is inextricably
bound up with what is termed pre-Raphaelitism, a
movement in art which has been variously described, but
which may be defined tentatively as a sincere treatment
of nature by the light of natural instinct. For the
Rossettis it meant very truly something which antedates Raphael: the mystic fervour of Dante and Peru-
gino, the religious art of the Catholic ages. Of course
neither was actually a Catholic; both were national
Italian Protestants, hot from the revolution and separated from the Church in every way excepting the
one which seemed most important to them, artistic

sympathy. Their strength lay in the power of their inheritance; their weakness almost directly in that which deprived them of a portion of it. With them to live was to be æsthetic, although in the case of Christina the flame burned almost too white for art.

The inspiration of Dante Gabriel Rossetti was neither constant nor sure of itself, but drew its glory from what was almost a perpetual dream. Considering life very much as if he were a stranger, this poet found in it strange deeps and heights, colours that seem unearthly and rhythms that are caught from the rising of the tide on an unseen sea. While he did not people the forests with nymphs or gods, he did commingle heaven and earth in a sort of intermediate dimness, a solid twilight, in which souls move heavy with perfume and weighted with golden garments. Rossetti may not have fully understood the symbolism of the early Christian artists, but he came nearer to reproducing it than most modern poets have come. Thompson is Gothic, masterly, structural; Coleridge more ghostly; but Rossetti the most colourful. The Blessed Damozel

> "lean'd out
> From the gold bar of heaven:
> Her blue grave eyes were deeper much
> Than a deep water even.
> She had three lilies in her hand
> And the stars in her hair were seven."

That is, as a matter of fact, how a soul would have been represented in mediæval art, plastic and gorgeous, with the beauty of life. No one can write thus unless he holds as indubitable, imaginatively at least, the existence of a soul, but the intellectual grasp is weak here. The later Christian artists, while preserving the bodily form, attenuated it, made the figure represent the urge of the spirit to be delivered from its prison.

Rossetti was by nature a man of riotous enthusiasms, but his work is too quiet and pictorial. He was utterly incapable of the intellectual rigidity of Dante. Nowhere is this defect shown more clearly than in the famous poem, "Jenny." Here the man who has accompanied a girl of the street to her lodgings sits musing upon her beauty as she, fallen asleep, is sitting beside him. Gradually the sensuous exterior, golden hair, and supple bosom, mirrors her soul, and he is led into a bit of really admirable moralizing upon what may have tarnished the brightness of her virtue. Rising quietly, he places a coin where it will look pretty in her hair and tiptoes out. This poem is no doubt romantically beautiful, but it remains futile because it is inactive; as a study of human nature it may be admirable but it is not human. There is something in it that comes near to silliness. Everywhere in his other poems also, Rossetti removes the eagerness and the passion of man to a tranquil environment and views them in two dimensions. Thus, in "The Wine of Circe" he hears the

"wail from passion's tide-strown shore
Where the dishevelled sea-weed hates the sea."

What Dante Gabriel Rossetti lacked was intellectual conviction, the sense of the reality of spirit as spirit and of body as body. Confusion robs his sacramentalism of the vitality which it possessed in Christian art; he tried to accomplish in philosophic twilight what must be done in believing day. A totally different stand was taken by his sister Christina who, in many ways, is the most interesting modern Englishwoman of letters. Consistently Anglican in her religious affilia- tions, her spirit was that of a cloistered nun dwelling humbly under the rule of Saint Clare. Intense religious conviction twice prevented her marriage; she visited Italy only once and never got over her sorrow at leav- ing the country of which she remained spiritually a native. Transplanted from the time and place into which she would have fitted with perfect contentment, she conveyed to English letters no note of rebellion but instead a song of perfect religious submission, of trembling eagerness to serve transcendently, mystically. Ford Madox Hueffer describes her person thus:

"This black-robed figure, with the clear-cut and olive-coloured features, the dark hair, the restrained and formal gestures, the hands always folded in the lap, the head always judiciously a little on one side, and with the precise enunciation, this tranquil Religious was undergoing within herself always a fierce struggle between the pagan desire for life, the light of sun and love, and an asceticism that, in its almost more than Calvinistic restraint, reached to the point of frenzy.

"The trouble was, of course, that whereas by blood and by nature Christina Rossetti was a Catholic, by upbringing and by all the influences that were around her she was forced into the Protestant communion. Under the influence of a wise confessor the morbidities of her self-abnegation would have been checked, her doubts would have been stilled."

Her life was a groping realization of the Catholic instinct. It is said that she was scrupulously careful not to tread upon a scrap of paper in the street, lest it should bear the Holy Name. Her writing might have been done upon her knees, and her verse is the forgotten song of Christendom, unusually plaintive, the delicate yet intensely passionate obeisance of the soul before the realities of the soul. Occasionally she could be romantic, as in "Goblin Market" with its two softly moulded girls:

> "Like two blossoms on one stem,
> Like two flakes of new-fallen snow,
> Like two wands of ivory
> Tipped with gold for awful kings."

But it was with the questions of life taken seriously—too seriously, in fact—that she was usually concerned:

> "Does the road wind up-hill all the way?
> Yes, to the very end.
> Will the day's journey take the whole long day?
> From morn to night, my friend.
>
> But is there for the night a resting-place?
> A roof for when the slow dark hours begin:
> May not the darkness hide it from my face?
> You cannot miss that inn."

Writing with a beautiful earnestness out of the sadness of her isolation, Christina Rossetti has made poetry almost too grave for song. Hers is the fancy of an abnormally solemn orphan child, distrustful of yet hungering after the laughter of life. She did not influence greatly the character of modern verse, but her individuality has a solid quality that will not brook neglect. And if she did not find her way into the body of the Church, she was united with its soul, an ascetic Keble with the eyes of a wanderer to the ancient places which are forlorn. Strangely different, it is together that the Rossettis belong. He with an etherialized conception of bodily form, colour and rhythm, she with a realistic understanding of the soul, unflinching, striving, are the two sides of the artistic tradition which superseded the pagans. Unfortunately their influence has seldom been felt thus, in unity, and the splendid earnestness of the Italian spirit has been mimicked by a group of muddling æsthetes whose veins, to use Kilmer's vigorous phrase, "drip scented ink." Perhaps their best disciple is that rather unstable Bohemian, Ford Madox Hueffer, pre-Raphaelite in the Rossetti sense while being both more material and less subtly suggestive. An enumeration of others would consume too much space. Let it suffice to mention the names of Katherine Tynan and John Masefield.

On the whole the literary force which came into English letters from a perception and partial expression of the artistic ideals of Christendom emphasized the beauty of the Catholic Spirit and rebelled hotly against the sordid monotony of industrial civilization. Of only one man concerned in it, Lionel Johnson, can it be affirmed that his life was Catholic inwardly and outwardly. Nevertheless, the others in their separate ways bore testimony to the vigour and sanctity of the Church. They were great minds and great hearts, and even in the failure of Ernest Dowson there is a great deal of strength; for it is by eternal hope that men live and by the constancy of their faith in the stars.

BOOK NOTE

See, in a general way, the "Cambridge History of English Literature" and Chesterton's "Victorian Age." The most noteworthy biography of Ruskin is that by Sir E. T. Cook; note also "Victorian Prose Masters," by Brownell, and "Philosophy of Ruskin," by A. D. Chevrillon, of the French Academy. Pater's biographers include A. C. Benson, Wright, and Greenslet. See also, "Pater: a Critical Study," by Edward Thomas; "Egoists," by J. G. Huneker; "Heralds of Revolt," by William Barry; and "The Æsthetic Outlook: Walter Pater," *Edinburgh Review,* 1907. In connection with Johnson, see "The Irish Literary Renaissance," by Boyd, and "The Poets' Chantry," by Katherine Brégy. L. I. Guiney's essay on Johnson is to be found in *The Month,* vol. 100. For information concerning the Rossettis, see "Ruskin, Rossetti, Pre-Raphaelitism," by Wm. M. Rossetti, and "Memories and Impressions," by Ford M. Hueffer. The best view of Christina Rossetti is that supplied by Mackenzie Bell; on Dante Gabriel, see the monographs by William Sharp, H. C. Marillier, and A. C. Benson.

CHAPTER ELEVEN

THE CHRONICLERS OF CHRISTENDOM

"The customary prejudices against the 'laws of history' cannot withstand five minutes of reflection; for, however little thought one may give to them, only the rules of mathematics are their superiors in certitude."

PIERRE VILLON.

THERE is something in every religion of eternity, but for Christians eternity is fundamental. Perhaps no one has stated more dramatically than Saint Augustine the mysterious fluidity of time—the imperceptible and awesome shading-off of the present into the past and forward into a future that is always an undiscovered country. Nevertheless, this thought which stresses so clearly the worthlessness of a moment is a powerful argument for the dignity of the year. The patient steadfastness of the past is our bulwark against the dismaying old Greek philosophy of perpetual movement. Studying it we shall understand the constancy of the human mind, the modernity of our progenitors in the dim ages when mankind was young. A great deal is being said in these days when supermen are scarce about the unity of the human race; of the common consciousness which despite all differences has moved men onward since the beginning and which will save them now if they recognize its power. And this will bring us at once to the consideration of a very

187

important truth: the only teaching which has insisted on and labored for the solidarity of the race is the doctrine of Christendom. Catholic civilization is alone in having worked on the assumption of a common origin and a common end; in having proclaimed the necessity for and the reality of corporate action, while providing an institutional scheme whose flexibility for the individual is as manifold as the separate courses of a multitude of stars.

The very nature of Christendom is historical. It is a civilization whose central act is a sublime miracle that keeps the past alive. No claim which it puts forth is philosophically so important as the assertion that it has remained historically unchanged; and while admitting the development of dogma the Church maintains that her dogma is of the Catacombs. The sublime fact that if the past were blotted out to-morrow Christendom would die, has been so well understood that we have even placed tradition on a level with scripture. There are, also, other subsidiary ways in which the Christian instinct for the preservation of the past has manifested itself. We have remembered, while others forgot, the progressive origin of our culture; its heritage from the society of Greece and Rome, its conquest of Europe and its mediæval kingdom. We have understood that by reason of the sanctification of the best that was thought and spoken in the gardens of Athens and on the seven hills of the Cæsars, Europe came into possession of the most equitable, energetic, and satisfying civilization known to man. Nor have we failed to discern the failure of the later ages to preserve the concord upon which society depends: we have seen the very idea of the past drowned in blood and error, as-

sailed by all the words of sophistry and scorn. But in
the light of the years whose splendour is part of our
creed, we have dared to hope in the future, and our
debt to the men, the historians, who have kept that light
burning is larger than we can easily pay.

I

Now there are, broadly, two ways of writing history.
The first is the method which, the mind searching carefully amid the chaotic records of the ages by the light
of general truths, divines the movements which dominate events; which observes the rhythmic yet designed
ebb and rise of the human flood; and which perceives
in the apparently disparate currents the single purpose
of the sea. It is a method requiring the highest efforts
of imaginative genius enlightened by a scrupulous regard for the most infinitesimal shred of evidence, and
withal lending itself, because of the magnitude of its
undertaking, to the likelihood of error. The second is
the method which strives to wrest from the details, the
melée, of life in the past the story and the lesson. This
is tireless in its inspection of records, of monuments,
of letters written with no eye to the future. Strong
imaginative gifts will save historians of such a kind
from the fate of the annalist by showing the pattern
of the past and by discovering the meaning of the mi-
grations of the dead. These two methods, inductive
and deductive, are really supplementary: both are
necessary and both are human.

Fortunately modern Catholic historians have grap-
pled with the problems confronting them in a surpris-

ingly able way. Before their work had been begun, even the writers of history in England had no conception of Christendom as a social organization. That was for them a buried city, ruined by its sins. The isolation of Britain's story, brought about by the exaggerated importance lent to the reigns of Henry VIII. and Elizabeth, had despoiled the popular mind of the sense of a common civilization which Christian Europe had espoused. Nowadays men, disturbed by the threatened dissolution of society, are eagerly seeking again the grounds of solidarity. What is it that mankind is trying to accomplish? What has it been doing in the past? These are burning questions, and we shall see the answer which the Catholic historian has brought.

To those for whom the Church is the central fact in the world, her progress and victory have seemed coördinate with the development of surrounding society. Rome, absorbing the intellectual and artistic forces of Greece, had built a working empire and laid on foundations of indubitable strength a government that was master of everything except the barbaric fringes of the world. Then had come the collapse—almost inexplicable—of the magnificent paganism of the Cæsars, and its fragments were carried away by generous Christian blood. Rome the empire died in cruelty and darkness, but Roman civilization was preserved by a now conquering Christendom and later carried to a length and across larger areas than had been dreamed of before. The meekness of the Gospel assailed the last and most formidable frontiers.

This was Newman's doctrine. In nothing is the intuition of the great Cardinal more remarkable than in his conception of culture as a common trust which the ages had conspired to save. He knew that the Romans had not forgotten Rome. The "Historical Sketches" and certain other books are marvelous examples of mind divining principles which all the facts substantiate. "When," he says, "the storm mounted overhead and broke upon the earth, it was these scorned and detested Galileans, and none but they, the men-haters and God-despisers, who, returning good for evil, housed and lodged the scattered remnants of that old world's wisdom which had so persecuted them, went valiantly to meet the savage destroyer, tamed him without arms, and became the founders of a new and higher civilization. There is not a man in Europe now, who talks bravely against the Church, but owes it to that Church, that he can talk at all."

Newman's realization of the central unity of Christendom is the only one of his doctrines to be recalled here. It is the sole theory which makes the story of man intelligible and purposeful while preserving the necessary realism; its worth has been recognized fully by modern historians, especially in France. In England it has gained many able protagonists, among whom are Sir Arthur Quiller-Couch, W. S. Lilly, and Hilaire Belloc, and it is the thesis of that very important book, "Europe and the Faith," of which more will be said in time. Nor should the work of another author, concerned during his studious lifetime with the dawn of Christendom, be overlooked. "The Formation of Christendom," T. W. Allies' large and imposing reply to the theories of Gibbon, is a monument of erudition and incisive criticism. The author's purpose was to show the unity existing amid the chaotic variety of the early Christian times and to outline a philosophy of history from the foundation of the Church to the reign of Charlemagne. His sonorous style and firm grasp of detail often remind one of the great skeptic who wrote the "Decline and Fall." In particular the last two volumes of the series, "Peter's Rock and Mohammed's Flood" and the "Monastic Life," are noteworthy for substance and dignity of expression.

No philosophic evaluation of history has been, or is likely to be, perfect in every respect. With the discovery of new sources of information some significant link in the speculative historian's chain of reasoning is sure to snap. Confident, however, that the general principles which Catholics believe to be reflected in history are correct, other able historians have contented themselves with the examination and correlation of evidence, and with the lucid setting forth of the human story simply as a story. The mere presentation of the truth, it has seemed to them, is the strongest argument for that truth. Of the high gifts and arduous labor demanded by such an undertaking, the life of John Lingard gives ample proof. His "History of England," which is today the acknowledged compeer of the best known chronicles of that country, was written by a man who retired from the executive activity toward which his earlier life had seemed to point, and who laid aside the offer of bishoprics and cardinalcies, in order to devote himself wholeheartedly to the scrutiny of documents. Only an unusually heroic man could have viewed the task without despair.

In order to appreciate fully the character of Lingard's achievement it is advisable to consider momentarily the life and environment of the man. He was

born in 1771, and having decided to become a priest
went to Douai where he stayed until, during the French
Revolution, he barely escaped the fury of a mob and
returned to England.   Here he assumed the responsi-
bilities of vice-president and professor in the newly established college at Crook Hall, Durham.   Having
become interested in Anglo-Saxon history, he wrote a
series of articles on the subject, which were published
at the instance of his friends.   The success attending
this work induced him to begin the monumental history
for which he is remembered, and he therefore retired to
a country curacy.   One must bear in mind the lament-
able condition of English Catholics at this time.   Recently freed from the penal code, their small handful—
60,000—was torn with dissension which separated the
laity from the clergy, and prelates one from the other.
There was no such thing as Catholic opinion.   Scorned
by the mass of Englishmen, accused of every kind of
villainy and more than occasionally threatened with
dire penalties, the faithful went their way, reduced to
an impotent silence.   It seemed scarcely the moment
for any kind of literature except the polemic pamphlet
or the horatory sermon; but Lingard boldly made the
resolve to write his history impersonally.   "The good
to be done is to write a book that Protestants will
read," he said with admirable wisdom.

The first volumes of the history were published without great stir; but as the successors neared modern
times, the reviewers began to take note of them; some
vituperation and controversy ensued, till finally the
approving dictum of Hallam, then at the height of his
fame, made the reputation of Lingard for accuracy
and fairness secure.   Edition succeeded edition, the

work was translated and abridged; but surely the best tribute anyone can pay its author is to say that he undermined a tradition which had been rigorously implanted in the English heart—the stupid assertion that a Catholic must lack character. Long after his death in 1851 men kept saying with Lord Acton, "Lingard has never been proved wrong."

The estimate was achieved by firm adherence to principles. In the Preliminary Notice to the final edition of his history, Lingard modestly remarked: "In disposing of the new matter derived from these several sources, I have strictly adhered to the same rules to which I subjected myself in the former editions, to admit no statement merely upon trust, to weigh with care the authorities on which I rely, and to watch with jealousy the secret workings of my own personal feelings and prepossessions." His success in doing these things is heightened by a style which is simple, very manly, and not at all elaborate. With his distrust of the "philosophy of history" he banned all imaginative portraits or that writing out of scenes which was Macaulay's chief delight. Extending as it does from B.C. 55 to A.D. 1689, Lingard's *History* affords plenty of opportunity for brisk narratives; this is seized but never for its own sake, so that the reader, trusting his reliable guide, is willing to forego the comparative glamour of another's conversation.

There were, obviously, many documents to which Lingard did not have access and the discovery of which will amplify the sketches of events given in his ever valuable *History*. The sifting of a vast amount of such evidence concerning the crucial movement in England's story, the Reformation, and that social order which preceded it, has been the life-work of a great Benedictine, Cardinal Francis Aidan Gasquet.   Voluminous as his writings are and great as his non-literary work has been, Cardinal Gasquet may be said to have focussed the attention of all right-thinking historians on an important period hitherto neglected and to have drawn conclusions as startling as they are incontrovertible.   His method is apparently a simple appeal to documents, but it is infinitely more, being in reality an attempt to reconstitute the life of a period in all its divergent manifestations, and to judge the men of past ages in the surroundings which circumstanced them.   Cardinal Gasquet has killed the old narrow straight-line historian by shifting the argument from the abstract to the concrete; to the probable amazement of many a smug maker of compendiums he has raised the dead to speak.

In that very fascinating volume, "The Eve of the Reformation," the reader is first told that the author is not holding a brief for anybody, but will allow the case to present itself.   Then one is favoured with an innocent-looking chapter on the revival of letters, which one closes with the impression that something has come out of the real past instead of merely from a library. Next the civil and religious governments are examined for their mutual relations; the mighty figure of Erasmus is unveiled of myth and walks the earth, a man; the institutional life of the time, the educational, parish, and guild characteristics of society, are reconstructed. One rises from the reading of this monumental volume impressed with the fact that here at last is history as it ought to be, stripped of conjecture and sophistry, and cheered, too, by the discovery that mediæval life is humanly most fascinating and that a million lies have been relentlessly slaughtered. For everyone interested in history there is no book in these days more valuable than "The Eve of the Reformation."

In an earlier book, "Henry VIII. and the English Monasteries," Cardinal Gasquet had undertaken to attack the long-established antipathy of Englishmen to the monastic institutions of the Church. His method, therefore, is one of resolute adherence to contemporary accounts examined by the most severe standards of scientific criticism. The reader's interest grows as the machinations of Henry are laid bare by the records of his reign. Old deposits of papers, which the easy-going romancer of an earlier date had ignored while polishing his periods, turn literally into bundles of truth. The actions of Wolsey and Cromwell, the gradual suppression of monasteries and convents for the sake of their spoil, the popular protests so altogether tragic and unavailing, the resultant martyrdom of the religious and the brutal impoverization of the people, compel the most reluctant reader to accept the conclusion that the story was vastly different from what he had fancied. The book, which began so demurely, has managed somehow to rise with the wrath of the avenger, armed with facts to which no answer can be made. The skill with which Cardinal Gasquet has managed the narrative is worthy of a novelist of the highest genius.

It seems safe to assert that such books will induce intelligent Englishmen to accept a fairer view of the Reformation, and to modify their opinions on other important matters. In time they may restore the sense of the singleness and continuity of European civilization, give social action a satisfactory leg to stand on, and restore the prestige of the Church with the common people. Having understood the possibility of rendering such service, the Benedictines of England have founded a veritable school of history, the fruits of which are large and important. We can do no more here than to recall a few names, primarily that of Dom Bede Camm, a charming writer who since his conversion has busily popularized some of the most appealing portions of English ecclesiastical history and whose "Lives of the Blessed English Martyrs" are the products of unusual care and sympathy. Then there is Dom Henry Norbert Birt, whose best known work, "The Elizabethan Religious Settlement," should remove many misconceptions and also win readers by reason of its honest ability, and Dom J. H. Chapman, whose various volumes are the creations of a refined and most diligent scholarship.

Truly the English Benedictines have deserved well of us. In passing, however, one should note the fine work of other priests—Thomas A. Hughes, of the Society of Jesus, for instance, whose historical researches into the past of his own order have gained such wide admiration, and Canon William Barry, whose brilliant analysis of the Papacy and its influence is known to a large audience. Nor should the student of literature neglect to consider the painstaking labors of Irishmen who, in Maynooth and elsewhere, have done such pioneer work in reconstituting the past of their own country, a past radiant with the blessing of the Church even if crowned so heavily with martyrdom. The Irish Dominicans have recently offered a few volumes which we hope are the forerunners of a series equal in value to what the English Benedictines have done. The lover of Newman will recall the introductory lecture on "The Idea of a University" with its entrancing picture of the ancient harmony existing between the neighboring peoples, and hope that a study of the past will reveal to both the means for a decently Christian adjustment of their difficulties.

We may turn back for a moment to an enigmatic man who stood close to Newman in many ways, but whose erudition was not of that patient sort which can wait for the day of its justification. Lord Acton, whose vast and somewhat arrogant learning spent itself largely on polemics of a journalistic character, was an admirable student of history (though his outlook was more than a little clouded by German metaphysics), but he lacked the impetus to a single, substantial work. His services to periodical literature were extraordinary in that he imbued it with a solidity of scholarship which had been notably missing. Again, as the adviser of many writers, as the friend of Döllinger and Newman, and as the designer of the "Cambridge Modern History," he left a name in English history not altogether written on sand.

The American Catholic contribution to the study of the past has as yet assumed no proportions of dignity. John Gilmary Shea, chief worker in this field, was a man of great ability but his lack of literary instinct gives his books a very colourless cast. As the author of a "History of the Catholic Church in the United States" Dr. Shea gathered a mass of precious information which, but for him, would probably have been lost forever. Nor is the story of the American Church a secondary affair, but rather a chronicle of unsurpassed heroism, of violent struggles against the odds of prejudice and poverty. Shea's researches into the story of the earlier missionaries and explorers have been of exceptional value; they aided Parkman in the making of his great if biased narratives, and have borne later fruit in the work of Father Campbell, S.J., author of "Pioneer Priests of North America." When the future historian of the unparalleled development of the Catholic Spirit in America shall proceed to write his narrative, it must be under a steady feeling of indebtedness to the scholarly, if unreadable, books of John Gilmary Shea.

On the whole, there is nothing of which we ought to be so proud and of which we are in fact so densely ignorant as the service of our historians. They are pre-eminently historical and not, like so many puny chroniclers, hysterical. If in their devotion to the work the gravity of some has been too grave, we may raise up other men to give the narrative the charm of Macaulay, or the piquancy of Taine. In fact, we have already done so in ways which will be considered later. As for the historical labor of Newman, Lingard, and Gasquet, it may be said that together they have given an impetus to a composite idea of civilization which men may not care to adopt at once but which, in the end, they will not gainsay.

II

However well unified our conception of society may be or however much interest we may feel in the popular movements and aspirations of the past, it must remain true that one of the greatest duties of history is to present the hero. While mankind gropes its way almost unconsciously to the Providential destiny, there are a few men in every generation who discern the march of events, in whom mind and will are stern enough to resist the apparently inevitable and to sway the multitude; there are other men also whose mental or moral excellencies raise up a silent bulwark against the swaying human flood, who direct the course of humanity by their majestic immobility. They are, respectively, the Napoleons who attack and the Wellingtons who refuse to move. Needless to say, the Catholic Spirit has been productive of both. The crowded galleries of the mediæval cathedral bear testimony to some; the biographies of literature and history chronicle others. Now the writing of biography is a surprisingly spontaneous thing, like poetry. It must be born of enthusiasm for the hero, it must glow with a realization of the necessity of that hero's message for the present age; and the best biography, like its subject, will be immortal. No one has needed to write a life of Nelson after Southey, or a life of Johnson since Boswell. Occasionally, it is true, the complexity of the theme and its queer involutions may render the task difficult, if not impossible. Where is the final story of Napoleon, Dante, or Lincoln? In general the most satisfying biography will have some of the impersonality of a portrait: it will show the artist's hand but the sitter's face.

A salutary preface to the consideration of work done by recent Catholic biographers is the "Lives of the Saints" by Rev. Alban Butler. Men of sanctity are models for all men, and although this contribution to their history was completed before the days of the

Catholic revival, it is the model for so much that is best in writing that it ought always to be borne in mind. Comprising as it does more than fifteen hundred biographies, each the result of deep study and penetrative analysis of evidence, it is difficult to believe that it was the work of a man engaged in many tasks and even the author of other books. Alban Butler was a professor at Douai when he conceived the plan of his *magnum opus;* later, missionary duties, the presidency of the college of St. Omer, and extensive executive tasks prevented the publication of the book, but did not dissuade the author from his high if almost sacrificial purpose. He set to work with as strict a regard for historical truth as the Bollandists strove for; but in addition he was fortunately gifted with a genial personality which delighted in sprightly narrative and did not allow either science or devotion to obscure the quest of beauty that is every writer's privileged business. Before his time the English saints had been lost in legend or in studied hostility; after him it was true to say that they had recovered not only historical existence but their rightful place in the popular literature of England.

That place, once so important, is being recognized again; and it is noteworthy that one of the scholars most interested in the subject, Professor Gordon Hall Gerould, should have expressed the highest regard for Butler. "The book," he says, "is the great classic of modern English Catholicism, and it is time-defying in the same way as the history of Butler's great contemporary, Gibbon. . . . Whether the "Lives of the Saints" be read as a book of devotion or history, whether by the man of doubting or believing mind, it cannot well fail to attract and give profit." The word *lore* is one of the most charming in the language, and Butler with all his calm detachment from mere ambition and his sincere piety understood it well. His sketches are alive, are written in the comely English of the eighteenth century, and are executed with the care of a most exacting artist. To what another writer would have made monotonous or heavy with moral teaching, he contrived to lend a greater allurement than Johnson threw about the poets. Butler made the saints live again just as a multitude of Englishmen were getting ready to pray, and he left them and their children a heritage of peace and light which is like a garden in Arcady. Of course, he had not seen many important documents and occasionally he made mistakes; but the substantial accuracy of his work cannot even now be challenged.

The fact that an important series of saints' lives was begun under the direction of Newman, brings us to his own biography. Without disparaging the volumes of Hutton or Meynell, it may be said that the task of interpreting the Oratorian Cardinal has been fulfilled most satisfactorily by Wilfrid Ward. This highly gifted man, the son of W. G. Ward and during many years the editor of the *Dublin Review*, brought to the study of Newman exemplary industry and enough tact to realize that his subject ought to be allowed to speak for himself. The "Life," therefore, consists chiefly of letters and utterances designed to show Newman's state of mind after he had become a Catholic. The biographer appears only in the arrangement of the material and in the making of what seem to him necessary deductions. The portrait thus presented

has not a little of the impersonality and deference of
good art.

Unfortunately the book, great though it is, admits of serious objections. Owing to the foreshorten-
ing of Newman's Anglican career, the public events of
his Catholic priesthood gain too much prominence.
Because the spiritual character of the man as he had
developed through the ordeal of his conversion is left
in the background, his reverses and temporary obloquy are given an inner importance which they surely
did not possess in real life. Newman dwells so much
in the shadow that one gets the impression that light
was generally shut off. "There was a wart on Newman's face," a wise and genial critic of Ward's book
once remarked to him, "and you have made it so large
that the face is hidden." To some extent the biographer realized the mistake which he had unconsciously
made and his "Last Lectures" are admirable interpretative corrections. Despite its limitations, however,
Ward's book has rendered a distinct service and an
accompanying *Vie intime* will some day be written.

In "The Life and Times of Cardinal Wiseman,"
Ward found a larger canvas and covered it with interesting figures brought together in a well-knit design.
The strong men who dominated the early days of the
Catholic awakening are set forth in the book with
freshness, vigour, and interest. Cardinal Wiseman
made up for what he lacked in genius by a fine vivacity,
a sterling talent for public affairs, and a deeply religious spirit. Not so extraordinary a man as Newman, he seems to have adapted himself more gracefully
to the biographer's requirements. But the best work
that Wilfrid Ward did was, perhaps, the bright and

informing "William George Ward and His Times." In this narrative of his gifted father the writer found opportunity to describe many fascinating intellectual characteristics of the Oxford Movement, and the eccentricity of his subject added a not unwelcome pungency. It cannot be said of such biographies that they are perfect works of art; but they are sane, earnest efforts to give common-sense views of great men and are saved by an ever-present critical instinct from rant and bias. No man has done larger work in setting before the world heroes who otherwise would probably have been ignored.

A student of life not so well known, perhaps, as Ward, but gifted to write one of the most masterly biographies of recent times, is J. G. Snead-Cox. His "Life of Cardinal Vaughan" served to make known a most profoundly spiritual man, who governed the ecclesiastical affairs of London with splendid success and quietly practiced a noble asceticism. With the sympathy and diligence of a true friend, Snead-Cox set to work upon a book that has the best qualities of intimacy with none of its superfluous gestures. "No interpreter was needed," he says modestly, "for the dead could speak, and far more convincingly for himself." But the Archbishop of Westminster, had he been in search of fame, could have chosen no better herald. Some of the chapters, particularly that on "Characteristics," are models, and the whole book is one that will be read with love.

A recent work of unusual interest is Shane Leslie's presentation of the real Cardinal Manning. That great prelate, so deeply inspired by the almost military zeal of the reformer, had neither the intellectual re-

ticence nor the single-spiritedness which makes for easy
approval of personality.   As a Churchman his interests were apt to take refuge in intransigeance of mood,
in the refusal to give his opponents a hearing; as an individual priest, however, he lived very conscious of his
unworthiness and consumed with eagerness to achieve
an apostolate.   Purcell in his biography of Manning
misread the evidence he examined and left a great deal
unread; unable to appreciate any but ostentatious motives, he made the surface of Manning's soul seem the
substance of it.   Naturally the injury done to Manning's character was very great, and the cynicism with
which the public came to view a leading representative
of Catholicism was extended to other representatives.
This regrettable impression was combated to some extent by various replies, but previous to the appearance
of Mr. Leslie's work the first impression remained extraordinarily persistent.

Hitherto unnoticed collections of letters, private
journals, and testimonials were unearthed and studied
with insight and fairness.   Shane Leslie is the master
of a style which scintillates with the intelligence of a
poet and, like the best of French prose, is quick to
reflect the nuances of imagination.   Possessing an unusual knowledge of the official life of Manning's time,
he was able to set forth the significance of the Cardinal's policy as a part of its environment.   Matters
that seem grotesque when viewed alone become intelligible when seen as portions of a pattern, and Shane
Leslie has made an admirable pattern.   The disposition of the work is so sincere, the analysis of Manning's inner life so calm and sympathetic, that the
moral heroism of the Cardinal is accepted by the reader

as a fact. Some of the conclusions reached are open to dispute, but the book is on the whole the most completely satisfying Catholic biography that has appeared in many a day.

Unfortunately we shall not be able to give other works the notice which they deserve. Our literature has been enriched by a large number of pleasurable biographies which have come like revelations of the energy of life. Agnes Strickland's "Lives of the Queens of England" preserve their charm for new generations, and may be read with profit even though the research upon which the narratives were based could have been much more careful. Canon William Barry's "Cardinal Newman" remains the best one-volume life, and its brilliant presentation of the Cardinal from a literary point of view is an excellent introduction to the study of his writings. In "Ernest Renan" he provided a searching study of an interesting if misled mind: here and in many other books Canon Barry has displayed critical strength and a ready understanding of the Continental spirit. Edwin de Lisle's "Life and Letters of A. P. de Lisle" is a serious and important account of a man devoted to the conversion of England; the biography of John Lingard, by Martin Haile, contrives to set forth clearly the personality of that great historian, and such other books as Richard Simpson's "Edmund Campion," Maisie Ward's "Father Maturin," Bernard Holland's "Kenelm Digby, a Memoir," Everard Meynell's "Francis Thompson" (a masterpiece of which a great deal might be said), and Father Martindale's "Robert Hugh Benson" are literary portraits of exceptional charm and significance. Theirs is a work whose reward is not often commensurate with the importance of the undertaking.

Is it necessary to emphasize again the importance of history in the development of the Catholic Spirit? We have already said that Christendom is inseparable from the past; that from an irrefragable presentation of that past opinions which have been as popular as they are false must be consigned to the dust-heap of prejudice.   Lingard, Gasquet, and their followers have done more to dispel unfairness than an army of missionaries; they have killed forever the myth of Christian oppression and Elizabethan virtue.   Catholic education and thought today can become solid only if they are built upon a firm understanding of the unity of Christendom; we must somehow realize the connection between ourselves and the Christian peoples of the Ages of Faith, and understand that Augustine speaks to us as directly as he did to the Carthaginians, that the voice of Jeanne d'Arc is a living voice, and that the Crusades accomplished what everyone today despairs of, the sanctification of the mob.   Good history is literature because it has power to inform the intellect, to arouse the gravest and most delicate emotions, to inspire us with that contemplativeness which is the goal of art.

BOOK NOTE

The best edition of Lingard is that edited by Hilaire Belloc. Some works of interest in connection with the subject-matter treated in this chapter are: "Saints' Stories," by G. H. Gerould; "Lord Acton and His Circle," by Dom Gasquet; Newman's "Historical Essays"; Mrs. Wilfrid Ward's introduction to her husband's "Last Lectures"; Belloc's "First and Last" (those essays which deal with the writing of history); and T. W. Allies' "A Life's Decision."   See also the "Catholic Encyclopedia."

CHAPTER TWELVE

ROBERT HUGH BENSON AND THE AGING NOVEL

"Every one on the earth should believe, amid whatever madness or moral failure, that his life and temperament have some object on the earth."

CHESTERTON'S "BROWNING."

THE novel, said F. Marion Crawford in an amiable moment, is a species of entertainment. Could anything be more diverting than a remark so incredibly old-fashioned from a gentleman whose cosmopolitanism was the marvel of his generation? Things have changed and the novel is no longer even new, if one remembers that age is seldom defined in centuries. A man does not have to be a contemporary of the pyramids in order to be thought elderly, and there are no living creatures in geology. When Richardson and his brethren began to issue lengthy prose narratives, they handled a literary form which was as vigorous and almost as incorrigible as a child. That to the stirring chain of incidents they added a moral was due to a convention which they inherited from all story-tellers since the beginning. The æsthetes notwithstanding, no stories of consequence anywhere have been told for the mere sake of narrative; not even Sir Walter, who held the moral effect of novels in low esteem, could escape being almost the author of an ethical revolution. Nevertheless, the ante-modern story, with its eye on the individual, made very little pretense at social lecturing; it probably did not think itself old enough to teach in public. When Dickens preached it was like buttonholing the neighbors and decidedly not like arguing with humanity; Thackeray said a great deal to the Gentle Reader but scarcely anything to the nation.

The later novel, however, is nothing if not social. What is the problem propounder from Victor Hugo to Patrick MacGill, what are the great Russians, if not reformers of civilization? When in the twilight of the great classic period of the English novel George Eliot veiled her characters in the sage and sad outlook of the Positivist, something happened to fiction the importance of which has never been sufficiently recognized. Henceforth men would no longer read a story and be bored with the moral; they would read morality and be bored with the story. The novel, bespectacled and sitting with the elders, would talk philosophy. It is possible to enjoy Richardson greatly and at the same time consider him an ass; it is, very likely, impossible to relish George Moore under the same conditions. Genuine enthusiasm for Joseph Conrad is probably limited to psychologists; for Mr. Wells to liberals in politics; for Gilbert Cannan and John Galsworthy to persons who are not enthusiastic about anything. In short, the novel is as wise in its old age as the Sphinx, and for the sake of decency the word ought to be changed. Of course there are honourable exceptions like Thomas Hardy, whose mournful views of life are inserted in the ancient manner and may comfortably be neglected. But in general there is no gainsaying the fact that the modern novelist is an educator; he may be expected to break off a love scene at any moment to write a history of the world or a treatise on business efficiency. In America he is vigorously exhorted to tell the truth and is often vehemently accused of—fiction.

Whether we like it or not, the modern novel is the great medium of philosophic propaganda, and should be accepted as such. One may speak indeed of the narrative art; there are even superior people who take down shelves of books to discover "how they are done." Still, it is for the public that novels are written, for a public which absorbs from them its ideas of history and politics, of sociology and religion. And the strange truth is that any story which makes a point for positive belief is cleverly termed a boresome tract, while the pseudo-scientific naturalism of Zola and Dreiser, the scented materialism of Gautier and D. H. Lawrence, and the pure skepticism of Anatole France are labeled unadulterated art. It is an important truth to remember, for so saturated with this principle is modern criticism that the course of Catholic fiction has been very effectively blocked by it. The orthodox novelist has quite generally come to be looked upon as a bothersome peddler, and while he has not greatly minded this, he has often been forced to beg. One does not find in Catholic stories the straightforwardness, the energy, and the beauty that are so manifest in our poetry, philosophy and history. More than any other art, fiction is dependent upon its reception and the Catholic audience has not been sufficiently appreciative or discerning. When these obstacles are borne in mind it will easily be seen that the presentation of Catholic life in modern English fiction has been surprisingly successful.

There is little to be found among Victorian novels
that has not already been considered. The ancient
popular traditions of Christendom were revived by
Dickens; Newman and Wiseman did something to
bring about a better understanding of religious history.
"Callista" and "Fabiola," with Miles Gerald Keon's
forgotten book, "Dion and the Sibyls," were able if
somewhat staid pictures of primitive Christendom.
Newman's "Loss and Gain" proved a witty, controversial narrative of a conversion and later there was a
similar book by Montgomery Carmichael. In the novels
of Georgiana Fullerton, English readers met with a
series of pietistic tales which were not well enough written to earn any large place in literary history. The
genius of the Catholic revival that grew out of Oxford
was too seriously concerned with higher spiritual issues to devote much attention to what was then a species of writing that aimed at amusing people.

If these books lacked the sparkle of modernity, the
defect was abundantly compensated for by the novels
of a most fascinating priest, Robert Hugh Benson.
His work, as we shall see, was prompted by peculiar
and special interests which may be summed up here as
curiosity in the borderlands of life and an appetite
for magnificence. Benson is the literary descendant
of two remarkable men who, while vastly different in
character, had a great deal in common. Joseph Henry
Shorthouse, author of "John Inglesant," was a mystic
Quaker who revivified in fiction the idea of sacramentalism. His novels are gorgeous pageants glowing with
a deep quest for spiritual realities and the instincts of
mediævalism. The story of John Inglesant, with its
colourful historical background and mystical subject,

probably influenced Benson more than any other book. His other master was Huysmans, the volatile convert-mystic of modern French letters, whose Catholic life was an intense preoccupation with the transcendental aspects of religion, and who surrounded the faith with the artistic pomp of a mediæval court. "En Route" and "La Cathedrale" deal with the arcana of belief but also with the gorgeous symbolism of worship, with music shuddering under dim cathedral arches or rising plaintive in Trappist chapels at break of day, and with the regal mysteries of architecture. Huysmans' life of Saint Lydwine, finally, is a ruthless dissection of a martyred soul fettered by a mission of expiation. These authors emphasized the things which Benson considered the realities of religion: God's hand on the unusual soul and the almost unearthly beauty of the Catholic ritual. All three were egoists, in varying ways of course, but serenely independent of the social life about them. Going their journey alone, of necessity they had no time for democratic fellowships. The average modern reader will therefore be perplexed by Benson's books, and certainly they do lack the large sympathy with which great novels are imbued; but that is the natural consequence of their modernity.

Some acquaintance with the character of Robert Hugh Benson will uncover an unusual individuality. The son of the Anglican Archbishop of Canterbury and born into a family almost all the members of which were devotees of pen and ink, he grew up knowing his own mind, not particularly scholarly, and innately artistic. Having decided finally to go into orders, he was ordained, given a mission, and suffered to enter an Anglican community. The story of his conversion to the Church, which was achieved quite suddenly during a period of two years, is the subject of his interesting book, "The Confessions of a Convert." It would seem that his motives were theologically rather ordinary, but individually most unusual. He sought the Church because his religious inclinations beheld in her dogmatic firmness and mystic character the only satisfactory support for his personality. No social considerations such as moved Bourget, no deep historical research like that which impelled Newman to make the step, no problems of modern religious criticism, were concerned. He became a Catholic quite independently of the intellectual currents around him, because he was himself.

Of Benson the Catholic priest and the Monsignor it it is not necessary to say much here. He proved an admirable pulpit orator and a successful spiritual director. Even so, he insisted upon going his own way and making those investigations into the fringes of the supernatural which engrossed his attention. Often he was dull about ordinary matters, but a ghost could have aroused him at any moment. The details of an apparition left him in a state of eager excitement. His books were written breathlessly and blithely, without any of the deep brooding which gives works of art an inward virility that is the pledge of immortality. It was an adventure to think them out, to write them down; and Benson preserved to his dying day a boyishness of temperament that, satisfying its zest in unfrequented places, had a truly Stevensonian relish for experience. He might have agreed with Cotton Mather about the reality of the witches, but he would have opposed him on everything else.

The vivid mind of Benson sought its first literary expression in the historical novel. What he tried to do, however, was not to outline a great movement or to study a period, but to present a striking individual who, borne down by the pressure of earthly circumstance, would seek refuge in religion. The past attracted him by the heroism, the splendid pomp, of its setting, and he labored hard to reproduce the actual colours. His admirers do not think that he ever wrote for the sake of history; he presented history because he wished to write and this inspired him. Almost all of Benson's novels of this sort deal with periods of religious strife—Elizabethan, Tudor, Stuart. "The Queen's Tragedy," perhaps the best among them, is a story of the futile career of Mary Tudor, made rich with elaborate description and fervent with religious sympathy. But the interest centers despite all extraneous incidents on the leading figure; we are made to follow closely the real character of Mary, to perceive how her weakness conspired to thwart all her hopes and to render her desperately unhappy. It is when the Queen is brought close to death that the horizon is lifted and made radiant, and the final scene, with its profound interpretation of the ritual, is a transcendently moving piece of writing.

"Oddsfish," probably one of Benson's most popular works, is the story of a youthful Papal agent who is connected with the court of Charles II. Here the character of the king remains somewhat in the background, but is the theme of the narrative none the less. Round about seethe the torrents of intrigue, the determined efforts to uproot the Jesuits, to annul Catholic influence, and to fetter the king. Charles, debonair,

intelligent, but debauched and weakened, is presented
with distinct skill, and manages to preserve his royal
allurement despite his fatal insouciance. In general,
the book evidences Benson's genius and its limitations.
There is a characteristic and regrettable weakness of
structure, together with a very conventional subordi-
nate narrative. The author's talent for description
leads him into paragraphs of detail which do not bear
upon the issue, and his failure to give the women in the
story reality makes such love interest as enters rather
banal. Still, it is the soul of the central figure which
is Benson's chief concern and he achieves its redemp-
tion with a glowing sympathy that wins the reader's
highest admiration. Charles seen in the light of eternity, with death upon him and the priest by his side,
is no longer a king but a frightened man; and the
author is superbly powerful in showing the comparative value of that manhood. Of various other novels,
"Come Rack, Come Rope" and "By What Authority?",
little could be said that has not already been implied.
As an historical novelist Benson analyzed certain characters of great importance from the Catholic point of
view, and succeeded by reason of imaginative artistry
and a grasp of the response of a harrowed and solitary
soul to the faith.

These two qualities were shown separately in stories
which gave their author something of an international
reputation, "Richard Raynal, Solitary" and "The
Lord of the World." Written with great care and
with an unusual understanding of word-color, the life
of Richard Raynal has a quiet grace that works into
the heart of the reader as its subject must have taken
possession of the author. Even if it be thought to

stand somewhat apart from life in an atmosphere of unworldliness, the book is vital and sincere. In "The Lord of the World," however, Benson sketched a brightly tinted picture of what he fancied the judgment day would be like. The story has vivid scenery and verve, but the imagination conceiving it is ostensibly a bit wild. There is something of Mr. Wells' scientific inventiveness about it—something which the Germans would term *kolossal*. It is a theme of tremendous possibilities, but Benson was not Michael Angelo and his work is melodrama. Let us risk boldly the statement that in these two volumes one will find their author at his best and at his worst, but employing all his powers.

Among the novels which Benson devoted to contemporary life, the discriminating reader will find two of especial interest. "The Sentimentalists" is able, healthy satire far above the average in ability. Christopher Dell, a dilettante redolent of Walter Pater and scented cigarettes, has the faith but no power of will. While he may be to some extent the caricature of a type, Dell is deftly and interestingly individualized. A healthy, common-sense environment having failed to save him, recourse is had to Mr. Rolls, a charming mystic too reflective and wealthy to be Patmorean, who redeems Dell by a surprising expedient. In this book Benson succeeds admirably with a group of fascinating men, fails utterly with a group of boresome women, and makes the point a little too obviously. But though the legerdemain is rough in places, it is a good book and will bear rereading.

The superiority of "Initiation" lies, first of all, in the selection of a daring and very modern theme: un-

merited suffering and its influence on the soul. Sir
Neville Fanning is a fine young landowner, not religiously enthusiastic but still thoroughly orthodox in
comportment. In Rome he meets Enid Bensington, a
beautiful egoist—unfortunately too beautiful and too
egoistic—who finally spurns his love with insane
cruelty. He turns to nature for solace, but soon dis-
covers that the disease which he has inherited from a
debauched father is fatal. Face to face with death, he
sounds the depths of the Catholic faith and draws from
it not only solace but truth. The exposition of his
decline is made with a realistic understanding and
imaginative sympathy almost too beautiful for praise.
Harrowing though the story be thought, Benson's
priesthood saves it from the tyrannical ruthlessness of
a naturalist.

These books will have indicated sufficiently the range
of Monsignor Benson's gifts. His novels, like Bourget's, are demonstrations but they are individual instead of social. The *milieux* in which the characters to
be analyzed are placed are nearly always conventional:
the entourage of royalty in the historical novels and
dignified country homes in the modern stories. Philosophically, Benson was an egoist who did not consider
sufficiently, perhaps, the nature and value of environment. Being concerned largely with spiritual cases,
he never wrote without a religious purpose, and his
books have some of the atmosphere of a "tract." Nevertheless, he succeeded in saying things which others
had neglected, in winning attention by his own interest
in the subject and by his brilliant skill. Never tire-
some, he manages in spite of his psychological preoccupations to be normal. A man of intense convic-

tions, he was not quite enough of an artist to attend to the finesse of craftsmanship, but he did honest work of which Catholic letters cannot be too proud.

The biographer of Monsignor Benson, Father C. C. Martindale, is himself an occasional novelist. In "The Goddess of Ghosts" and "The Waters of Twilight" he has written two very striking studies of religious temperament, which the average reader may find dull but in which the discerning person will rejoice. It must be borne in mind that Father Martindale is a stylist of the school of Pater, writing sentences that turn round queer corners and manage to say things by suggestion rather than by statement. There is about his two little books a subtlety of conception and a richness of meaning that are surprisingly educative without being in the least unctuous. "The Goddess of Ghosts" studies the differences between the Catholic and the Greek spirit in action. The author, who is a famous classical scholar, succeeds in giving to his delicately rhythmical prose the odour of distant schools of thought, and brings together in a quiet Breton garden the ends of the spiritual earth. Pater, had he been a Catholic, might have done this very thing, but it would not have been better work than his disciple's. "The Waters of Twilight" is an interesting résumé of a phenomenally clever Englishman's religious opinions. They exhibit nuances of spiritual sensibility which cannot fail to delight the lover of such things. It may be an error to speak of Father Martindale as a novelist, for his books adhere to the vague form set by "Marius the Epicurean." Painstaking in their treatment of almost intangible ideas, they occupy a corner of their own in modern Catholic letters.

It is almost disconcerting to descend from these lofty
rooms of thought to the honest commonplaceness of
John Ayscough, who is, as everybody ought to know,
Monsignor Bickerstaffe-Drew and despite his priesthood the literary brother of Anthony Trollope and
Archibald Marshall. The author of a formidable
array of books, John Ayscough is often guilty of writing for the sake of penmanship or rather for money
to be expended philanthropically. His best work,
however, is blessed with genial qualities that Alphonse
Daudet or Mrs. Gaskell would have hastened to endorse.
Marching comfortably along in the realm of platitudes,
he describes the scenery and the people with soft, easy
sentences that succeed by reason of a genuine whimsicality and shy humor. If it is necessary to present
some exceptional person, saint or sinner, one may be
sure that the author will render him quite tractable
before the chapter is done. The hard egoism of modern letters seems to have fostered in John Ayscough
the praiseworthy desire to be childlike; only, like all
plebeian things, this is apt to prove a little dull at
times. One is afraid that Monsignor Drew, despite
his valiant priesthood, has retreated from the modern
turmoil to a charming position that no longer exists.

Such a book as "San Celestino" may be termed a
novel because it is a picture of manners, but it is really
the life of a saint. Considered from the hagiogra-
phical point of view the book is admirable, for it emphasizes just what the average saint's story fails to
present: the amiable humanity of the subject. Petruc-
cio, the mystic Italian lad who becomes Fra Pietro
the hermit and finally Pope Celestine, is made very un-
derstandable, though the iron in his soul is not melted

away. As a study of society, however, "San Celestino" leaves much to be desired, despite the painstaking historical accuracy and picturesque charm of the narrative. The fierce Italian spirits of that riotous century are softened until they nearly blur. The best of the characters, like the best in Ayscough's other books, are those whose foibles make them subjects for quaint satire. What deftness the author's hand shows here! Pompous little ecclesiastics, so sure of their learning and position, provoke the most charitable of smiles. Written without the faintest trace of cruelty, the book is delightfully kind and yet spiritually intense. It is easily John Ayscough's most impressive achievement.

In "Fernando" and "Gracechurch" we are given two partly autobiographical studies of English country life. Not many stories of boyhood are so quiet and devoid of noisy pranks as "Fernando." The lad grows up in the midst of a leisurely environment which does not conduce to thrilling adventure, but does provide a host of odd, interesting people. They appear, one by one, for a moment and then disappear, as in a dream. This languid haze tempers their characters, but they all have character. Fernando's mother is an exquisite Victorian woman even though she is Irish. "Gracechurch," a sequel, chronicles life in a small town with the fine taste of "Cranford," but rambles disconcertingly and draws attention to its author's woeful inability to construct narrative. There is absolutely nothing in it that resembles an adventure or an intrigue. What gives the book colour and interest is the genuine, delicate humour of the telling, a humour that is like a smile, without a touch of boisterousness

or a desire to be brilliant. In addition, the story is
spiritualized by a temperate vision of the faith which
gains the hero's heart. Keble might have written just
such a book had he possessed the twinkling spirit of
Charles Lamb.

It would seem that John Ayscough served a long
apprenticeship in the craft of writing, during the
period of which he sought advice from the leading
novelists of the modern time. "Dromina," at all
events, is a book resembling so closely George Meredith's "Harry Richmond" that one suspects the likeness of having been deliberate. Gypsies appear from
Romany with beguiling ways and mysterious customs;
there is an eccentric if delightful Irish father, and a
family of entertaining young people. The adventure
leads to the establishment of a surprising West Indian
kingdom and the martyrdom of the idealistic young
ruler. Improbable and incoherent as the story is, the
romantic atmosphere has the flavor of Meredith's
happy book, its smell of woodland smoke and strange
enchantment of scene. "Hurdcott" strikes the reader
as a rather poor approximation to Hardy's "Tess
of the d'Urbervilles." There is a queer young shepherd whose antecedents are unknown and who is sus-
pected of undesirable qualities. Though he is a child
of nature he manages to win the affections of a charming young lady, but is falsely accused of murder and
sentenced to death. The mystic resignation of his
fiancée is just a little too exalted for reality, and the
catastrophe is too exactly the opposite, in spirit, of
the grim finale of Tess. The book has fine rustic
scenes and characters, but it is evident that the author
gasps for air.

John Ayscough merits attention as the representative in literature of an attitude towards life that is both humorous and deeply religious. Fascinated with the spirit of rural Italy, as several of his books show, he applied its standards to the English life he knew and loved. It is unnecessary to say that he moves outside the busy currents of national affairs. No one would fancy from a reading of his books that there are such things as industrialism, an East Side, spiritism, or eugenics. His way of revolt against these details has apparently been to ignore them. Coveting peace, he looks at the world where it is bathed in a beneficent twilight, busy with little, heart-holding comedies and tragedies, conscious of no economic or social problems and content to be, simply, the world. It is a philosophy which can be scorned, but which is redeemed from commonplaceness by its firm hold on the now uncommon art of laughter.

It is significant that the three novelists just considered should have been clergymen and converts who brought their Oxford training into the service of the Church. Few other men would have mustered sufficient energy to undertake the difficult and slightly rewarded task of Catholic fiction. They were aided, however, by an intelligent and artistic woman, Mrs. Wilfrid Ward. Moving freely in cultivated circles and interested in the work of her husband, she brought to novel writing a thorough acquaintance with the environment with which she wished to deal. Religious influences are never lost sight of, although she treats them as social forces and not as matters of controversy. Gifted with a great deal of Jane Austen's skill in unfolding the intimacies of a situation, she has

Bourget's view of the worth of the novel as a critique of institutions. "Out of Due Time," like the "Robert Elsmere" of another Mrs. Ward, is a study, from the Catholic point of view, of the relations existing between theology and the positive sciences, and has the limited merits of all stories written about and during a "movement." Her latest novel, "Not Known Here," is in many ways her best: it is a sincerely poignant narrative concerning a man of German extraction who lives in England and is ostracized during the war. The theme is one which has the sort of possibilities that may easily be bungled; to say that Mrs. Ward has succeeded is to restrain praise to the freezing-point.

Many critics are of the opinion that while she is not one of the most widely-known Catholic novelists, she is almost the best of them. For delicately devised situations, subtle and strong characterization, and fine, sharp-pointed style she is notable; her books have been *done* while so many others have merely been written. Probably the most popular of her tales, "One Poor Scruple" may seem a study of marriage from the Church's point of view, in which Madge O'Reilly is tempted to accept Lord Bellasis in spite of his living and disreputably divorced wife, but it is really a diversified and remarkably perceptive study of modern woman. Janet Riversdale and her budding daughter Hilda, Laura Hurstmonceaux, the manipulator of social alliances, Cecilia the thoroughly modern, and Mary Riversdale the mystic, are not figures in black and white wood, but living creatures with emphasis on their minds rather than on their hysterics. Some of the men are charming, too, but one feels that Mrs. Ward has done her best with women and proved them to have souls, a matter which a dispassionate survey of recent fiction would seem to deny.

No list of the English Catholic novelists would be complete without a mention of Francis Marion Crawford who, by reason of birth, belongs really to American letters. Nevertheless, because of his cosmopolitanism and essentially narrative gifts he shall be suffered to intrude here where there is room for him. Crawford, a hard student of history and Sanskrit, tumbled into fiction quite by accident, and while undervaluing the art paradoxically succeeded in it. Religion was the most serious concern of his life and he did not often talk of it in work which he believed was intended for idle-hour amusement. It may be that the lack of passion so apparent in his novels was due to this strange and misguided reserve. An admirable romancer, able to conjure up an atmosphere with amazing skill, and familiar with so many sides of cosmopolitan life, Crawford failed just where the best novelists succeed: in the creation of dynamic characters. Dickens, for instance, could present people who might reasonably be expected to go on doing equally entertaining things outside their book; Thackeray's Becky, we are sure, had many an adventure which her sponsor did not find it necessary to relate. In short, the masters of fiction have given their creatures enough life to carry them through life. Crawford's people seem to lack this abounding vitality, to be fit for books only. When this has been said, however, criticism of his craftsmanship must cease, and one bows to the miracle of his narrative instinct.

As has been stated, his artistic effort was not often concerned with his Catholic belief. Such stories as "Greifenstein" and "Mr. Isaacs" touch no philosophy of life very closely, and numerous others are pastels of love or some other passion. The great Saracinesca trilogy may be considered a contribution to the literature of Christendom, as a romantic presentation of the collapse of the Papal power. In addition to the splendid intrigue of the narrative there is a world of really valuable social information: the viewpoint of the great Roman families, the religious atmosphere of the ;ity, and the industrial changes which came in with the new era. Unfortunately, the power of the first book, "Saracinesca," is not maintained, and while it stands a good chance of being read for many years, the others are already forgotten.

Nor is one likely to be deeply impressed by such books as "Marzio's Crucifix" and "The White Sister," into which Crawford ventured to inject considerable Catholic sentiment. The spirituality of these volumes is unmistakably deserving of the word "pretty"; and the effeminacy of their outlook is a denial of the stern position which Christianity occupies in modern life. The tirade of a somber man like Huysmans against the insincerity of doctoring the faith for popular consumption is relentless but also irresistible. How much better, both as a story and as a view of life, is that romantic novel "Casa Bracchio," a work of consummate narrative skill and insight into life! The dark moods of the Italian temperament burst into livid fire, nature is aglow with responsive gleams, and the whole story moves to its conclusion with the masterly unison of Hardy's best tales. Crawford did nothing better; it is a memorable novel.

It would seem that Marion Crawford was a man who knew exactly what he was expected to do, rather than a genius striving to impress upon the world the things he had been born to say. A fine, tactful student of men, his scholarly instincts made for absorption rather than transcendent analysis. No one knew more of Italian life than he did, although he thought it unnecessary to repeat everything he had found out. A manifold reflector of the pageant, he selected with nice discrimination what he fancied the public would like to hear. His readers were generous, graceful, and tolerant of convention; he believed it quite sufficient to entertain them without emphasizing his individuality in the manner of Stendhal. Crawford failed to be the great Catholic novelist because he did not foresee the social power that the novel would come to exercise and because he practiced too rigorously the discipline of the secret.

While these names are the most important, there are others of interest to the lover of the Catholic note in fiction. The brilliant work of Canon William Barry, an essayist with a startling synthetic grasp of history, is best shown in "Arden Massiter" and "The Two Standards." Written about a time when strong social forces were ebullient and unsteady, these novels view history as the reflex of human passion, as a record marred by desire. The ambitious verve of such books is easily contrasted with the quiet, comely art of Leslie Moore, whose "Peacock Feather" is fine vagabondish romance and whose other books, such as "The Desired Haven," have the natural piety of De Vere and a tranquil humour that recalls the work of Peacock. Something interesting might also be said about the work of John Oliver Hobbes, and a score of eager writers like M. E. Francis (Mrs. Francis Blundell), Isabel Clarke, and Enid Dinnis.

English Catholic fiction has just begun. Now that the novel has taken on a new meaning and become the conduit of social speculation, it must not be allowed to fail as a weapon in the battle for Christendom. Our authors must learn how to respond to the impulses stirring in the present world, how to freshen their art with unfettered vitality, and above all how to dramatize their philosophy. The upheaval upon which contemporary life is based, the seething of delusion and the rolling of rebellious drums, must not find Catholic art in a distant upland country whence the din of these things is barred by convention. We are born of sterner stuff than that. There must be an eagerness for the heroic in this wilderness where all but the mightiest valour quails, and a concern for beauty even in the mire of a tumbling civilization. Story-telling merges ideals in life, and the common people have loved it because they have always followed leaders rather than abstractions. No novelist can be great until he has become an artist; and no artist is worth talking about unless he can rebuild his dreams from the stuff of life.

There is one thing more. The great writer is naturally not made to order, but he cannot appear unless there is a demand for him. Readers must learn to read with discrimination, not to praise a book merely because it is Catholic and also not to heed the silence of hostile criticism and ignore a book because it believes in the soul. It is consoling and salutary to remember that in the background are the great Christian masters of modern Continental fiction—French,

German, Spanish, Italian, Polish—who have solved the problems of an inimical environment and who have much to say that we can use to our great profit. To release our fiction from provincialism of outlook and parochial feebleness of handling, to make it truly representative of the Catholic pulse in the world, is the task that confronts both our creative art and our criticism.

BOOK NOTE

Robert Hugh Benson is noteworthy also as a religious essayist; F. M. Crawford has written charming volumes of history; John Ayscough is an essayist as well as a novelist; William Barry and C. C. Martindale have done much work of a scholarly character. Reviews of fiction by the writers discussed in this chapter may be found in quantity in the *Tablet,* the *Athenœum,* the *Dublin Review,* and the *Catholic World.* For information concerning Benson, see "Hugh: a Memoir," by A. C. Benson; "Robert Hugh Benson," by C. C. Martindale; and his own "Confessions of a Convert." On Crawford see "A Diplomat's Wife in Many Lands," by Mrs. Hugh Fraser; "The Art of Fiction," by Bliss Perry, and "The Cambridge History of American Literature."

CHAPTER THIRTEEN

THE ADVENTURES OF A JOURNALIST: G. K. CHESTERTON

"A sword, a spade, and a thought should never be allowed to
rust."   JAMES STEPHENS.

IN these days we are so accustomed to the melancholy remark that the journalist is making the
library obsolete that we often overlook his really
stupendous effort to create a library. Defoe was a
journalist and so was Dickens; Steele, Goldsmith,
Johnson, Thackeray, Kipling—one after another the
fathers of large families of healthy books have been
inseparable from the newspaper. They have seen no
reason why writing that is new to-day should not be
just as surprising on Doomsday; they have remembered, with a chuckle, that the word "press" may mean
a receptacle in which to keep things of price. This,
however, is not the place to discuss journalism in general, or even that service of the Catholic Spirit which
has been the aim of a devoted and constantly improving
press. We have instead the much more difficult task
of inspecting the testimony of a single man, who is a
person of such divergent activities that summarizing
them is like trying to put the adventures of a normal
boy into a paragraph.

Gilbert Keith Chesterton is too very much alive for
anything like an estimate of his genius; a coherent im-

pression of his utterances would in fact have the same simplicity as a panorama of the birds of the air. But just as the birds are subject to a few general laws, so one may assert without temerity a number of facts about the writings of Chesterton. First of all, he is popular: his remarks are common property, his portrait needs so signature, and about none of these things is there an attitude of disdain for the opinions of the mob. Chesterton has talked religion to enormous audiences with the understanding that he himself is in the audience; having learned that citizenship is a mixture of action and thought, he has spoken of literature and politics in the same breath; finally, he has changed the romance into an editorial and the leading article into a fairy tale. In the second place, he is an Englishman fighting for England. This means so many things that we shall content ourselves here with stating what it does not mean: conquering heathens or Irishmen, forgetting that history was once contemporary, and believing that an intelligent man is never seen on the street. Both of these primal principles have led to the acceptance of a more important third, the championing of the Catholic Spirit with surprising vigor and freshness.

The result of such comparatively simple things is a tremendous influence which nobody will deny. Fundamentally, of course, it is not an influence which settles anything, but rather one which unsettles everything; for Chestertonian literature is a protest. It arose from the midst of a crowd which, having accepted the modern dictum that there are no natural laws, began to feel the iron laws of nature; it spoke out at a moment when the stoical agnosticism of Huxley had been weakened by the plague of decadence; it laughed aloud on the very evening when the intellectual world was on its way to a philosophic funeral. The missing link had made the London skeptic feel the weight of all the years and all the glaciers of science, and talk began to circulate about various drugs that might be applied to senile society. Those were days when, in the mystic shadows which no eye can pierce, the later War of Europe was brewing like a shuddering storm; when men decayed in the midst of the poisonous philosophies which they had planted round about them, yet dreamed that they had never been so secure or so remarkably right. The challenge of Chesterton was a recruiter's trumpet sounding the things for which men would later stand and die. Those things were right at the critical moment because they are eternally right; and it is not improbable that the future will base the fame of Chesterton primarily upon this service and this discovery.

As has been suggested, the career of the man is sufficiently well known to dispense with a detailed biographical note. Chesterton was born in Kensington in 1874 to a father who painted and wrote poetry in a minor way. The son contributed art criticisms and poems to the magazines, and in 1900 "The Wild Knight" was published. His real activity began, however, when he joined the staff of the *Daily News* as an editorial writer; here he remained until the fact that his opinions were exactly opposed to all those championed by the paper became too obvious for his conscience. Beyond the routine of a literary life, Chesterton has been active as a debater on social topics, as a traveler, and, during the war, as a moral force rather

than as the tower of physical strength which assuredly
he wished to be. His enormous figure has been cari-
catured and admired in every part of the world, and
those people whom he had not forced to thought he
has at least stirred to laughter. Finally, his journey
towards and into the Catholic Church has seemed to
many a spectacle of a modern pilgrim's progress—a
twentieth-century edition of the experience of Newman,
rich in wisdom and awe.

The literary output signed by the famous initials
G. K. C. is so enormous that the limits of this chapter
would hardly suffice for its enumeration, but a great
deal of it is journalism, well-made but fashioned
frankly for the moment. Conceive of Shakespeare as
the author not only of the plays now attributed to him
but also of various occasional pieces which a producer
might require for a performance or two and which,
while revealing the master's hand, would be comparatively unfinished. These might well have lines of beauty
and passages worth noting, but one could arrive at a
knowledge of the poet's principles and moods without
referring to them. So it is with Chesterton; his representative books reveal the man sufficiently to justify
an estimate that is based exclusively upon them.

He was and is chiefly a poet, although the bulk of
his verse is not large. Your true singer is always
democratic, whether he be Dante engrossed in popular
politics, or Verlaine who cannot keep away from *les
gens trop indulgents*. What enabled Chesterton to
discover the beauty of common things and to pierce
the mummery of the cultivated egoist was first and last
his poet's gift, and this has kept him fresh and free.
Learning from such divergent masters as Whitman and

Macdonald the democracy of miracles, he found them plentiful in England. The challenge, the satire, of "The Wild Knight" is a voice from the streets in a drawing-room where everybody is bored to death. Chesterton in this book was something like one of those fiercely brilliant young men who began the Revolution in France: he did not quite know what he wanted, but he was certain of what he did not want. This instinctive rebellion against smug intellectualism and smug squalor is responsive for many later poems, such as the delightful songs of Roundabout in "The Flying Inn," and the more satiric "Ballades Urbane." In these one finds the Chesterton who stands for beer and merriment, the Chesterton who is never so gay as when his enemies have hedged him round.

"The Ballad of the White Horse" is an ambitious poem that contains a great number of the best things its author has to say. Founded upon the popular traditions of King Alfred, the tale becomes symbolic of the contest which Chesterton is most interested in: the constant battle between Christendom that came from Rome and the heathens who have remained outside. The inspiration and the vigour of expression are alike remarkable. A simple ballad stanza is deftly interwoven with supple rhythms and iridescent diction, while the sweep of the narrative is sustained by a series of lyric stanzas that are strong or tender, that snatch at the heart or carry it aloft. More important even is the characterization. Alfred the Great, anxious to reconquer his kingdom from the invading Danes, goes for aid to three men—Eldred, a Saxon, Mark, a Roman, and Colan, a Gael. The three represent their races as the Danish chieftains are made to typify theirs, and the interpretative sympathy of the author marks the poem as the one great English epic of the twentieth century. The symbolism inherent in the story will not escape the attentive reader. It reveals the character of the eternal contest between heathen and Christian with the subtle insight of perfect music, giving to each side its due but deciding the victory with magnificent fervour. "The Ballad of the White Horse" is a poem to love and even to sing, which are more important matters than putting it on a shelf and calling it great.

There are many people, however, who will continue to find Chesterton's most interesting poem in "Lepanto." This foreshortened epic, rich with lines that are lyrics in themselves, is made of haunting battle music through which runs a prayer. It might be termed the story of Mahound's defeat and the Christian victory, or it might be called a simple battle ballad. The great and the small are here found side by side, under the symbolic banner of Don Juan of Austria, whose chivalry dominates the struggle with the magic glamour of Roland. Here is a new verse-form, too— organic rhythm employed with a mastery that no other poet has achieved. English literature has little to compare with it and the strange, elemental effect of many lines rivals the best efforts of the French symbolists. But Chesterton is a love-poet and a religious poet also, some of whose lyrics achieve the lowly loveliness, the towering abasement, of Donne and Vaughan. Always and everywhere he is the singer who gains the crest of song because he has seen the little things among which he wanders; who chants the wassail in a world that seems young because he himself is a boy.

Yet Chesterton's verse, genuine and fascinating though it be, is only a fragment of his work as a poet. He has carried the same imaginative gifts into prose and, in a series of romances that are virtually allegories, has drawn pictures in paragraphs that resemble stanzas. "The Napoleon of Notting Hill" is the earliest of them and in many ways the most beguiling. Auberon Quin, a genuine humourist, has been chosen king in 1984 by alphabetical rotation, and his first official order is to the effect that all the boroughs of London shall be surrounded with walls and guarded by mediæval-looking provosts and their halberdiers. Adam Wayne, the Provost of Notting Hill, is enough of a fanatic to believe that his borough, and indeed his little street, are matters of sovereign importance. He refuses to permit the destruction of the street, wagers battle in its behalf, and by a series of ruses actually manages to set up the Empire of Notting Hill. Later this waxes fat and insolent and is crushed by neighbours who have emulated its example. Auberon Quin and Wayne then set forth on a tour of the world. Thus proceeds the Chestertonian story, not fiction in the ordinary sense of the word, but rather a series of thoroughly extravagant incidents which end in a riot. Nevertheless, the tale seems, for the time being, perfectly plausible, and the lesson which underlies it is startlingly simple. The author has made of the romance an extended paradox, and the reader has only to apply the theory of Adam Wayne to the French Revolution or the revolt of Ireland to discover how true it may be in the world of reality.

The later romances do not depart widely from the method of the first. "The Man Who Was Thursday"

is perhaps the most brilliant and difficult of them all.
The last chapter, which should have explained, really
jumbles up everything, and the baffled reader is likely
to cry out in protest. The best thing to do with such
an one is to send him speedily to "Manalive," one of
the wittiest and most human books in the entire Chestertonian repertoire. Innocent Smith, though not
quite so fascinating as Father Brown the innocent
detective who enjoys great popularity, is a very charming person. The story of his fantastic adventures in
an attempt to make his wife fall in love with him repeatedly, is really a study of the transcendent adventure of matrimony and of the modern failure to understand it. This and the other romances, yes, even the
detective stories, ought to be issued with a commentary
and footnotes by, say, Mrs. Chesterton. As it is, the
average person is ready to admit that it must have been
great fun writing them, but also to wonder why he is
expected to read them. On the other hand, "Magic,"
a short story which turned into a play, is clarity itself.
Nothing could be more quotable or in many ways more
obvious. The Duke is genuinely "a gentleman though
an ass," the minister a critic of religion, the doctor a
skeptic, and the conjuror a mystery. The illusion is
perfect though, as the author explained in the *Dublin
Review*, it really hasn't a leg to stand on. "Magic"
makes the point so admirably that one cannot help
wishing that other short stories had turned into plays.

Chesterton the poet is, however, primarily a poet
with a sword; a poet who is a debater. No man ever
had a greater fondness for argument or managed it,
on the whole, with such outstanding success. The
point about the famous book of protests, "Heretics,"

is that the world is full of enemies worth fighting. That is probably the most satisfactory reason for being a philosopher, or, at least, for worrying about philosophy. One of the most characteristic modern ideas is that it really doesn't matter what a man believes; and were he to believe in nothing whatever it would generally be supposed that his happiness was complete. In his book Chesterton "pointed out" (a favorite phrase) that it does make a great deal of difference what opinions a man holds, particularly if he wishes to be happy. The leading exponents of the age are analyzed and their limitations set forth with a vividness that has made many a reader gasp. Of the method with which the argument is conducted something will be said later; it is enough to remark here that it was by this series of negations that Chesterton arrived at an affirmation.

That "Credo" is uttered vigorously in "Orthodoxy," a book that has been largely misunderstood. It is not a philosophy but a statement of preference; not a handbook of apologetics, but an apology that might have been made in a tavern where atheists interrupted the speaker constantly. The answers come in flashes and are astounding because they are overwhelmingly obvious. One of the strangest things about "Orthodoxy" is the fact that its case for dogma hinges on the acceptance of Papal Supremacy, which Chesterton has not in practice accepted. The most striking thing about it is the fervent conviction of the conclusion which is easily the most simple and sincere, as well as the most impressive and torrential, passage that its author has ever written. The later Chesterton is less vivacious and more reflective in making his plea. "The

New Jerusalem," which under the guise of a trip to the Holy Land makes an historical voyage from London to Calvary and stops off for a lengthy visit with the Crusaders, is a supplement to "Orthodoxy." "St. Francis," finally, is an effective statement of the truth that the greatest of virtues is charity.

Conviction, too, has governed the vast amount of literary criticism signed by Chesterton. His books on Browning, Cobbett, and the Victorian Age have taken their places among standard works of the kind, have been appraised favorably and otherwise, but have all been distinguished by resolute determination not to dissolve the art of utterance from the thought that must precede utterance. They have taken boisterous issue with the æsthete. Perhaps the most characteristic of these volumes is "Notes on Charles Dickens," virtually a series of prefaces to the novels. With the author of "Pickwick Papers" Chesterton has much in common: in fact, it often seems that when he speaks of the "mob" he has in mind a great crowd of Dickens people rather than any assemblage that might really gather in London today. Nobody has ever said so well the things which actually matter about Dickens; and one could go further and declare that these "Notes" are almost indispensable to a proper understanding of their author himself.

What has been the central purpose of this giant literary enterprise? Many people have replied that the Chestertonian attack on beliefs so tranquilly entertained by modern *illuminati* is simply reactionary and perverse. On the other hand, hundreds of young men not too reactionary or perverse are sure that it is actuated by a firm and high resolve. To begin with, Chesterton's success may be attributed largely to his amazing discovery of the ordinary. While the intellectuals were talking over their books of progress, efficiency, the Inner Light, and the higher this or that, the "man in the street" was talking about life. He remembered the forgotten and invaluable truth that two and two are four; he was gay with the obvious and joyful things, like wine and prayer, while his cultivated neighbour was sitting with great seriousness in a melancholy library. It was Chesterton's luck as a poet to meet this common man; like Socrates he went down the road asking questions which the professors had declared unanswerable and discovered that everybody could answer them. The earth turned out to be a palace of awful beauty wherein a man should go down on his knees before a glade of grass. It was a gay business, too, that had its root in laughter; for mirth, as well as awe, is an announcement of the discovery of the unexpected, and the distance between the two is proverbially slight. Thus a man laughs when a girl loses her garter but is dumb when, like Hardy's Tess, she loses her head. Chesterton, afire with the reality of this forgotten world, puzzled the educated alike with his jollity and his worship: many of them shook their heads and asked him to be serious and others smilingly called him a fool. It was another case of class-conciousness.

What all these people really saw in the author of "Heretics" and "Orthodoxy" was something hard to see, something that for lack of a better word is called mystical. Every sort of theosophic nonsense has been associated with the term, but for Chesterton it means understanding by analogy, something like reading the advertisements of God. It is the reasonableness which unseats reason, the common sense which transcends the sensible. The mystic, believing in God, sees the world as a garden bright with flowers that are tokens of His love, but he need not forget that it is the world. Chesterton finds that the universe is democratic, and mankind "the million masks of God." The elusiveness of every natural thing emphasizes the will, almost the willfulness, of The Master and the man. Philosophy becomes a gay sacramentalism, making joyous obeisance to wonder and to war.

Impelled by this insight into the forgotten mystery of things, Chesterton has been a life-long defender of the Faith. He fights for liberty by relying steadfastly on dogma, just as a patriot might struggle for his country from ancient battlements of stone. Because the democratic society, the many-sided life, and the full religion demanded by the manifold temperament of man have been the ideals of the Church, and because civilization was saved and sanctified and brought to its best bloom by her efforts, he upholds the Church and her history, particularly the magnificent history of the Middle Ages. A common error avows that being a mediævalist implies of necessity a retrogression, whereas it is simply a straightforward assertion of confidence in human progress. If society as it was formed by Greece and Rome had any goal, manifestly it was the thirteenth century in which all the elements of antique culture were made socially effective. The alternative is to believe that the worth-while history of man began with Martin Luther and not with the Saviour, that Christianity was founded for the sake of

higher criticism and wireless telegraphy; it is to assert
that society is now sane and that the ages have yearned
for the culture of Henry Ford and Hugo Stinnes. It
has seemed impossible to the religious and democratic
mind of Chesterton that the modern course is right,
primarily because nobody really believes that it is
right; but here again he is too much of a fighter to be
intimately concerned with the details of the reëstablish-
ment of Christendom. His social program is as hazy
as a revolutionary patriot's idea of the constitution
of his liberated country. Chesterton feels that Socialism is wrong because it is a negation of freedom and
therefore of a fact; that German philosophy is wrong
because it denies the reality of Rome; and that Irishmen are right because they affirm the existence of
Ireland. He has blazed the trail with laughter and
battle, but is content that the land of promise shall
remain the land of dreams.

It is interesting at this point to consider the relation of Chesterton to other defenders of the Catholic
Spirit. One cannot resist the impression that he is
deeply indebted to Newman, despite the gulf which lies
between the style of "Orthodoxy" and that of the
"Apologia." Both are concerned primarily with the
skeptics, whose principles they can state with remarkable clearness, and both wage war with evidences that
are personal and complex but none the less realistic.
Newman's almost instinctive attraction to Catholic life
and history is, when one makes the necessary allowance
for differences of vocation, very similar to the religion
of Chesterton. The two are alike once more in cease-
less effort and versatility of form. Naturally there
are divergencies; Newman, ascetic and meditative,

craved celibacy and contemplation, stood even in his writings at some distance from the crowd. Chesterton, akin to the robust, democratic spirt of Dickens, has believed in love and song, has cherished the lusty bravadoes of the mob. It may not stretch the distinction too far to say that while Newman venerated the Christian Fathers, Chesterton has been fascinated by the fathers of Christians.

Another sort of relationship is discernible between Coventry Patmore and the author of "Manalive" and "The Man Who Was Thursday." In these books Chesterton is perhaps nearest to being a mystical poet concerned with understanding the tumultuous pursuit of God's love, which is the consuming theme of "The Unknown Eros" and particularly of the kindlier lyrics like "Toys" and the "Departure." Neither would it be extremely difficult to trace a parallel between "What's Wrong with the World" and "Religio Poetæ," although the fierce democracy of the one is at war with the intense egoism of the other. To select an instance in point, there is the hostility of both to prohibition. Patmore detested such meddlesome popular legislation because it infringes on the liberty of the superior man; Chesterton, because it is an attack, by another kind of superior man, on the liberty of the populace. For both it is not so much the drink that matters as the freedom; not so much the reality as the symbol. Here is only another instance of the remarkable unity of principle which the Catholic spirit may achieve among men of diverse temperaments: Patmore was high and narrow, Chesterton is low and broad; together they occupy satisfactorily the three dimensions of belief.

No one, however, has influenced Chesterton so profoundly as his bosom friend, Hilaire Belloc. The opinions of this combative historian will be considered in the next chapter; it need only be suggested here that in numerous ways Chesterton has found them good. If his philosophy is wider in "The New Jerusalem" than in "The Defendant," it is because the social views of Belloc have also developed. The abilities of the two men are so remarkably complementary that the term, "Chesterbelloc," facetiously employed by Bernard Shaw, really stands for organic unity, for impulsive intuition linked with cold empiricism. The matter may be put briefly by saying that Belloc proceeds by straight lines, like Roman roads, while Chesterton goes to the same place by rainbows. For one, life is law; for the other, something like lawlessness. Their interdependence will be seen more closely when we examine the work of Belloc.

These comparisons have been made for the benefit of those who make the facile assertion that Chesterton is not original in ideas. Nobody is, and the only claim to superiority is superior company; what the accusation really means is that his literary method is not honest, although it is the delight of the present generation. This judgment seems quite unfounded. Chesterton's perennial ability to see an obvious thing which everybody has overlooked is extraordinary because it is sincere. No verbal trickery could fashion rows of lamp-like sentences that really illuminate (and here is the vital matter) not only one side of a question but both. The older literature had mastered this secret, which is the sum and substance of Shakespeare's genius. Cordelia, for instance, is a victim but also a victor;

Shylock is a villain but also a man; interwoven with the sanity of Hamlet is a thread of unreason which leads him to his death. Now Shakespeare, who was a humanist and concerned with the world as a stage, is reflective and inexorable; his reading of life was the accepted version, there was no need of proving it to the pit. Modern literature, however, is combative, is chiefly interested in establishing a philosophy, and Chesterton has no other purpose. If he is dealing, say, with defeat and wondering why men are often so deeply impressed by it, he runs across a maxim which declares that if a thing is worth doing it must be done well. The answer to his inquiry flashes upon him: "If a thing is worth doing it is worth doing badly." This is the source of the famous paradox, which may become simply a mannerism but with Chesterton is usually a manner—a way of arriving at truth by looking over the shoulder of logic. Again, in "The New Jerusalem" there is a discussion of the relation between St. George and the Dragon, between faith in moral principle and fear of the Demon. Chesterton sees that while science has pretty well stripped the Saint's history of legendary glamour, it has, by psychical research, given a new realism to the Dragon; and he is moved to question the general adequacy of complacent logic. The answer is again given in a flash: "We never find our religion so right as when we find we are wrong about it." How well that reveals both sides of the problem! The people who accuse Chesterton of being a mere master of the paradox are really implying that he is an author of the inferior caste of Shakespeare; a philosopher of the second-rate quality of Newman.

But the paradox is only one characteristic of the Chestertonian style. This is what might be termed an early Gothic prose, bedecked with imagery that is both lifelike and grotesque, and rhythmical in a way that startles and yet pleases the ear. No modern prose writer, it may be affirmed, has understood so well the power of figurative language. If the making of metaphors be indeed a birthright like the ear attuned to immortal music, then Chesterton has been blessed abundantly; the whole course of our literature cannot show writing that is more closely akin to illuminated manuscript. Despite the transient themes and the modern ring of the laughter, it is difficult to see what contemporary prose is destined to live if it is not Chesterton's. Boys dipping today, for the first time, into "Heretics" or "Orthodoxy" find them as fresh as we did when they were first published. And it seems not at all unlikely that the young people of the future will do the same, without bothering very much about whether Mr. McCabe or even Mr. Dickinson is a real or a fictitious personage.

Chesterton is, moreover, a writer sufficiently in demand to be an imperfect, at times even a glaringly imperfect, writer. The point here is not so much that his epigrams are frequently overworked, that he misses being effective by becoming affected. Nor are we concerned immediately with the lack of clarity which muffles so many of his stories and essays in a kind of tangled dusk. He has never tried to be that master of construction who is the ideal of French stylists and their disciples. Almost every one of his books is a scrapbook, and his unity of composition is best in his natural medium, verse. No one can quarrel justly with the construction of "The Ballad of the White Horse" or "Lepanto."

His most noteworthy fault goes deeper: it is a very natural overworking of the symbol. When a man believes that such and such an institution is a sacrament, every detail about it will acquire the character of a mystic ceremonial. If one is convinced that marriage and the home which it builds are more wonderful, more sacred, and more important than an empire, and if one sees that woman is the awful goddess of that shrine, one cannot help viewing with alarm even the slightest compromise between the spirit of these things and the world. Therefore Chesterton opposed woman suffrage and seemed to many, even among his admirers, stupidly conservative. It must be admitted that such opposition was close to mere antipathy; but he meant that the whole trend of such movements is wrong, that suffrage was only a rung in the ladder which would bring down Juliet from her bower and Peggotty from her kitchen into a business which in itself is unworthy and which will have to be carried on in a better way than by passing round bushels of crisp ballots. Chesterton was here opposing divorce, eugenics, race-suicide, state control of children, the dozen capital sins of domestic life which are the result of a false ideal of government and the abandonment of Christian morality. Nevertheless one feels strongly that the connection between suffrage and these things is not so obvious or necessary as he would have us believe, and there are other instances in Chesterton's journalism of the same stubbornness of opinion.

Other widespread criticisms seem to be based on a

failure to take the man for what he professes to be. When "A Short History of England" appeared, it was gravely handled by some critics in a spirit which would have been altogether proper for a review of a monograph by Lord Acton. They queried very gravely whether the author had seen a learned dissertation by So and So, a certain bundle of manuscripts in the British Museum, and the theories of a Heidleberg savant on the genuineness of an early date. Such criticism may display the writer's historical learning, but it proves him ignorant of history and Chesterton. This book, like everything else that its crusading author ever wrote, is a summary of the reasons why a man should find the national life worth talking about. Abstruse familiarity with the exactness of a text is useful; but it will never induce anybody to sing "England, My England," and surely that also is important.

Chesterton would say that it is most important. His service, when one looks at it broadly, has not been to add to the erudition of the wise, but rather to subtract from it. With commendable gusto he has removed heaps of learned rubbish that had blocked the windows of the world, and has been one of the first to rediscover the immemorial scenes, like starlight on the seas, for which men have been glad to live and to die. Surely there has been enough of pessimism in modern life and men are sated with despair. The merriment of the English, older than the walls of Rome or the crests of Norman kings, has stood in real danger of succumbing to the last and most ignoble of influences, the pride of foreign savants. Chesterton has restored, or at least helped to restore, the laughing humility of the common citizen, which is not servitude nor yet pride, but the virtue of freedom for which Christendom was founded, the virtue of the symbol of Resurrection. In him, though the world was going astray with the blind philosophy of the Germans and the too perceptive art of the French, the Englishman came back with the best thing he ever possessed. He came back with a laugh.

BOOK NOTE

In addition to the published work of Chesterton, see the files of the London *Daily News*, the *New Witness*, and the *Dublin Review*. Noteworthy criticisms include the following: "G. K. Chesterton," by Julius West; "Chesterton: a Biography," Anonymous; and "G. K. Chesterton," by J. de Tonquedéc (French). See also, "Victorian Prophets," by Slosson; "On Contemporary Literature," by S. P. Sherman; "Uncensored Celebrities," by Raymond; "The End of a Chapter," by Shane Leslie; "Chesterbelloc," by Theodore Maynard (*Catholic World*, 1919); and a Review of "Orthodoxy" in the *North American*, vol. 189.

CHAPTER FOURTEEN

THE ADVENTURES OF AN HISTORIAN: HILAIRE BELLOC

"The founder of the Christians has put into their heads the idea
that they are brothers."   LUCIAN.

THE mirthful crusading of Gilbert Chesterton
seems inseparable from a gallant trade like
journalism; it does not fit in so naturally, for
instance, with the studious pursuit of history. And
yet without this pursuit, especially as it has been undertaken by one of the friends of his bosom, the author
of "Orthodoxy" could scarcely have conducted his
campaign. Let it be granted that the historian is
usually a mole in some library, enchanted or otherwise;
but it is not at all necessary that he be a mole. The
past justly remains for most people a land of varied
adventure, crowded with places and people that are,
above everything else, interesting. The historian may,
therefore, consider himself a benevolent detective whose
business is just as much human entertainment as it is
the quest of truth. If, for example, one were to arrive
for the first time in the city of Chartres at the lonely
hour which just noses out the dawn, one would see,
standing like an awful throne in the luminous darkness, the form of Notre-Dame. It is likely that as the
bell, which surely is of gold, whispered the time, the
neighboring streets would fill with the majestic and unfathomable people who once gathered from the sur-

rounding country to build the cathedral; it is even probable that if one's historical imagination were satisfactory the structure would seem just to have been completed. "Is it not an enormous business merely to stand in such a place? I think it is," says Hilaire Belloc.

And here is the first reason why this historian has a right to his own corner in modern letters. Belloc has looked upon the past not as a record but as a reality, as something like a gigantic novel which the peoples of the world have actually lived. His outlook and method are as fresh and concrete as those of any healthy business carried out in early morning. He goes to work upon some knotty question much as a man might sit down to a puzzle, with a good-humoured intentness on solving it. History is a matter of personalities and of *ésprit*, at least, if not of the spirit. Because of his philosophy, which will be considered briefly later on, Belloc brings to the analysis of the past what every sane person ought to instil into his life: a sense of humour. Perhaps we can bring out this side of the man best by recalling the coincidence that he was born in 1870, the year when Dickens died and France fell. The great novelist divined the truth of popular tradition; it is Belloc who verifies it by refusing to believe that France has fallen. Both are ample and robust, but both are quite unflinching on the issues for which they really care.

The next thing to note about Belloc is that he believes not only that truth is stranger than fiction but that what passes for truth is often more fictitious than fiction. His work generally assumes a critical attitude and he is forever hammering the sophist. This,

too, is in the real spirit of the adventure, for battle is
what lends zest to the careers of Ulysses and d'Artag-
nan. Belloc writes history because he is defending the
central tradition of Europe with the one irresistible
weapon of experience. Just as his presentation of the
past is convincing by reason of his sense of its con-
temporaneousness, so he writes with a constant eye
on what Professor Perry calls "The Present Conflict
of Ideals." A large share of Belloc's best work is not
constructive history at all, but inspection of someone's
opinions: an inspection made sharply and often accompanied with stern reprimand. There is no compromise
in his blood.

Such a manner is natural to the man and his creed.
Hilaire Belloc is of mixed French and English ancestry,
and is descended from people who were soldiers and
artists. As a boy he attended Newman's school at
Edgbaston, and it is significant that he has defended
many of the great Cardinal's views. Being a French
citizen, he served for one year as a driver in a regi-
ment of artillery stationed at Toul, in northern France.
After a varied tour of Europe and the United States
(like Stevenson he married in California) he entered
Balliol College, Oxford, taking honours in history, to
the study of which he had intended to devote his life.
There were reasons, however, why no fellowship was
awarded him, and after a period of waiting he journeyed to London for a try at journalism. Very fortunately he got a foothold, made a friend of great
value in Chesterton, and found a publisher for his
earlier books. Some of these, it will be remembered,
were illustrated by G. K. C. Belloc, now a naturalized
British subject, decided to enter politics and was

elected to the House of Commons in 1906. His sturdy liberalism made a strong impression and he seemed on the threshold of great success; but other principles, such as a pronounced anti-Semitism, a radical labour policy, and an uncompromising Catholicism, could not fail to ruin the career of any modern statesman. Belloc retired from the arena, founded the *Eye Witness* (which has since become the *New Witness* under Chestertonian editorship) and wrote extensively. A large part of his ablest writing has been journalistic in character and must be sought out in magazines. During the war his articles and lectures on the military aspects of the struggle gained him a wide reputation, although as the years dragged on and strategy blurred in the labyrinth of trench warfare, this subject was stripped of the dramatic definiteness which Belloc is most successful in presenting. Of late years he has become simply a journalist and literary man who, despite opinions which are not commonly shared, is looked upon as a leading spokesman of English Catholicism.

What, then, have been the central beliefs of Belloc's philosophy? First of all, it would seem, there is a strong, confident grasp of the Catholic idea of civilization. We follow our ancestors not in straggling groups or individually, but rather socially: we have come out of the past in a body. History, therefore, is coherently human and not a vast museum of isolated specimens. A synthesis of early European civilization had been successfully completed in the Roman Empire, whose social discipline had steadily pushed back the boundaries of barbarism. The Catholic Church, not a vague philosophy but a compact organization, preserved the culture of Rome while the rule of Cæsar

withered away. This Church also undertook the reformation of Europe by insisting strongly on religion and
democracy, and succeeded better than any other agency
in history at the attempt to unify the Western world.
That unity, however, has been broken up and a number of evils have resulted. The obvious thing to do
is to return to the older faith and to the older social
order. Acceptance of these must be based in turn
upon a full recognition of liberty. It will mean the
end of capitalistic industrialism and the collapse of
bureaucratic government. It will mean that property,
which is the pledge of freedom, will be held by the great
majority of citizens whose rights will be protected
against class aggression by a strong and popular central
government. Such a return to mediæval social practice cannot, Belloc is convinced, be wrought by any
kind of legislation, but must be the result of a new
state of mind, the *will to freedom* of a spiritualized, a
Catholic democracy.

It will be observed that all this stands in rather vivid
opposition to the general direction of modern English
thought. But although Belloc is hardly miserly of
words in attacking contemporary politics and historical doctrine, he is not romantic in any sense of the
term. If anything he is too rational, too devoid of
emotion, in his dissection of motives and movements.
The ordinary man will find in this appeal for a new
social order much that seems dry and disenchanting.
Belloc's French mind and training are thoroughly different from what Britain has become accustomed to
during the last century. But although he must rank
with Swift, Patmore, and Samuel Butler in the class
of writers who cross the grain of the English mind,

Belloc views social institutions with much of the calm common sense and firm reliance on tradition that were displayed by Napoleon in the making of the *Code Civil*. It will be recalled that the Emperor decided against large estates and for many small ones; that he upheld firmly the Church and such moral institutions as marriage, and that he smiled at philosophies of the State which did not rest squarely upon experience. All of this was the view of a *bon Français*, but Napoleon lacked the religious conviction, the spiritual selflessness, that would have made his scheme a revival of the Christian age. In teaching the lessons of the past Belloc, however, is consistently a belligerent defender of Catholic ideas. He understands England, too, with the clarity of love; no one has written more discerningly of her tradition and her beauties, and no one is more sincerely concerned with her future.

The manner which Belloc has chosen for the expression of these views is individual. To a great versatility —he has mastered nearly every literary form except the drama—is added a style that belongs to no one else, which combines the wit and clearness of Voltaire with the logic of the schools. Invariably he begins by stating a thesis which in these times is sure to be warlike, much as a revolutionary patriot might hoist a strange flag. Not concerned with the ideal as an apostolate, he champions it simply because it is true; where Newman, for instance, would have been eager to arbitrate, Belloc opens fire. The thesis is then established step by step, with a remarkable ability to make each point concrete. Nothing drifts into the realm of theory, but is tied to time and space, is fastened by a vivid and steely empiricism. Facts, the stock in trade of the rationalist, are also the weapons of Belloc's apologetics. There is never a dearth of satire, which is always directed at those who have failed to observe how facts cohere and establish principles, but great verbal brilliancy, or rather eloquence, is rare. The diction has the ring of swords on armor; it is never soft and seldom tender. Belloc's work is Napoleonic in the sense that it is done in the belief that an army of words must travel on its stomach—on something substantial and very evident. Moreover, the argument is conducted to win, and there is no pretense of concession. Very often it seems dogmatic in the extreme; and it must be admitted that wherever Hilaire Belloc loses his sense of humour he is likely to become pompously stubborn, like a pre-Revolutionary pamphleteer.

Since, however, he is generally something of a pamphleteer, it is difficult to examine his work in detail. Let us begin with the histories, for the excellent reason that Belloc himself began with them. A Frenchman born into England would naturally, if his mind concerned itself with the past, turn to the great epic of the Revolution, so significant as a popular and dramatic effort to change the face of the earth. A little book on "The French Revolution" will seem to many Belloc's most fascinating narrative; it has the glamour of Carlyle, a much better grasp of the situation, and the indispensable French logic. Compact though it is, this volume manages to cover much ground and is not the off-hand essay which its brilliant style might suggest. Nevertheless, the author's skill is based upon a previous diligent study of personalities who dominated the Revolution and who are still largely misunderstood. "Robespierre" and "Danton" are dramatic biographies, but every chapter is visibly the product of scrupulous care. Taken alone they are sufficient evidence for Belloc's genuine historical ability—his exactness and narrative skill—but as life-stories they do not equal the later "Marie Antoinette." The author is sympathetic with the unfortunate queen but does not spare the truth, and the result is a portrait that convinces and moves like great fiction. Even Taine, whom Belloc resembles by reason of crisp, unemotional intelligence, could not have surpassed the psychological insight of this book or equaled the splendid art of its final chapters.

Taken altogether, these books present a more accurate account of the Revolution than is given by any other work in English, and their value lies precisely in the circumstance that they were written with the British public in mind. If there is any part of modern history which that public has failed to understand and profit by, it is the amazingly democratic uprising of the modern French. Characterized by excesses, the Revolution nevertheless blocked the progress of capitalism in France just when its power was most tranquilly being established in England. It is hazardous to assert that Belloc set forth this history as a prologue to his attack on the British social system, but certainly he could have found no better matter for an introduction. Here is the parable; the commentary will follow. From the technical point of view these books are uneven and betray, despite their general vividness and individuality, the hand of one learning to write.

Belloc is not a master of style like his brother-in-arms, the incomparable Chesterton. His writing is calmly scintillant, seldom contagiously emotional, and his horseplay even is not always mirth. "The Path to Rome," however, is a book which challenges attention to its craftsmanship. Here is a perfect travel record, set down with the shrewd insight, the kindly sympathy, and the odd whimsicality of an ideal if unusual voyager. The flavour is so rare that one can suggest it only by means of an outlandish comparison: it is a blend of the modern Samuel Butler and the mediæval Brother Bozon. For the benefit of those who have not traveled to Rome with Mr. Belloc, it may be stated that the book claims to be an account of a pilgrimage, made on foot and without notable deviation from a straight line, from Toul on the Meuse to the city of Rome. With the exception of the mountainous vistas (curiously the only tedious matter in the book) one does not see much of the landscape, but rather a great deal of the Catholic spirit of this elusive and altogether delightful country-side. The traveler arrives in quaint towns, converses with simple folk, gathers entrancing legends, drinks wine, and goes to Mass. Finally, before one really understands what has happened, pilgrim, staff and scrip have reached the city of the Popes.

The author is attempting, of course, to uncover the mediæval walls upon which modern Europe rests. He laughs with the Catholic peasant at the expense of the modernist; he joins eagerly in the dozen democratic things which people who are free in practice think it natural to perform. The observations, while not paradoxical, are none the less satisfying, and one drifts out of industrial society without the least semblance of a shock. Meantime the author is going about his business very skillfully and actually does reconstruct a social environment that may be called mediæval. "The Path to Rome" is a polemic in disguise, like some gentle, ancient allegory, and the disguise is admirable. The style has spice and vigour, but above all things a kind of ruminative reasonableness which needs a reader just the least bit sympathetic. For the truth about Belloc is that his arguments are almost never adorned with smiles for the enemy, are militaristic. This book is also the manifesto of its author's mysticism, a joyous but rational discernment of the Truth in the little things of life. None of his other travel sketches, among which "Paris" and "The River of London" may be mentioned, seem to reach the level of "The Path to Rome," although their eye for the adventure of history is interesting and fruitful for the mind. Hilaire Belloc is a master of travel literature because of his instinct for the poetry of places, which lies not so much in the scene that makes a picture as in the history that makes a song.

The books mentioned so far may be considered the foundations of Belloc's journalistic career which, opening about the time of the Boer War and amid the triumph of imperialism, had for its purpose the restoration of the idea of liberty. It is impossible, of course, to review the whole of this endeavour, so much of which was dedicated to a particular hour and to a select audience. For instance, the files of the *Dublin Review* contain two of the most striking papers that their author has written: one on Bury's "History of the Freedom of Thought," and the other on H. G. Wells' "Outline of History." For the purposes of the present discussion, we shall practically confine the matter to

Belloc's most important book on social problems, "The Servile State."

When this volume appeared it made clear to everybody that there is a solution of the social injustice which cuts across the positions which leading modern schools of thought have drawn up. Previously any discussion of industrial economics had seemed a struggle between Capitalism and Socialism, though either of these might assume peculiar forms. Belloc, however, boldly declared that Capitalism is an imperfect, a transitory, social condition, and that the real struggle lies between what he called the Servile State, wherein 'so considerable a number of families and individuals are constrained by positive law to labour for the advantage of others as to stamp the whole community with the mark of such labour,' and the Distributive State, wherein the ownership of property is divided among the great majority of citizens. The purpose of this book, however, is not to make a brief for the distributive ownership of property, but rather to show that the Servile State is the easiest solution of our present difficulties and is, in fact, the one which is gradually being adopted. The historical chapters explain how paganism was complacently servile and how the Christian civilization which superseded it almost proved successful in setting up the distributive state. Some of these declarations have long been commonplaces in France, but the temper of England is still quite foreign to them.

It was expected that the book would be attacked and it was built to offer sturdy resistance. Written and arranged with the logic of an able schoolman, its case rests stubbornly on facts which are difficult to conjure away. History is the soil upon which Belloc's sentences stand like trees, well-groomed and scornful of puny blows. They defy criticism of the ordinary sort because they do not plead for anything, but simply state the situation. While there is never any doubt of Belloc's preference for the freedom of the Christian State, he realizes very fully that its restoration is everywhere dependent upon the regaining of a free mind, which is the social aim of the Catholic Spirit everywhere. One sees at a glance that this book crystallizes into a few phrases the basis of the instinctive opposition of the Church to Socialism; that Chesterton's championship of "peasant society" is built upon it, and that dozens of others have profited by the definitions and conclusions it presents. Belloc himself undertook in several essays to outline more completely the distributive state and to suggest practical measures by which it could be promoted. In "The Party System" (written in collaboration with Cecil Chesterton) he exposed in a telling way the secret and venal political combines by which the British government is actually administered. The book does not seem of sufficient general interest to be called more than a brilliant pamphlet.

Belloc's social criticism, akin to the Code Napoleon in many of its legal principles, suggests his writings on military subjects. A year's service with an army is not ordinarily a reason why a man should be credited with an understanding of strategy, but granting his natural gifts and studious preparation for the writing of history, it will supply him with a directness of perception and an understanding of details not easy to obtain in other ways. In many essays written before the war Belloc proved an astute discoverer of clues to military mysteries, and in his account of the battle of Valmy unearthed what seems to be a satisfactory theory to account for the strange outcome of that struggle. During the war his analysis of the First Battle of the Marne attracted wide attention and seems to have been a remarkably correct bit of deductive reasoning. It is quite evident that he enjoys exploring battlefields which, the pacifist notwithstanding, are the cradles of new eras.

Underneath all of this, however, there has lain the deeper and more permanent earth of Catholic tradition. Every page of Belloc's work bears the imprint of the Creed, but in what seems his most important book after "The Path to Rome" the Church is the immediate subject-matter. "Europe and the Faith" adopts for its thesis the proposition that the soul of European civilization, the inner power which has purposefully shaped it and given it a cogent unity, is the Catholic Faith, and that a return to this Faith is the only possible escape from social ruin. Belloc proceeds to show how Europe was originally welded together and civilized by Rome; how the Church preserved and transformed the culture of the tottering and sunken Empire; and how the unity thus established was dissolved by the Reformation which, originally concerned with ecclesiastical abuses, ended, by reason of the defection of Britain, in the disruption of Western civilization. Most of the elements of this doctrine are not original; many have been taught by Saint Augustine, by Bossuet, by Newman, and various others. But they have probably never before been set down so symmetrically and arrestingly in one book.

Criticism of the historical data of "Europe and the Faith" must be left to competent historians. No one else is able, for instance, to offer an opinion on the validity of Belloc's theory that the Anglo-Saxon language spread over England because the missionaries sent from Rome adopted it. The manner in which the book is written may, however, be legitimately commented upon here. In the first place, the tone is characteristically belligerent. What of it? If history is worth troubling about, surely one is permitted to attack error savagely. If records and common sense show plainly that the Church was not despotic, surely a little harshness is not out of place with people who assert blandly that she was more tyrannical than a Cossack chieftain. There is nothing that prejudice fears more than to be called prejudice. Next, there is no unfairness in the book, excepting perhaps a somewhat abnormal and unfortunate antipathy to the Germans. The evidence for Belloc's theory is stated without any subterfuge, is put so clearly that one is never in doubt of the concrete testimony upon which the case rests. There is question of nothing except history; the argument is concise, scholarly, and manly. If mistakes have been made they are obviously not intentional. One may state without hesitation that "Europe and the Faith" is not only a challenge, but also an honourable and respectable challenge, worthy of attention.

The book is important enough to make an examination of the style interesting. Throughout the language is simple and direct, the language of a man earnestly addressing a thoughtful audience. No word has been set down for the mere sake of literary effect, and if there are metaphors it is because the argument requires them. The most interesting trait of style is, however, the manner in which the distant past is made real by simple pictures of the daily life of the time. As the exposition proceeds, propositions to which we have perfunctorily assented, as one does to abstractions of comparative aloofness, become as plainly sensible as if they were incarnate in our own day. Belloc must have learned not a little psychology from Newman. Never before has the formation of Christendom been so succinctly and realistically set forth or made to seem so genuinely the Divine Adventure. "Europe and the Faith" is unique and necessary because of the clarity, the logical power, of a very great historian. Into a few staunch chapters he appears to have compressed all that an honest observer can say about the continuity of Christendom.

It is somewhat remarkable that so diligent a student should have what may be termed the finer gifts of poetry. Nevertheless, in "Verses" Belloc has collected stanzas that admit of comparison with the finest of modern English lyrics. They are, as might have been expected, distinctly French, resembling Beranger much more closely than Tennyson, and masculine in form and verve. Belloc is not a conscious, brooding artist begetting inspiration from the sweat of his brow, but rather a jovial singer whose tunes come to his lips quite naturally. As a general rule, the note is satirical, with a stanza or two of sheer wisdom, whimsical, tender, and yet not romantic. Perhaps, however, such poetry will be admired rather than loved.

"The South Country" sings the praise of Sussex with a haunting refrain through which peers the melancholy of life:

> "A lost thing could I never find,
>   Nor a broken thing mend:
> And I fear I shall be all alone
>   When I get towards the end.
> Who will be there to comfort me
>   Or who will be my friend?"

This looks far off from the downs of England into the lonely stretches of human mystery, a gaze that is the secret of Belloc's grip on the heart in such other poems as "The Prophet Lost in the Hills at Evening," "Courtesy," and "The Rebel." There is excellent satire in "Dives" and keen burlesque in "Newdigate Poem," which is attributed to Mr. Lambkin of Burford, who has chosen for his subject, "The Benefits of Electric Light." The attack, however, is never local or personal but directed always at the vagaries of modern thought. Even Belloc's poetry is belligerent, but then soldiers have been known to make verses. It is an interesting fact that his favorite form is a compromise between the lyric and the ballad, a form admirably befitting a man of action in whose nature there is a saving touch of reflection, of human sadness, of kinship with the earth and its beauty. There can be no doubt that Belloc is a good poet, although one is not ready to believe that his verses deserve the extravagant praise that some of his friends have buried them under.

If Belloc the poet merits attention, Belloc the novelist and essayist is probably more interesting. The word "novelist" must be used reservedly here, for his

books are not great social outlines of life but rather
satiric allegories that have to do with politics. "Emmanuel Burden" is diverting and incisive symbolism,
between the contours of which lie buried a host of first-
rate leading articles for a somewhat revolutionary
newspaper. Englishmen in general do not seem to have
taken to it kindly, and Americans are too remote from
the scene to be deeply interested. Belloc the essayist,
on the other hand, is a universal figure. A man who
has written "On Everything" and "On Nothing" may
reasonably be expected to be dull occasionally, but the
average Bellocian essay is a stimulant. Many of the
papers gathered in "First and Last" and "Hills and
the Sea" are shrewd comments on historical writing,
quaint travel sketches, or interpretations of human
nature made in a fresh and unusually thoughtful mood.
The essay is a prose lyric that is saved by its flavor of
didacticism from the excessive influence of romantic
imagination, and it seems, in fact, the avenue that leads
to classic art. No literary form could be better suited
to the natural gifts of Hilaire Belloc, and this he has
not failed to discover.

In speaking finally of the great service which he
has rendered to Christendom in these days of its partial
revival in England, one may say that Belloc has found
that service difficult but not discouraging. By nature
a good fighter, he has not feared to battle against odds.
Freedom, the distributive state, and the Catholic conscience of history are Christian ideas, but they are
acceptable to few even among Catholics. To assert
them dogmatically, to make practical issues of them,
and to accompany their defense with barbed arrows of
satire, is to invite hostility and to limit one's audience.

It is characteristic to Belloc that he has not thought of these consequences. Resolutely conscious of a mission to assert principles, he has left to others the task of popularizing and discussing them. Fortunately, Chesterton, the man best fitted to undertake such a task, has performed it with a success that need not be dwelt on here. The two men have leaned on each other and have drawn proud strength from their alliance. The truth of the Chestertonian maxim, "Two times one are not two, but two thousand times one" has never been more fully proved.

Belloc is a man of no illusions, and one might almost say of no dreams. There is no Utopia in his philosophy, although he would agree with Ruskin that the saddest thing which can happen to people who see how bad matters are is to believe them incapable of betterment. Only, he insists that only one system of life, only one principle of action, can effect a permanent betterment because in fact only one has done so. The logical French mind that has fed on Bossuet, Pascal, and Taine will not be weaned from the experience of history. And it is characteristic of that French mind again that it should, for all its common sense, love both truth and laughter. The mirth of Belloc is not the humour which is the meat of English literature, but rather the wit that is the kindly wine of France's thought. Two men more different in philosophy than Stendhal and Belloc cannot be imagined, unless one takes into account their mutual admiration for Napoleonic methods. And yet in instinct and manner they are strikingly alike. Stendhal's analysis of love is no more empirical or incisive than Belloc's dissection of modern politics, and the verve of phrase is similar in both authors. If Newman is like Ernest Renan, is it out of place to say that Belloc resembles the elusive Henry Beyle? Many, of course, will prefer to find a counterpart in Joseph de Maistre.

Belloc has aroused Catholics to a better understanding of their ancestry and their duty. Not everything he champions will be accepted, and not everything ought to be accepted. Nevertheless, he has done more than any other living Englishman to uphold steadfastly the social principles of Christendom and to restore these to a position of public importance. Philosophies to which Catholic opposition was instinctive but scarcely well organized have now become unmasked and human adversaries. The renaissance of Catholic social action in English-speaking countries has accepted his distinctions and his phrases. It has been an honest career, noble in its inspiration, selfless in its motive, and human in its preoccupations.

BOOK NOTE

Several of Hilaire Belloc's most interesting volumes have now been reprinted. Many of his finest essays must be sought out in the files of the *Dublin Review, Studies, The New Witness,* and *The Catholic World.* See "Chesterbelloc," by Theodore Maynard (*Catholic World,* 1919); J. Kilmer's introduction to "Verses"; "Socialism and the Great State," by H. G. Wells; and several articles in *The Living Age.* It is useful to compare Belloc's historical position with that assumed by various French authors: Bossuet in the "Discourse on Universal History," Louis Bertrand in "Saint Augustin," and P. Imbart de la Tour in "Histoire Politique." Of interest as bases for comparison are Stendhal's "Napoleon" and J. de Maistre's "Soirées." The student of history proper will, of course, see the influence of Guizot, Fustel de Coulanges, and Charles Maurras.

CHAPTER FIFTEEN

THE VOICE OF IRELAND

"It is when night prevails that it is fine to believe in the light."
ROSTAND'S "CHANTICLEER."

THE appearance of Ireland as a distinct creative
force in English letters is the outstanding literary fact of the post-Victorian age. It is
like the sudden, stalwart entry of a giant into a room
where none of the company has imagined his existence
or been prepared to welcome his society. There is a
bit of boldness about it and some resultant dismay.
Our admiration is tinged with bewilderment; we succumb to the stranger without feeling quite at home in
his presence. And yet, what a glorious stranger he is!
"The Celt," says Mr. Shane Leslie, "struck the an-
cients as the only folk who would lend money on a
note due in the next world." This perplexing concreteness of religious belief remains, indeed, with the
Irish, but they strike us primarily as a people without
money to lend, a people whose voice has, after all, been
spared by misery and martyrdom from the trade of the
auctioneer. Liberty and fairies are still real things in
Ireland, and it is more than a coincidence that a civilization believing in force will have nothing to do with
any of them. The insanity of the armies that hounded
the peasant patriot to his hovel is a tragic mystery

for all who love the virtues and traditions of the English people; but it is no more tragic or mysterious than the gradual disappearance from Britain of familiarity with the elemental things which to the Irishman are like next-door neighbours.

Whatever the future may hold in store, the past has spanned a gulf between the two races. The Britisher fails largely to understand the Celt and Celtic literature because he no longer quite understands himself. He has forgotten about England, his modern books are mostly of the Empire; but all of Irish literature is about an island. The two are separated by the difference between a man who has lost himself in his conquests and a man who has never been conquered; between the hard and greedy sea and the land which it has surrounded but is powerless to engulf. We rediscover in Irish letters as they exist today a surprising, long-lost freshness, tenderness, spirituality; and so we naturally find them unfamiliar. An attempt at appraisal must deal with mysteries and beauties alike, and it has every reason to be modest.

The voice of Ireland in English literature is, to begin with, an anomaly, a heaping-up of coals of fire upon the oppressor's head. This music and message antedate the Saxon and are largely foreign to his nature. That Gaelic is beyond a doubt the natural language of Irishmen becomes more evident as its revival progresses. English rhythm, idiom, and metaphor are alien to this people, and the sources of their fancy and meditation are in no way Anglo-Saxon. The development of Irish expression in English has been contemporaneous with the restoration of the ancient tongue; and it is likely that if Gaelic were rooted out by law

or accident, the greater portion of the individuality
which makes the writing of Ireland priceless would
disappear. There is a mysterious law which decrees
that a people's soul and its language are inseparable.
Still, we need not believe that Gaelic will ever prevail
to the exclusion of English; Anglo-Irish literature will
(let us hope) continue to develop, drawing inspiration
and originality from the ancient tongue. If not, the
future voice of Ireland would be as foreign to Englishmen as Russian.

Another matter that distinguishes the Celtic utterance is strong national feeling, an instinctively emotional protest against bondage. The older Irish
authors in English literature frankly adopted the British point of view, even if they did retain their natural
gifts. Dean Swift, Edmund Burke, Richard Sheridan,
and Oliver Goldsmith had the genius of their exotic
ancestry but they were not exiles. They looked upon
the world from the windows of London as from a home.
During the nineteenth century, however, the Irishman
rediscovered his tradition: the legends and history,
which the peasant had tenaciously preserved, appeared
publicly in Dublin and took possession of art. The
picture of Ireland as a nation, as the Black Rose or
the radiantly beautiful Kathleen, seemed drawn everywhere on the high walls of the sea. This vision begat
a literature that cannot be separated from patriotism
in the healthy sense, and is accordingly baffling for even
the sympathetic alien. "This 'terrible and splendid
trust,'" says Thomas MacDonagh, "this 'heritage of
the race of kings,' this service of a nation without a
flag, but 'with the lure of God in her eyes' has endowed

some of our poetry with meanings that must be lost to all but those baptized in our national faith."

None the less, there is a difference between national feeling and nationalism, between writing that is inspired by indigenous tradition and that dictated by the political policy of the moment. Some of the most highly gifted men in Ireland have failed in art because their duty, as they saw it, was to make propaganda. The misery of the fatherland, the sting of the invaders' lash, memories of famine and destitution, goaded them to frenzy but scarcely to fine frenzy. This almost eighteenth-century concern with abstract ideals, a noble concern but fatal to letters, helps to make the Irish renaissance difficult to set forth. The battle is still too noisy for the tranquil enjoyment of song. Yeats is a great poet but a weak patriot; MacDonagh was a glorious soldier but scarcely a master-poet. The Irish will probably enshrine this soldier and forget this singer; and no appreciation of literature is honest unless it takes into account the attitude of the people directly concerned.

Since we shall limit ourselves here to the literature of the Catholic Spirit, we must confront another great difficulty. What is the nature of that Spirit in Ireland? It is not very essential that there are so and so many Catholics in the island or that the parish priest is a popular figure: the important thing is to learn how far the Celtic mood has been influenced by the traditions of Christendom, and what it has contributed to the establishment and interpretation of these. Everyone knows how gloriously and at what cost the Irish have held aloft the light of the Faith. In the centuries immediately following the arrival of Saint Patrick, scholars and poets from Celtic monasteries carried the gifts of Christian civilization over the northern parts of Europe; great names succeeded one another like emeralds on a gleaming chain—Alcuin, Columbanus, Erigena. Nevertheless, circumstances conspired to leave Ireland comparatively unaffected by the later triumphant efflorescence of Christendom. She stood of necessity aloof from Rome and romance. The native mythology was probably never fully merged in the symbolism of the Church; art did not rear many magnificent Gothic monuments on the island of saints. Moreover, an even wider separation from the culture of Europe was the result of the modern persecutions under which peasant and priest adhered with miraculous tenacity to the Faith which they could not make social, which was shadowed by the repressive influence of the Puritan invaders. It must be admitted also that the rulers of the Church did not always understand the Irish situation, and from Pope Adrian to Cardinal Cullen there were found ecclesiastics to succumb to English influence.

None of these things can, however, minimize the essential fact that the Catholic Spirit in Ireland has meant as much as even the national impulse. The Celt had beautiful gods when Saint Patrick came and he was converted without the shedding of blood. Since that time, numberless generations have gone the thorny path of faith with full confidence in the sanctity of their martyrdom. Christianity has become so domesticated that it is part of the daily speech, of the "furniture" of life. That the Irish are primarily a nation of peasants, that they lack the artistic sensibility of the mod-

ern æsthete and cherish poetic stories about the pagan
gods, surely does not diminish the power of the spirit
of belief within them. If they have not built edifices
like those which are the testament of mediæval France,
or if Dublin is not a city of colour and form and manifold music like Bruges, it is surely retort enough to say
that no people has ever created a satisfactory social
life while burdened by oppression. The Irish creed
will wear beautiful garments when it is given liberty
to make them. Our cursory examination of the utterance of the Catholic Spirit in Ireland will show that it
is nothing slight or mean, but instead a crown which is
the more beautiful and symbolic because it is, in many
ways, a crown of thorns.

Thus with a background that is Gaelic, national,
partisan, and uniquely Catholic, the Irish literary
movement has attained the proportions of a renaissance
which impresses the reader by its young robustness,
which seems to have linked hands with the morning of
the world. It has delved into numerous strange things:
the poetry of the Celtic gods, ancient hero-lore, and
mysticism of several kinds. The relation existing between this revival and the English tradition was, however, made possible by a group of writers whose inspiration was more conventional but who were sufficiently
in the current to merit being called precursors.

One of the most famous of these is the story teller
William Carleton, whose slightly pessimistic genius
made the common life of his people a matter of literary
interest. Although he is known chiefly for many
spirited tales, there also stands to his credit a novel
of unusual power, "Fardorougha the Miser." Somber,
rather Gothic in mood, it is scarcely representative

Irish fiction. Of the two Banims, John and Michael, little is remembered today excepting the intriguing "Tales of the O'Hara Family." Here, as in Carleton's stories, the sense of form is lamentably undeveloped, nor is there any outstanding concern with actual life in Ireland.

The most representative early novelist, both as an Irishman and a Catholic, was beyond a doubt Gerald Griffin. He was typically strong in moral character; having come to London in search of literary fame, he lived down extraordinary hardships and temptations without damage to his spirit, although his body broke under the strain. Griffin was strong and serene, a soldier of the soul, even to his modest death as a Christian Brother. These qualities are finely reflected in his only enduring work, "The Collegians," where there are imagination, delicate humour, and loyalty to the ideal. The form is sufficiently good to hold the story over to new generations. Griffin's success was the success of character, a matter which the Irish demand in poet and patriot. They value in their leaders what a primeval people would consider worth while in selecting a king: moral grandeur and a temperament not too mystical to lack the iron upon which the success of causes is wrought.

With Thomas Moore the poetry of modern Ireland begins. And what poetry it is! Hundreds of songs and ballads, the authors of which are unknown or forgotten, bear the unmistakable stamp of Celtic sadness or laughter, belief in or acceptance of life. No people has ever set its imagination so readily to music; and the greatly gifted men and women among them have taken care that the melody should be rich and radiant.

Moore, vagabond of many lands and moods, was generally superficial and not very faithful to his own country. Nevertheless, his Irish melodies, caught up here and there and set down in faultless English which manages not to rob them of spontaneous pathos and fancy, are great in spite of the poet's subsequent "Lalla Rookh" and "Epicure." Earliest of Ireland's poets, Moore was also her first æsthete and uncovered a tendency in the Celtic character which modern times have seen develop.

If Tom Moore gave to the genuine Irishman a kind of staginess, in the "Reliques of Father Prout," the stage Irishman very nearly became real; his was the poetry of the sprightly ballad, the jovial jest, and the whimsical reminiscence. It is indicative of this poet's personal character that he should have been a Jesuit who neglected his calling and a native of Cork who died in Paris. "The Bells of Shandon" has become folklore, and other verses of the same sort are known around the world. The mirth of Father Prout is offset by the sad, sensitive spirit of Jeremiah Joseph Callanan, who died young but not before he had discovered the enchantment of the Gaelic saga. In general the poetry of the early Irish writers was a series of experiments that sought to adjust Celtic notes to the English scale. It was a generous struggle, for the victory came of necessity to their inheritors.

Side by side with this fashioning of story and verse the immemorial struggle for the country was revived, and stirring spokesmen pleaded for the treasured cause. Of eloquence and the literary graces which accompany it the Irishman has never stood in need. Verve and beauty of address are his by right of birth, and half the great modern English orators are Celts. Among them all there is none who sums up so majestically the virtues and faults of his race as Daniel O'Connell. He is the only modern conqueror of Ireland, and he subdued her with the loving power of his voice, in which there was tenderness and fear, wit and quiet faith, the noblest kind of patriotism, and yet a blindness to the real position of his country. England beat him to the ground in the end, but Samson-like he shook the walls of her palace in his collapse. Had the rulers of Britain known the future, could they have foreseen the surge of outraged sentiment rising from one end of the Gaelic land to the other, they would have listened to O'Connell. His life was a splendid performance, with the action, sparkle, and pathos of a brilliant play. But the modern Irishman has grown too desperately in earnest for the theater and the curtain has gone down on the glory of the greatest among Celtic orators.

With the foundation of the *Nation* by Charles Gavan Duffy, in 1842, Irish leaders began to abandon the idea of conciliation with England and to dream of independence. This paper, glowing with enthusiasm for a country "beautiful and sacred," whose history and cause seemed as radiantly attractive as the shores of a rich and undiscovered country, reached everyone from judge to mechanic and gained their hearts. Duffy was himself a poet and the idea of publishing national songs and ballads met with enthusiastic response. It was not poetry in the strict sense, but rather verse of passion and sentiment written by able men and women after the day's work had been done. Chief among the writers of this fervent national hymnody was Thomas Davis, a man who seems to have embodied all the virtues of ideal Irish manhood. As a result he stood, during his short life, as close to the hearts of his people as any man of the time. Davis was first of all a patriot, and his verse lacks the meditativeness of the poet whose only mission is song. One loves him for the stirring ballads of battle, like "Fontenoy" or "The Sack of Baltimore," in which the martial rhythm is quickened by burning emotion and the rhetoric is abundantly redeemed by splendid earnestness. In a few other poems, notably the "Lament for Owen Roe" the inspiration of Gaelic originals is more sensible, and these are considered, therefore, superior by many. In general, Davis' poetry is the revelation of his own spirit rather than the record of a contemplative brooding over life as a whole; its energetic manliness compensates for a manifest unripeness of handling. His influence is visible in the work of other *Nation* poets such as John O'Hagan, author of the stirring song, "Ourselves Alone," and Ellen Downing, whose religious and patriotic verse has the naturalness and simplicity of bird-song.

In James Clarence Mangan Irish poetry beheld its first authentic genius. Viewing life with an artist's detachment he found the key to ancient Gaelic hymns, to rhythms of exotic loveliness, and to the heart of the modern world. Like Thompson he followed Coleridge and was in turn beloved of Poe. Thus, more than any other poet, he synthesizes the Irish and English traditions. Personally Mangan was a failure, a poor and melancholy man, whose dreams were often clouded by opium and drink; but there was nothing base in his soul. He was, says Miss Guiney, "a solitary young golden-haired figure, rapt and kind" and "his speech was full of sudden witticisms, shy fooling that drew no blood." Forced to his daily labor as a clerk, this poet went arrayed in outlandish clothes that included a small brown cloak and an absurdly large hat. However, the umbrella which he carried constantly, to the great amusement of his companions, was the symbol of the sword he might have borne in an ancient epic contest with the brood of evil. As it was, he made war only upon himself.

Mangan's great poems gleam with the splendour of the past, but it is always a sad or embattled splendour, with scarcely a touch of the gayety with which the Irish have so often gone to death. His best work was done in adaptations from the Gaelic where the old songs lay ready to his hand; alone as he was, little moved him to original work. Yet, though such a poem as "Dark Rosaleen" is almost as old as the Celtic race, the weird beauty of Mangan's English version is the creation of his own genius. What marvelous conformity of emotion with the rhythm of words! The poem opens, plaintive and consoling, deepens its note of tragedy, and stifles pain in tears and vows of devotion; then finally becomes insurgent, facing the pitiless foe with a desperate battle-cry:

> "Oh! the Erne shall run red,
>   With redundance of blood,
> The earth shall rock beneath our tread,
>   And flames wrap hill and wood,
> And gun-peal and slogan-cry
>   Wake many a glen serene,
> Ere you shall fade, ere you shall die,
>   My dark Rosaleen!"

Who does not know these lines that burst with passion, that are musical but scorn the bonds of traditional verse? It is the master-song, thus far, of Ireland. Nevertheless, Mangan's adaptation of "O'Hussey's Ode to the Maguire" is alive with the same reckless emotion and has some of the most haunting lines in English:

"Though he were even a wolf raging the round green
    woods,
Though he were even a pleasant salmon in the unchain-
    able sea,
Though he were a wild mountain eagle, he could scarce
    bear, he,
    This sharp, sore sleet, these howling floods."

And yet the poet who triumphed thus over the limitations of his art was also the scribbler of second-rate stanzas galore, the victim of rhetorical eloquence and willful rhyming, the counterpart of Father Prout. Mangan's career is, in fact, the index to the artistic development of Catholic Ireland in his time. That Ireland was at once enthusiastic and uncritical; unable to follow the poet when he was a seer, it acclaimed him boisterously when he was a clown. But it is probable that nothing could have saved Mangan; in the end he lost control both of himself and his craft, carrying to a dark tomb the darkness of his dreams, a pathetic king of a land of shadows. The poets nearest to him in sentiment are two who belong to the English tradition —Lionel Johnson and Aubrey de Vere.

Modern religious poetry in Ireland may be said to have begun with Katherine Tynan (Mrs. Hinkson). The daughter of a robust, intelligent country gentle-

man, she lived and studied in modest retirement until
the appearance of her first volume, "Louise de la Val-
lière," which, as the title suggests, followed pre-
Raphaelite conventions and was enthusiastically received by Ruskin, the Rossettis, and a large share of
the general public. Since then new books have been
issued frequently, for this poet is almost fatally facile.
Two among them are especially noteworthy—"Sham-
rocks" and "The Wind in the Trees." Devotedly Irish
in spite of more sympathy with the English tradition
than most young Irelanders display, Katherine Tynan
is a patriotic poet interested in the Gaelic past. Nevertheless, her distinctive quality is a devotional naturalism, a blending of delight in the beauty of the earth
with loving, joyous worship of God. No matter how
intimate her knowledge of the world may have become,
she is firmly Franciscan in spirit. In "The Flowers of
Peace" she gathered the best of her devotional poems
as a magician might gather sunshine that flits through
the windows of a country chapel. Hers is, indeed, a
sunlit Irish faith, confident, sad, with none of the
bitterness of disillusionment. To such gentle lyrics
as "St. Francis to the Birds," "Cor Dulce," and "Sheep
and Lambs," the world will turn almost as gladly as
to the "Fioretti." Where the same note is in disguise,
as in "An Island Fisherman" and "Larks," it is no less
effective. Naturally one may object to many of
Katherine Tynan's lyrics on the ground that they are
scarcely more than fluent stanzas done in a hurry, but
the best of her work is the very voice of the Catholic
soul of Ireland.

Quite like this poet in sentiment and manner was
Rose Kavanagh, a girl poet who died before her genius

had been formed. The little book she left is singular
in promise and melody, and makes her name a poignant
recollection. Sadness of a different kind is evoked by
the name of Dora Sigerson (Mrs. Clement Shorter)
who died heartbroken after the Eastern Uprising in
1916. She is the poet of neither convention nor laughter, but instead a brooding spirit weary of the bonds
of modern life and impassionedly responsive to the
primitive call of the Gael. The ballad proved the most
successful medium for the expression of her emotions;
the ballad fashioned on a Celtic bias, unfamiliar therefore to English ears, but often reminiscent of Continental masterpieces like Goethe's "Erlkönig" or the
truest stanzas of Grillparzer. This affinity with a
certain type of Teutonic poetry is, surely, very evident
in Mrs. Shorter's work and is the more remarkable
because she was so completely, sensitively Irish. No
woman has ever felt more deeply the tragedy of her
race or borne it with greater fortitude. Such ballads
as "Cean Duv Deelish," "All Souls' Night," and "The
Woman Who Went to Hell" are perfect in form although, unfortunately, the greater portion of Mrs.
Shorter's work is marred by inadvertencies of technique. She who cared so much more for the spirit of
life than for its conventions, adopted the same point of
view in art.

Two other Irish women to write poetry were Moira
O'Neill, author of "Songs of the Glens of Antrim,"
and Ethna Carberry, who is remembered for "The
Four Winds of Eirnn." Neither volume has the verve
of great poetry or the fresh devotion of Katherine
Tynan's best lyrics, but both taste of the country and
are the forerunners of that robust peasant song with

which the name of Padraic Colum is now so closely identified. Colum, a playwright and the author of "Wild Earth and Other Poems," represents the Irish farmer as a stark primordial man with his hands on the plough. Whereas Dora Sigerson approached the Germans, Colum is almost a brother to the Russians; there is in his poetry very little direct religion and almost no sense of inherited tradition, but one feels the surge of elemental faith, the strength of soul which the Irish peasant really possesses. His verse is rugged, almost uncouth, though its powerful imagery scorns the insinuation of crudity. Very different is another poet of the country who died a British soldier in Flanders. Francis Ledwidge, a boy whose sense of the beauty of nature is akin to that of the "Shropshire Lad," made simple songs that are both wild and sweet, vagabondish in spirit and form. "Songs of Peace" probably contains his best work. Ledwidge remained, however, somewhat aloof from the official central purpose of modern Irish literature, the Gaelic revival so strongly emphasized by men of letters like George Sigerson and Douglas Hyde.

While the true leadership in Celtic poetry passed into the hands of William Butler Yeats, a pure poet who viewed all the traditions of his country as literary materials and employed his own mysticism, the patriotic fervour of his companions, and the ritual of the Church to fashion lyrics, other men reverted more closely to the idea of Davis and placed action before words. Thomas MacDonagh, Patrick Pearse, and Joseph Plunkett, shot by order of the British after the Easter Week uprising, bore with mystic, elemental fervour the sword of Ireland's freedom and the shield

of her faith.   Together they seem three tragic Horatii
going down together.

Joseph Plunkett was a young man of distinction and
promise rather than a finished poet, but his book,
"The Circle and the Sword" seems to foreshadow the
approach of Celtic poetry to the inner Catholic world
where Francis Thompson lived.   Plunkett himself was,
enthusiastically, Thompson's disciple in deliberate
shunning of the commonplace, in spiritual exaltation,
and in sense of form.   His sonnets speak confidently
of immortality and seem themselves immortal.   This
boy is no trivial rhymster, but the master of space and
time, another poet for the elect:

"You must walk the mountain tops where rode
Gabriel, Raphael, Michael, when the stars
Fell from their places, and where Satan strode
To make his leap.   Now bend the crackling spars
Athwart the mast of the world—and five deep scars
From that strong Cross call you to their abode."

MacDonagh was a learned, gifted man with a taste
for study, but he felt that "it is well that here still
that cause which is identified without underthought of
commerce, with the cause of God and Right and Freedom, the Cause which has been the great theme of our
poetry, may any day call the poets to give their lives
in the service."   It is enough, perhaps, to say of Mac-
Donagh that he was a poet and that he gave his life.
"Songs of Myself" and "Lyrical Poems," his two finished books, are respectable, if not very great.

It is for Padraic Pearse, of the three, that one naturally reserves the highest homage.   He was first of all
an educator who dealt lovingly with little children and

then took up as an apparently natural consequence the spiritual leadership of his folk. Pearse's stories, poems, plays—diverse in character and done originally in Gaelic—have almost the gentle sublimity of Plato; he was a man with a halo in a group of unusual men. Irishmen he idealizes as no one else has dared to, idealizes, though, because he is fundamentally a child "trailing clouds of glory." Accordingly most people will find him in the work he did for children—"Iosogan," "The Roads," and "Eineen of the Birds." A deep admirer has said: "He is a man with the heart of a child. He sees with the eyes of a child and speaks with its lips. His stories are not children's stories, they are stories of children and so they are read with delight by children of all ages. Old Matthew's words to Iosogan, 'among the children it was that I found you' might well be applied to Mr. Pearse himself." But this "child" had also the heart of a man whose martyrdom was previsioned and sternly met, whose high dreams were kingly in a way only kings can understand.

Tom Kettle died for Ireland in a different fashion than the three men just mentioned; he died leading a charge in Flanders, with the uniform of a British officer on his body. He is placed here among the poets because he was able to glorify his death in the lines:

> "Know that we fools, now with the foolish dead,
> Died not for flag, nor King, nor Emperor,
> But for a dream, born in a herdsman's shed,
> And for the secret Scripture of the poor."

But in reality this man, who felt that his nation must bleed not only for its own freedom but for the liberty of peoples everywhere, was almost, if possible, more

than a poet. Only one little book, "The Day's Burden," remains to tell us of Tom Kettle's sanity and
remarkable sensitiveness, of his honour and wisdom,
but its words are unforgettable. He recalls Sir
Thomas More in ever so many ways. Is it too much
to say that the attainment of Ireland's independence
is not nearly so important as the fact that Tom Kettle
lived for it?

We shall conclude this cursory examination of Irish
verse with a mention of only one book among several
recent ones. In "Arrows," by George Noble Plunkett,
there is present once more a high, reverent mysticism
and an unusual spiritual serenity; the author does not
lack either a noble sense of form or a ready devotion
to ideals. There are other poets, but enough has been
written to indicate the richness and variety of a body
of verse which has appeared in a surprisingly short
while. Its many-sidedness is especially noteworthy;
there has been no single manner, although lyric and
ballad measures predominate, and no monotony of
mood. The peasant has spoken, the soldier has answered, the voice of girl and mother has been heard.
Here our purpose has been to set forth those who have
spoken for the Catholic body; but we have beheld Irishmen always, glowing with enthusiasm for the national
idea, gathering round the fount of Celtic tradition. So
distinctly individual is this poetry that fondness for it
will depend considerably upon one's ability to sympathize with the aspirations of the Irish people. For
us their heroes, their gods, their visions are strange
and often fantastic, but an honest effort to understand
must fulfill Yeats' prophecy that Anglo-Irish verse
"will lead many that are sick with theories and with

trivial emotion to some sweet well-waters of primeval poetry."

If the modern verse-writers have thus successfully carried out the work of their predecessors, the story-tellers have not fallen behind them in diligence. Irish novels, on the whole, are not stormy. The contrasts, the stirring drama, of Irish life have never been adequately set forth, because these things seemed too common-place and men craved idyllic fiction. The success of Canon Sheehan's "My New Curate" was due to the simple charm of the people it talked about. The parish priest is a character to reckon with in Ireland, and his exploits and quandaries have helped to make Canon Sheehan's book thoroughly delightful. "My New Curate" was followed by others, especially "Glenaraar," "Lisheen," and "Luke Delmege." These manifest an ambitious habit to which their author unfortunately became addicted—the study of queer characters in cultivated society. It was a *milieu* of which he knew almost nothing, whereas his gift for making realistic sketches of village life was genuine. The man himself was genial, scholarly, and in every way a priest whose life was perhaps as much of an inspiration as his books.

The art of Seumas MacManus is concerned with the kindly, humorous aspects of daily life, the lore and ready fancy that colour the speech of the Irish peasantry. His early work was exaggerated humour that naturally failed to adopt the serious-minded, realistic point of view so much lauded by intellectual critics. "A Lad of the O'Friels," on the other hand, is a novel that is the result of deep brooding and exceptional interpretative sympathy. Knocknogar awakes to life and hides nothing of its soul from the keen if affectionate observer. The greater portion of MacManus' work consists, however, of short stories, two collections of which are especially deserving of attention—"Yourself and the Neighbours" and "Top O' the Morning." Here and throughout his writings the author is an intense patriot who loves the traditions and inhabitants of his country so well that he may be inclined to neglect the shadows. While his treatment is much like that of Jane Barlow, he is intimate where she stands aloof. Ethna Carberry (Mrs. MacManus) wrote stories which are preferred by many to those of her husband.

Three women whose novels are attempts to amalgamate the Catholic idea in Ireland with the national principle are M. E. Francis (Mrs. Francis Blundell), Katherine Tynan, and Rosa Mulholland. All have done good work, although none is even approximately a great novelist. "Dark Rosaleen" is probably Mrs. Blundell's most impressive performance. Two boys who grow up side by side are made to represent, respectively, the tendencies of the North and South of Ireland. The women, really impressive epic figures, symbolize the suffering and the immortal hope of their country. It is with regret that one is forced to admit the technical gaucherie of "Dark Rosaleen": a very poignant story has been turned very nearly into melodrama. Miss Mulholland has grace and sprightliness, but an obviously sentimental mind. Katherine Tynan's fiction is readable, sprightly, and superficial.

Unquestionably the outstanding Catholic master of contemporary Irish narrative is Daniel Corkery, who sums up also the spiritual results of the Rebellion. Corkery is a story-teller, as has been said; he is also a poet and an effective playwright. To perceive the range and quality of this man's genius one may select from his rather ample list of books a volume of short stories, "The Hounds of Banba"; a brief poetic play, "The Yellow Bittern"; and a prose drama, "The Labour Leader." There is prose-poetry in "The Hounds of Banba" of a breathless vitality, combining the fiery idealism of Pearse with the elfish fantasy of James Stephens. Naturally there is no laughter, for Corkery is writing down here, with an awesome sense of definiteness, the soul of the rise of yesterday's young Ireland—an Ireland whose lips were set sternly and whose heart was high, where the banners breast the winds. Quite amazing is his fairness in the drawing of the picture: his ability to realize the dramatic value of opposition, which must have some human qualities to make the battle worth while. The prose here is the most delicately wrought Irish-English, if one may use the term; there is the eerie rhythm, the strenuous, magic phrase, the semi-barbaric virility of a strange new texture in our letters.

"The Yellow Bittern" is only one of Corkery's poetic plays, but its tenderness would seem to be more acceptable to us than the fierce accents of some of the others. This story of the comfort which the Mother of God brought to a dying culprit has the lovely, sympathetic understanding of a tale done in the Ages of Faith. There are phrases here that catch at the heart and keep it fast, but in addition there is a very much greater thing—human nature dealt with humanly. If one goes now to "The Labour Leader" it is almost like proceeding from the poetry of Shakespeare to the dramatic action of Shakespeare. Mr. Corkery has not yet learned how to combine the two things, but this

play is a noteworthy performance. Davla, the Leader,
is a man and a genius who dominates the stage, by reason of his innate reality, as one of the most vital personages in recent dramatic literature. All in all,
one is satisfied that Daniel Corkery has not inherited
the vision of young Ireland unworthily. He has creative instinct and power, splendid artistry, and delicacy
of thought as well as of feeling. Of course, his writing
may seem odd and in more ways than one a little savage; but the Irish mind of today is no resting-place for
classic decorum.

One is glad to note in many writers not professedly
Catholic a kindly appreciation of the dominant religious feeling in Ireland. The folk-lore of Lady
Gregory, the older fancies and narratives of Fiona
McLeod, the tales of Stephen Gwynn, and the novels
of Emily Lawless are splendid tributes, even though
they emanate from comparative outsiders. An even
more affectionate discernment seems to have guided the
hand of Amy Murray, in whose "Father Allan's
Island" the soul of western Ireland is caught up with
its atmosphere. Miss Murray has not tinkered with
her material, and unlike Synge has been unhampered
by literary theories. To sum up the matter, one may
express admiration for the novels that have come from
Ireland without forgetting that their authors have
largely lacked a guiding sense of form. The Celtic
story-teller must learn to look at his country without
tinted glasses and above all he must remember that,
since the novel is not a primitive literary medium, failure to conform to its traditions cannot be condoned.

Since we have asserted that the Irish spirit is at bottom Catholic, some mention must be made of the artists

who have elected to depart from it. George Moore is a great and gifted writer, but he is also a dead writer. For years he has been issuing successive farewells, in beautiful prose, when his *Vale* was in fact uttered early in his career. He chose to turn up his nose at the mother country and to follow, with rhythmic ease, the æsthetic dilettantism of the French decadents. As a result he is neither a decadent nor an Irishman; he is simply George Moore who has gone to the devil. It may be interesting to write impressionistic adaptations of the great French naturalists, but readers who find that sort of thing entertaining have scarcely exhausted the originals. Mr. Moore is not, as is often supposed, the living proof of the failure of the Irish literary tree to produce anything better than wild crabs, but instead a perfect demonstration of its fruitful vitality. He is the lovely dead branch.

Moore's indubitable genius has, however, influenced many of his younger countrymen, and not the dullest among them. In "The Portrait of the Artist as a Young Man," James Joyce has rewritten the youngster's confessions from a lower depth than Moore ever reached—one of the most wretched depths, in fact, that English literature has as yet revealed. Without doubting the genuineness of the narrative, one may permissibly recall the fact that there have been quite a number of similar confessions from people like Baudelaire, most of whom, grown older and wiser, counseled their friends to write in other strains. But while a great deal of recent Irish fiction is decidedly somber and pessimistic, it cannot be accused simply of imitating the French naturalists. The average Irishman has looked upon himself and his compatriots a little too complacently, perhaps; and a certain type of thinker, studying the facts by the light of alien literatures, has gnashed his teeth and sat down to tell the "truth." Such fiction as Brinsly McNamara's "Valley of the Squinting Windows" and Conal O'Riordan's "Adam of Dublin"—to mention only two striking books—are unpleasant, but who shall deny their veracity? Where there is exaltation there is bound to be depression as well; where there is concern with art there is sure to be æsthetics. By a probably wise dispensation of nature not all men are idealists, and some of these break their hearts against the eternal stone of the world. In our emotional age the depression may easily become too deep, and the æsthetics too æsthetic. Something of the kind has manifestly happened to Eimar O'Duffy, whose "Wasted Island" is quite too much of a travesty to mislead anyone. The case of Patrick MacGill, author of "Children of the Dead End" and "The Rat-Pit" is obviously different. He has grown absorbed in the social degeneration, the horrible unfairness, of modern life, and has managed to say certain things we ought to know. Unfortunately he himself has become unfair. It would be easy to select from his books examples of what seem perilously like deliberate falsehoods. In consequence, as MacGill admits, he has been spurned by the Irish and driven to ally himself with a little coterie of English radicals.

The literature of Ireland will be formed by Irishmen as they elect. No pandering to outside preferences will aid the writing of the noble and sincere record of national life which some day will be found complete. Still, though she is a primeval, glowing, individual country, Ireland cannot hope, and should not desire, to stand spiritually alone. Her literature must undergo formative influences; her place is in the world for the world. This has been very keenly appreciated by most writers who, like Synge and Moore, have applied decadent methods and standards to Celtic material; and the danger from similar grafting is not to be brushed aside lightly. Oscar Wilde, too, was a fine Dublin temperament corroded by evil literary affiliations. We feel that for Irishmen nothing is of such very great importance as thoroughgoing alliance with the Catholic tradition of Europe, with the tradition which reared the soul of Ireland as well as the spirit of Western civilization. Tom Kettle had this firmly in mind always. "Ireland," he wrote, "awaits her Goethe who will one day arise to teach her that, while a strong nation has herself for center, she has the universe for circumference. . . . My only counsel to Ireland is that to become deeply Irish she must become European." It is towards the fulfillment of this wish that all lovers of Ireland will look forward hopefully, awaiting the increasingly fascinating revelation of the grandeur and the misery, the sorrow and the song, of the island which is the magnet for hearts in every part of the world. And we shall remember as a pledge that this island has been for centuries the training-ground of saints.

BOOK NOTE

The works mentioned in the text are only an indication of the wealth of modern Anglo-Irish literature, and many more might be added—Colum's "The Land," MacSwiney's "The Revolutionist," Mrs. Shorter's "The Dark Years"—were our canvas not already too crowded. Good literary references are: "The Literature of Ireland," by Thomas MacDonagh (an interpretation of the spirit of Irish letters) ; "The Irish Literary Renaissance" (modern criticism tending to æstheticism) ; "A Literary History of Ireland," by Douglas Hyde (concerned chiefly with early Gaelic writers) ; "The Celtic Dawn," by F. R. Morris (a study of the revival of Irish tradition) ; "Studies in Irish Literature and Music," by Alfred P. Graves; and "Nova Hibernia," by Michael Monahan. A study of the Irish mental background may be prefaced by the reading of such books as "The Middle Years" and "The Dark Years," by Katherine Tynan Hinkson; "Celt and Saxon," by Shane Leslie; "Evening Memories," by William O'Brien; "The Soul of Ireland," by William J. Lockington; "Irish Impressions," by G. K. Chesterton; "Ireland," by Francis Hackett; "My Diaries," by Wilfrid Blunt; and "Canon Sheehan of Doneraile," by Alan Heuser.   Almost indispensable poetic anthologies are: "Love Songs of Connaught," by Douglas Hyde; "A Treasury of Irish Poetry," by Brooke and Rolleston; and "A Book of Irish Poetry," edited, with a splendid introduction, by Wm. Butler Yeats.   Miss L. I. Guiney prefaced her edition of Mangan's poems with an interpretative essay; "Poems," by Joseph Plunkett, has a foreword by Geraldine Plunkett and the poet's own paper on "Obscurity and Poetry"; "The Ways of War," by T. M. Kettle, has a charming "Memoir" by his wife.   The periodical literature on the subject of Irish letters is extensive.   Note especially, "The Literary Movement in Ireland," by George Birmingham, the *Fortnightly Review,* Dec., 1907; and "The Irish Literary Movement," by Padraic Colum, the *Forum,* Jan., 1915.

CHAPTER SIXTEEN

THE AMERICAN CONTRIBUTION

"Keep the young generations in hail,
And bequeath them no tumbled house."

MEREDITH.

THE study of Catholic opinion in the United States has characteristics that would not appeal to the proverbial cautious angel. One may calmly say that no words are sufficiently powerful to describe the energy, the determination and the sacrifice which have brought the Church to its present dignity and influence in the Republic; but certainly the times have been out of joint for the creation of intellectual leadership able to mould and guide Catholic opinion, nor has any large public been ready for such leadership. Emerson, speaking a kindly word for the "Romanist," classed him with the negro; and if the American Catholic has learned anything thoroughly it is the art of making apologies. He has issued libraries in refutation of the astonishing charges that his priests have cloven feet and that his churches are stocked with ammunition. He has even proved triumphantly that the Papal fleet does not contemplate swooping down upon Chicago! It is hardly surprising that such deference to environment should have precluded a satisfactory telling of his own story, or that the literature which has arisen under the shadow of the American Church should largely be the work of converts.

Linked by a thousand beautiful memories—the vow of Columbus, the French and Spanish missions, the widespread dedication of places to the saints—with the tradition of Christendom, we have been forced to let others preserve them. Parkman is still, very likely, the best missionary historian, and the discovery of mediæval society has been carried farthest by Henry Adams and Ralph Adams Cram. Hand in hand with this inarticulateness of the Catholic body has gone a corresponding deafness. The long, desperate battle with poverty and social inferiority left our ancestors, splendidly sturdy though they were, little time and opportunity for other things.

But a great and significant change has taken place during the past few years. At length the leaders of the Church have seen the possible victory of the multitude they represent and have begun to talk plain, martial English which is being more and more widely listened to and understood. The opportunity for Catholic ideas grows larger, the obligation to emphasize them much more impressive. We are living in a new land that has changed its character and become old: the institutional clothes which fitted so snugly during the pliant era of development are found irksomely small, and the resultant democratic derision has almost imperiled the wearing of any such clothes whatever. Secure in her possession of immense economic power, closely combined and efficiently managed, America is mentally a wriggling mass of conflicting opinions. Nobody, for instance, seems to know what the aims of our national existence are, though many persons tell us rather frantically what they ought to be. Our variegated philosophies and religions do not merge, like colours, in clarity, but remain motley. Our citizenry, rushing here and there for some rule to go by, is the easy prey of blatant advertising and extravagant shams; in so many cases is the American's intellectual history a series of scalps that one is not surprised to hear him say honestly, in the end, that he has lost his own. Accordingly, there is some genuine cause for alarm, lest a nation whose search for ideals is so evident, so eager and so unsatisfactory, should rise in anger and break the shrines while cleansing the stables.

Under such circumstances Catholic thought, no longer speechless, and released from provincialism, has a stirring opportunity to address the nation. Whatever people may say, Americans deeply respect traditions and Catholicism is the Great Tradition. For a long while, representative thought in this country has followed in the wake of what has seemed the mental policy of Europe, provided that a certain element of "progressiveness" attended it. The New England transcendentalists walked behind the early German idealists when these were already old-fashioned; today our liberals are abreast of Mr. Wells in his youth, and our æsthetes are trying to create a naturalistic literature after the fashion of France at a moment when that country has made an act of contrition. None of these matters has, however, satisfied very many people. For the great majority the prevailing idealism offers nothing substantial to build on, at least nothing that they can feel sure may not be blown suddenly into the middle of next week. And so disillusionment darkens very frequently the honest effort to escape materialism, to accomplish the primal task of hitching the wagon to a star. Eager though men may be for the freedom of a definite faith, it is not in the market-place that they will acquire the sense of eternal things, the sense of beauty, for instance. Our examination of ourselves will, therefore, be of practical value. It ought to make clear the causes which have led to the present condition of affairs, show what influence Catholics have exerted in the past, and uncover certain possibilities which can be made use of.

Now the formation of American opinion is not a neatly catalogued affair, but it may be said, roughly, to fall into three divisions. First, there is the Puritan influence, a long-continued and largely successful exercise of power by a group of hard-mouthed and close-fisted Calvinists with a determination to conduct their part of the world as they saw fit. New England at first identified beauty with hell, so that while Cotton Mather was picturesquely augmenting the terrors of the damned, the prettiest girl in Salem was hanged as a witch. There was an admirable iron in the Puritan soul, but iron is not an artistic medium. The various annealing influences which stole in from Europe softened and moulded, but did not altogether succeed in transforming it. Ralph Waldo Emerson, the disciple of Fichte and Swedenborg, sounded the first strong note of romantic rebellion, by assuming the existence in nature of a universal spirit which, because of his paradoxical individualism, he probably did not even care to prove. Moreover, one side of his mind looked to the future and he became the prophet of scientific pantheism without ever really believing in it himself.

Emerson's neighbour, Nathaniel Hawthorne, dwelt

spiritually in another country. Brooding over the relation between good and evil, he preached the moral retribution which is at the centre of Shakespeare's doctrine, but removed his pulpit to a chillier region where no sun dispels a certain eerie twilight. In other words, Hawthorne awoke to beauty as Emerson to life, but neither shook off the dreamfulness of slumber. With the entry of two poets, Longfellow and Whitman, into the lists, a different struggle with Puritanism had begun. The author of "The Village Blacksmith" had an understanding of democracy, but no great vision of it; the author of "O, Pioneers" had a vision of democracy, but understood it not. And Longfellow, the most cultured of poets, was also the most plebeian; Whitman, scorning civilization, was its autocratic aristocrat. Both contributed to a sorely needed renaissance of wonder, the one with memories of a blessed past, the other with a pæan to the future. To sum up the matter, it may be said that the trend of Puritan thought as expressed in letters was toward a romantic idealism and away from realism. Based originally upon a denial of the world, it drifted with the lifting of the horizon out to the paler stars.

It is a long way from the cold equality of Massachusetts to the provincial Toryism of the early South. According to all the rules, a literature should have been born to Virginia: there were both leisure and culture, a fondness for the literary traditions of England, and a certain gayety of spirit to which art is not averse. Nevertheless, it was just this culture and this leisure which diverted the energies of the best men to abstract questions and to action. The Southern colonies began to bloom during that strange eighteenth century

when there was nowhere any great art, but instead a
universal concern with the principles of government
and the possible reconstruction of society. This was
the age when the ripest minds tried to keep abreast of
Rousseau and Voltaire, of Gibbon and Hobbes. Thus
the guiding spirits of the Revolution were Washington
and Jefferson, the one the highest type of honest business man, the other absorbed with a dream of democracy
in the abstract which stamps him in many ways as the
greatest genius in constructive theory that America
has produced. There was something in the fiber of
Virginian society which saved it from excess; it was
preserved from ruin by the resiliency of another typically eighteenth century mind, Benjamin Franklin. All
of this, which suffered the eclipse of the arts with la-
mentable tranquillity, did in the end make for the appearance of a very individual and abstract literary
genius, Edgar Allan Poe. The whole point about this
strange man is that he was a rationalist almost to the
verge of insanity, while the New England that viewed
him askance was irrational both in its Puritan repression and in its idealistic escape. Nobody but a dullard
would urge against Poe's art that he had no strength
of character, for surely he had as much as Villon or
Verlaine, but it is very true that he made no characters, no people, to fill those haunting parallelograms
that he built of horrors. The same conception of literary material appears in the verse of Sidney Lanier, a
totally different man. If any American poet is authentic it is the author of the "Symphony" and "The
Marshes of Glynn." Still, in these and more clearly
in his poorer poems, the pressure of the abstract idea
is present: concepts of a better social order, of a purer

democracy, of a spiritually conducted commerce. To this day the South has not shaken off its eighteenth century characteristics.

With the migration of thousands to the West, however, the attitude of America towards its own destiny underwent a stimulating change. Straggling little villages in which the primitive communal instinct was strong, the long, lone trails to the gold mines, and the stirring venturesomeness of a life under elemental conditions produced a race of men whose chief mental trait was a sort of twinkling sadness, an ability to dispel profound melancholy with titanic laughter. It is significant to note that the two men whose instinct for realism was the sharpest descended from Virginian people—Lincoln and Mark Twain. The superlative common sense of the great President was mixed with intense sympathy with the common man; Mark Twain was little except a common man until the end. There were dozens of Westerners in days gone by who could have told the story of "Life on the Mississippi" with gusto and understanding, and who had shared generously in boyhood the exploits of Huckleberry Finn. Unfortunately, the chief virtue of Samuel Clemens, self-reliance, is powerless against the tragic history of the ages and is no bulwark against the flood of honest thought. He learned in the end that life which he had jested with so merrily could laugh last. And he had found nothing to soften the cruelty of its smiling lips.

On the other hand, William Dean Howells and Bret Harte, who sponsored most successfully the delicate and idealistic qualities in the temperament of the rising West, were of Puritan ancestry. They did not rail at existence or drink it down with gulps of laughter, but

accepted it tranquilly, with a geniality often close to
tears. In Bret Harte's best work there is the honest
sentimentality of a pioneer with a taste for Victorian
fiction; in Howells the idealism of a frontier doctor
who has been reading Tolstoi. All this literature of
the expanse, which came out of the Civil War, resembled
it in the inner conflict between Northerner and Virginian, between the older provincialism and the coming
nation. It is significant that the style of every one
of these authors should have been modeled on the Bible,
which was the older America's literary and spiritual
food; this explains both the domination of the Puritan
teaching and the limitations of American culture. In
such ways, with additions made from all sides, by Tho-
reau and Holmes in New England, by Cooper and Irving in New York, by Cable and Simms in the South, by
Joaquin Miller and Artemus Ward in the West, the literary tastes of the Republic were formed.

Now it is apparent that the influence of the Catholic
idea on the shaping of American literary destinies had
necessarily to depend upon the conversion of able men.
The early missionary efforts of Frenchmen and Span-
iards had been rendered neglible by the Anglo-Saxon
advance, and the hordes of Irish and German immi-
grants were not yet ready for self-expression. In general, literary converts were attracted to the Church
by one of two things: a firm solution of intellectual difficulties or the beauty of Catholic faith and worship.
They discovered in the synthesis of the Christian past
either an answer to questions which had become central in their lives or strong support for viewing the
world as the lovely garment of God. It was natural
that in the East the Catholic writers should be those

for whom philosophic inquiry guided life, and we confront at once the puzzling figure of Orestes A. Brownson. This man of logic, adept at debate and scornful of the trivial, underwent almost every kind of religious experience open to Americans. Successively a Presbyterian, a Universalist, an associate of Robert Owen, a Unitarian minister, a Saint-Simonian pamphleteer, a religious disciple of Matthew Arnold, and a spiritist, when Brownson turned Catholic at the age of forty-one, he came armed with vast empirical knowledge to do battle with his foes. During the years when Brownson conducted his famous *Review*, Emerson was at the height of his renown and Emerson accordingly became the target. There can be no question about the victory of Brownson, but the Concord sage is safe from oblivion because he was a poet and because he took the trouble to write well. Brownson was probably incapable of a quatrain and his style has that aridity which is the curse of all mere pamphleteering. His best work is "The American Republic," a thorough and subtle analysis of the principles upon which this government is based and also a study of popular rule in the broader sense. Some of his philosophical discussion has the same sort of value as Jonathan Edwards' "Freedom of the Will"; the two men had much in common that is admirable: verve of intellect, devotion to spiritual causes, and relentless abnegation of self in the search for truth. Brownson lacked the amiable qualities of the artist, and though his name is held in reverence, only his staunch admirers save him from oblivion.

Great literary renown has likewise passed by the interesting figure of Father Isaac Hecker, an idealistic man of German descent, whose share in the Brook Farm

experiment and other diversions of the more emanci-
pated Puritans had been large. Upon becoming a
Catholic and a priest, Hecker spurred the most promising of his friends to literary activity, being convinced
that the idea of Christendom as a system of thought
and belief could sway the hearts of millions in America.
His personal eagerness to engage in this task left small
room for writing of his own, although he is the author
of at least one book that can still be read with pleasure,
"The Church and the Age." One knew that Father
Hecker grasped things and understood the times in
which he moved; from England Newman wrote to him
as to a kindred spirit, engaged in the same apostolate.
Together with Brownson he typifies the response which
a great many intellectual New Englanders made to
Catholicism: the recognition of dogma as an escape
alike from unbalanced idealism and materialistic despair. Unfortunately neither of them possessed the
literary gifts which would have made their testimony
irresistible.

Among the men who gave expression to the spirit of
the American migration, surely none is more charming
or more neglected than Charles Warren Stoddard.
This most gentle of all Bohemians, who sent Stevenson
off to the South Seas and was beloved of Harte, Clemens,
and Miller, was so oddly and delightfully himself that
the common streets of literature have never led to his
domain. Where is there a more fascinating book of
essays than "South Sea Idyls," which are scented with
the perfume of the choicest flowers that open to a tropi-
cal sunrise? Its gossamer pages were surely written
in fairyland to the music of the Hawaiian paradise.
Lafcadio Hearn has no more poetry and a great deal

less of other things. Then there is "The Island of
Tranquil Delights," "Poems," and "A Troubled Heart"
—the lyric, moving story of Stoddard's spiritual life.
More than any other Western writer, perhaps, he was
responsive to the elusive voice of beauty. Without any
noticeable concern with the problems of civilization, a
wanderer through the misty valleys of the world, he
served the melody of the heart with chivalric tenderness. Pilgrim to the West, voyager to the distant and
then mysterious islands of the Pacific, and wayfarer
to Europe, he was moved to delight by all. If there
is tender loveliness in his memories of Wai-ki-ki, it is
matched by the dream-vision in Anne Hathaway's house,
of which he tells in "Exits and Entrances."

Stoddard was born in Rochester, New York, educated
in the East and suffered to seek a literary career in
San Francisco. What repelled him from the various
forms of Puritan belief to which he had been introduced
was simply the crudity of their spiritual appeal. A
man born to culture and sensitive to the mystic voices
that speak to the soul, he found his place ultimately
within the ancient confines of the Church. There lay
about the man an aura, intangible and elfish, which
even the greatest of his contemporaries bowed to,
which inspired Stevenson to unbend in loving doggerel,
moved Clemens to read the book of Ruth with tears in
his eyes, and enthralled the pupils—for fifteen years
he taught English literature—who sat under him.
During the last years of his life, mystical things absorbed his attention more and more; without ever
abandoning a whimsical interest in life, he drew closer
to the saints and sought out with care instances of
superior devotion and even of communication with the

world beyond. How has it happened that a man so
innately a genius should be for the majority of his
countrymen scarcely a memory?

To some extent the answer may be found, perhaps,
in the fact that Stoddard's art was unconnected with
the giving of highly moral lessons, while Americans are
nothing if not ethical, spending their time prodigally
in reforming the modes and methods of society. The
Puritan whose hand has guided the national life still
insists that man lives for the betterment of his neighbor's habits, that uplift must be accomplished somehow by "getting" religion, money, isms, or dynamite.
Now Stoddard was perversely opposed to all of this—
to lugubrious psalmody and store clothes for heath-
enish islanders, to politicians and platforms, yes even
to professional uplifters, for the rest of the world. It
is to be feared that he believed the pursuit of beauty
and the salvation of the soul quite similar and of individual concern. Again, he was not a novelist, a critic,
or even in any important sense a writer of verse, but almost exclusively an essayist. But an essayist must
rely for his success chiefly upon style, and Americans
have grown quite indifferent to that in a search for
mammoth ideas and epoch-making phrases. Stoddard's
art is like the laughing spray that leaps from a woodland waterfall. Modeled upon the rhythmic weave of
English Bible diction, the sentences of such a sketch as
"The Island of Tranquil Delights" combine Oriental
dreamfulness with the bright, optimistic humour of
western America. Stoddard's spiritual nature shrank
from the slightest taint of coarseness and his pen wandered among the savages "who came as they were created" with the jovial innocence of nature. That verbal

rainbow "South Sea Idyls," is a-twinkle with points of golden laughter; within its tropic colours burn the American street lamps. In the deeper melody of "The Lepers of Molokai," with its majestic prose hymn to the melancholy surf, in the tranquil intimacies of "A. Troubled Heart," there is the same delicate realization of beauty. No one in that famous brotherhood of Californian humourists had so subtle a sense of fun; his work was made for the ambrosia cells of memory, priceless for those who prize it. Stoddard accepted the Catholic tradition humbly, because it is beautiful; and since he had been a captive, he became in the end a willing and exalted soldier.

In the older South, where the beauty of ancient chivalry was followed in spite of the crime of slavery and the languour resultant from too violent a concern with pure politics, there was much to smile at but also a great deal to admire on bended knees. Warriors in whose veins ran kindness, like blessed wine; a genuine, if somewhat sentimental respect for beauty; and poets like Lanier to overhear the whispers of life: these were the best things in a pleasant civilization that found its apogee and its defeat in Robert Lee. With the appearance of a reticent priest, John Bannister Tabb, the Catholic Spirit found expression in lovable form. Father Tabb, who was a convert, had served with the Confederates and been the friend of Sidney Lanier; somehow he learned how to take care of his soul and how to write. It is scarcely necessary to describe poems that everybody knows—tiny lyrics of six or eight lines which are more like bird-notes than songs. Yet what fulness of melody there is in the cry of the lark and what long colloquies in the quatrains of

Father Tabb! He speaks from "the primal tone," making what one may call miniatures of infinity. The religious tenderness of such poems as "The Christ Child to the Christmas Lamb" and "The Old Pastor," the Franciscan sympathy with natural things so evident in "The Shell" or "The Haunted Moon," baffle analysis because they adhere to the simplicity of a very simple genius. His life was plain, too, and spent in the routine of the priesthood or in teaching boys the rules of rhetoric. Of course he had a shy, playful humour that smiled at long days and befriended the stars. Having found serenity in the faith to which he was a convert he could say, in the words of his poem,

"A life of exile long
Hath taught thee song."

We have said that Father Tabb's verse, being *minimum in minimo*, mocks at dissection; and yet one cannot help trying. This poet always retained so much of the boy that no matter how many years of reflection he might give to the turgid flood of information supplied by experience and learning, the song that resulted finally was certain to select only those things which are everlastingly human. A decade passed sometimes before the lyric he wished to make had hardened, cameo-like, under the impress of his spirit, but it was sure in the end to seem perfectly spontaneous. Take for instance that most arresting poem, "Evolution." People had been talking very much about Evolution—talking so freely, in fact, that man's relation to the theory was quite forgotten or hectically misstated. Now Father Tabb succeeded in condensing the human interest of the scientific hypothesis into four little lines, each one of which is, however, of almost mountainous spiritual hugeness.

> "Out of the dusk a shadow,
>   Then a spark";

What an image of light creeping out of chaos and standing suddenly, feebly, over the void! Then

> "Out of the cloud a silence,
>   Then a lark."

Life, with all its beauty, activeness, aspiration is expressed by a single word; and the marvelous characteristic of these verses is the fact that "lark" and "spark," in each of which there is a cosmic image, seem accidental, almost comic, rhymes. The next four lines complete the cycle by applying "Evolution" to the earthly and then to the eternal life of man:

> "Out of the heart a rapture,
>   Then a pain"

A rapture and a pain—these indeed are as good a summing-up of our existence as any sentence from Pascal. Finally,

> "Out of the dead, cold ashes,
>   Life again!"

Note the positive thrill of those two lines. Men cannot in the end fail to surrender to such poetry, and the fame of Father Tabb has, as a matter of fact, risen by such leaps and bounds that we need say nothing more about it. His art smiles, a little satirically perhaps, at the gush of free and easy versifiers.

Quite different in character are the poems of Father Abram Ryan, whose identification with the Southern cause gave some of his best stanzas a martial rhythm and a rugged pathos. "The Conquered Banner" is one of the truest of American patriotic songs, even though it was written for a broken cause. One turns, however, with greater eagerness to the plain but resonant stanzas of "The Song of the Mystic," a hymn that praises contemplation with no touch of merely literary ecstasy. Nor could anyone excepting a poet originate the haunting figure of Uncle Remus. Although none of Joel Chandler Harris' work is distinctly Catholic, it developed from that genuine charity and kindly faith which he crowned with his conversion.

Thus, in diverse ways and in the face of stern popular opposition to "Romanish perversion," these representative Americans came to accept the Catholic idea and to give it a place in letters. While their isolation from any large and appreciative audience and their limited understanding of tradition deprived their work of much influence, it will remain significant as the powerful and unsolicited testimony of native Americans to a view of life which was then thought foreign and absurd. Soon, however, the power of a vast immigrant population would make itself felt; while the Germans remained silent, guarding their customs and language, the Church came to be represented largely by Irishmen whose literary work is something like an interlude between older and modern days. In John Boyle O'Reilly an ancient and oppressed people spoke. Exiled to Australia as a Fenian, O'Reilly escaped to America and began a successful journalistic career with the development of the Boston *Pilot* to a great and representative

Catholic newspaper. He was a man of verve and mental resiliency, with a strong undercurrent of poetic feeling. This found expression in four books of verse, among which "Songs of the Southern Seas" is the best. There is melody and experience in his lyrics, but their glaring imperfection of form forestalls any generous appraisal of their value. Vastly better, it may be thought, is the novel "Moondyne," forgotten now, but well-done and invaluable as an account of strange life in Australia.

O'Reilly, like Meagher and other Celtic revolutionaries, showed a buoyant readiness to adopt American views, but a much more striking grasp of national conditions was displayed by John Ireland, Archbishop of Saint Paul, and counterpart of Manning. Educated in France and given spiritual charge of the great Northwest, Ireland understood that a rapidly changing world presented opportunities that must be seized vigorously. Viewed as the response of a great constructive mind to the problems created by an expanding civilization, "The Church and Society" is a remarkable book. It takes rank beside Webster's "Orations" and Roosevelt's "Americanism" as an appeal to the American spirit, and to Catholics it gives, in spite of a tendency to chauvinism, a needed tonic. A more purely literary blend of the Celtic spirit with the American background is seen in the work of Maurice Francis Egan, poet, essayist, and novelist. The sonnets of his earlier career are not altogether unworthy of comparison with those he translated so gracefully from the French, and his essays, while uneven, have a charm of style that compensates for a general superficiality of thought. Egan's besetting sin has been complacency with his gracefulness; gifted with the rarest qualities, he has shirked the mental discipline which alone can give writing its sea legs.

While these Irish writers represent the period of mental adjustment, it must be remembered that peculiar conditions—the indifference of the general public and the absence of strong, cultivated Catholic opinion —continue to enforce modesty upon the majority of our authors. Miss Guiney retreated to England and Crawford became a cosmopolite. Nevertheless, there remains a group of writers to be regarded with pride. In the essay Agnes Repplier rules supreme; conservative but decidedly not old-fashioned, she applies to the romantic effusions of popular thinkers the acid test of intelligence. In her hands the essay becomes a weapon quite like a corrosive chemical. It has wit, boundless learning, a calm common sense, and perfect form; it dispels shams as some caustic insect powder drives away gnats, and takes up a position not likely to be molested. Miss Repplier is the ghost of Jane Austen wedded to the spirit of Montaigne. An entirely different standard was adopted by James Gibbons Huneker who, while not a consistent Catholic, did interpret for Americans some of the finest religious writers of Europe. He was a Bohemian with an ultra-impressionistic mind that worked like a furiously active motion-picture camera. Without the solid grasp of principles which lifts the philosophic critic above the fashions of the hour, he proved an admirable reflector and brought to the attention of many critics tendencies which they would otherwise have overlooked. Huneker was Pateresque, but more human and less humanistic.

Catholic fiction has suffered from the same ailments that have afflicted the American novel in general. Obsessed by abstract ideas, schemes of reform, and a theory that art is designed for our weaker-minded sisters, we have given, at best, only a mediocre version of American life, a version that has satisfied so well the tastes of the great majority of readers that nothing else is likely to be commercially successful. The great bulk of American Catholic fiction is unintelligent and unreadable. There are, however, a few redeeming names which may give us counsel and hope for the future. In "Robert Kimberly," by Frank Spearman, one finds a study of a moral issue in modern life that is done with finesse and dramatic power. It has the *feel* of reality and a rounded organic structure that connotes mastery in story-telling. The earlier works of Richard Aumerle Maher, especially "The Shepherd of the North," are strong, colourful, and appealingly Catholic. The novels of John Talbot Smith have many faults, but also virtues like plot and crisp brevity of narrative. Such a story as "The Art of Disappearing," probably Father Smith's best, fails by an inch of being great; there is too much straining for effect, too little real charm of diction, and an overdose of the bizarre. Christian Reid has endeared herself to thousands by such stories as "A Light of Vision" and "The Coin of Sacrifice," tales of spiritual struggle that miss being effective by becoming too spirituelle. The reader is likely to compare her books with those virtuous but underfed virgins who preside over charity bazaars. These authors have, however, done much to present the Catholic idea, and others have been kind enough to second their efforts. What book, for instance, could be more Catholic in tone than Mrs. Jackson's moving story of "Ramona," surely one of the few great romances in American literature? There is now a real opportunity for genuinely conceived fiction. A vigorous resolve to spurn, as unworthy of a great artistic tradition, the trivial and technically abominable books now so prevalent, and a patient deference to the masters of the art in other lands, will do much towards giving the Catholic novel in this country an honourable reputation.

What we may honestly be proud of, however, is the poetry that has been written in our name. At a time when verse making, too, has turned into tractarian or naturalistic channels, the Catholic singers have insisted on song. Not in murmuring melodies from nowhere, but in finding their voices in the turmoil of today, have they grown beautiful and reputable. They have come together, Heaven knows how, like a band of troubadours. Joyce Kilmer, Thomas Walsh, and Thomas A. Daly have stood abreast in an unusual conspiracy of song. Kilmer was probably not a great poet, but he was great enough to be thoroughly alive. Writing and living with the intensity of a chevalier, he put to music the simple things around him so that they were no longer simple: trees became instinct with the soul's tenderness and the delicatessen store was almost the ante-room of Paradise. Kilmer the humble succeeds always, but Kilmer the ambitious occasionally fails. "The White Ships and the Red"—which is Chestertonian in theme—seems a little too lurid for life, while "A Blue Valentine"—which is Patmorean—is almost too good to be true. Of his final service in a cause which he visioned clearly, everyone will speak with reverent sadness, thinking of the many songs that went with him to death.

For Walsh, however, the commonplace is not an inspiration; he finds the source of melody in Spanish gardens and the courts of kings. No other American poet writes blank verse so full and melodious, so charged with brooding and beauty. He has visioned the minarets of the Faith and sung of splendid memories that are American because they came with Columbus and the missionaries of Spain. The verse of T. A. Daly, delicate and whimsical, is quite different in character; couched in dialect or written in smooth English, it hides under the simple pathos of an Irish or Italian lyric cry the perfection of technique. Then there are others: Father O'Donnell, whose poems reflect the mystic delight of Thompson; J. Corson Miller, calm and classic in manner; Sister Madeleva, who is rapturously mystical and yet exquisitely artistic; Aline Kilmer, who sings of the joy and pathos of domestic life; and last, John Bunker, who burns incense to the nature with whose moods he is lovingly familiar. For these all may God be thanked; through them whisper the hymns of faithful ages that wrought miracles of song, and the praise of virtues that have almost been forgotten.

Our survey of American Catholic literature has revealed no list of giant names, no magic success in the wresting of beauty from daily life, but it has brought to light noble effort and artistic discernment. What gauge these are for the future no one can tell. It is quite generally admitted that the close of the war opened a new page in the history of America. The total collapse of Puritanism as a force able to guide popular thought, and the discovery of materialistic

murk at the basis of our civilization, has set the immense national caldron of unassimilated minds to seething ominously. With a thousand problems to solve,
Americans are confronted with ten thousand answers.
The smug complacency of the money-lenders, the glare
of foul advertising, and the decay of religious standards were commonplace matters before the war, but
now are extraordinary. In the face of the call to
death, men discovered how little there was to die for.
There will be no peace until the philosophy which is to
dominate America has been settled upon to the satisfaction of the multitude. Captains may dicker with
their subjects, and generals give orders; but surely
none of these dare hope to deceive, in the end, the intense scrutiny of the mob.

Catholic social action has come forward, speaking an
earnest word and rousing to united action a mighty
army that has slept. For the first time in the history
of America, the tread of the Church has been heard
in the market-place. What we have to say is neither
new nor bizarre: it is simply our determination that
the primal beliefs of America are not to be bartered
away, that the spiritualization of democracy is fea-
sible, and that there is such a thing as the right to daily
bread. We have remembered our heritage from the
society of Christendom. It is a splendid protest, splendidly spoken, but we know that it is not enough. Somehow the instincts of the soul are instincts of beauty,
and the things that men love are useful but also topped
with glory. During the long past of Christendom the
sun has fallen on towers that are like cataracts of
stone, on cities radiant with the splendour of our idea
of heaven; always and everywhere the Catholic artist

has labored to image the majesty of the kingdom of God in the simple things which surrounded him. Our task is to do the same here: not to rear occult and extravagant edifices or to write books of subtle and dangerous colour, but to transfigure the life around us, ugly though it may seem and weak though we may be, into an existence which is worthy of man. Our place is not merely in the politics of the world, but also in its spiritual abundance; ours are the spires of Notre-Dame and the tables of the Lord.

BOOK NOTE

The following general works may be found useful: "The Cambridge History of American Literature"; "American Literature," by W. P. Trent; "American Literature since 1870," by F. L. Pattee. For the special point of view offered in this chapter, see "Father Tabb," by Francis A. Litz; "The Life of Orestes A. Brownson," by Henry F. Brownson, and "The Convert," by O. A. Brownson; "The Life of Father Hecker," by W. Elliott; and "Steeplejack," by J. G. Huneker. For information about Joyce Kilmer, see the introductions to the three volumes of his "Works," by R. C. Holliday; about Stoddard, see "Apostrophe to a Skylark," by G. W. James; "A Troubled Heart"—Stoddard's religious autobiography—and the *Ave Maria* for June, 1909; about Archbishop Ireland, see an article by J. Talbot Smith in the *Dublin Review*, January, 1921. The "Catholic Encyclopedia" may frequently be consulted with profit.

CHAPTER SEVENTEEN

"While Kings of eternal evil
Yet darken the hills about,
Thy part is with broken saber
To rise on the last redoubt."
LOUISE IMOGEN GUINEY.

I

THIS book has been written—if it must be weighted down with a purpose—to make clear that a portion of modern English literature is definitely Catholic in spirit, that it represents the Catholic mind; and a general view of the subject will, therefore, not be out of place here at the end. We have seen, first of all, that it was essential, in a country where the ancient traditions of Christendom had been discarded or discoloured, that the past should be brought to light again as it really was, with no disparagement of the truth and beauty of its culture. While the romantic movement, particularly as represented by Scott, may be said to have become acquainted with the people of the Ages of Faith, it was on the whole too superficial and fanciful to revive the reality of their society. The characters evolved by the romanticist were, so to speak, galvanized into a modern attitude. Kenelm Digby was the first great English

317

writer to see the Middle Ages as they ought to be seen, to group the picturesque qualities of the time round the profound social unity which they coloured, and to understand the soul of Europe as a Catholic would understand it. Even if one cannot say that the author of "Mores Catholici" was a literary genius, surely it is not wrong to call him a genius simply, by reason of his remarkable discernment of a buried world. Others would exploit the discovered country; and John Ruskin preached a comely gospel of beauty from the texts of his master.

But no Catholic who is really alive would spend much time dreaming of the reign of Saint Louis or the heyday of the Schools, solely for their own sakes, or because he believed them models after which society could be refashioned. The point of the mediævalist is simply this: the spirit which informed mediæval life is latent and can be made effective in modern life, a philosophy which really worked out should again become a working philosophy. It was the great service of Newman, the most scientific mind in modern England, to have understood this truth in its myriad ramifications. With a grasp of history that seems amazingly acute and complete, Newman went to work upon the spirit of his age by analyzing its horizons. Moving a full step ahead of the time he guessed its limitations; he went from the equator of English thought to the poles and left no intermediate land unvisited. His work was, of course, mental and aimed at the conversion, the renovation, of the English point of view. The more immediate and concrete matters he was willing to leave to others.

Those others were not wanting. A great body of poets engaged in the very practical business of song

with gifts that will in the end be ranked with those of
Wordsworth and Browning. The impetus given to the
action of the Catholic Spirit upon social problems by
Cardinal Manning was accepted with devotion by
many other able men. It became also the chief interest
of a powerful group of pamphleteers at the head of
whom have stood the Chestertons, W. S. Lilly, and
Belloc. History has been written from the Catholic
point of view by some of the ablest among its masters;
fiction has taken on the allurement of faith; eloquence,
philosophy, journalism—the multiform endeavours of
the modern literary movement have engaged the powers
of notable Catholic writers. There is not a department
of English letters that has not profited by the expression of the spirit of Christendom. All this has been
accomplished in a country which a hundred years ago
scoffed at the name of Rome and which scorned nothing
so deeply as the memory of the Faith which had once
crowned England with the glory of its handiwork. Add
the fruitful appeal of the Catholic voice in Ireland and
the growing power of its utterance in America, and
you have a magnificent force, creative of truth and
beauty for the world.

Seen thus in its entirety, the literature which we
have examined is a most impressive spectacle. Let us
use the word "spectacle" because it implies ʻthat the
matter is quite visible, although it has been overlooked
often enough. In no weapon has the philosophy which
is anti-Catholic seen such power as in silence. And yet
we have become too tall to be ignored; we have talked
too much to be termed mute; we have stood in the
market-place too long to be thought hermits. Clearly
the Catholic presence is quantitatively important; and

the only thing we still have to do is to consider briefly
its inner value, the worth of its principles as standards
in art. We recognize very fully that Catholic letters
must not be separated from the world at large, or limited to a body of thought which is not directly concerned with the life of the time. The pages of this
book have shown, it is hoped, some of the relations
which have actually existed between the current we have
been following and the surrounding domain of English
literary art. The creative power of the Catholic Spirit
has worked with the materials of the age and has been
subject to its influences, joyfully and in the spirit of
service.

Now what have been the conclusions of the modern
time concerning the purpose and nature of art? We
naturally think broadly of literature as expressing first
the individual and then society. We feel that what
distinguishes it from mere writing, is creative sincerity. An artist must know and be able to express
human nature as it actually is. Unless he has divined
correctly the mixture of aspiration and perverse instinct that constitutes an individual; unless he understands concretely the dream, the resolve, the prayer,
and the effort that lead to heroism or towards it, as well
as the inner egoism so seldom subdued, the reverie of
passion, the urge to lust, and the petty misery of unfed
mentality that induce ugliness and spiritual subser-
vience, the artist is not in the end accepted by humanity. The false ring of his coinage will betray his
counterfeiting, and nothing will save him from the derision of the stocks. In a similar way, literature must
be based upon a recognition of elemental social truths.
The artist need not be a scientist or even a strict phi-

losopher, but he must comprehend intuitively the realities of collective life. He must see, for instance, that Arcadia is not situated just twenty-four miles outside any large city; that the success of marriage as an institution is not based entirely upon an exchange of kisses by May moonlight; and that all ladies are not immediately susceptible to all traveling men. In short, literature must adopt not merely the common language, but also common sense.

These things are simply the result of intelligence looking sanely upon the world it seeks to express. That expression cannot, however, be purposeless, simply because there is no such thing in human life as intelligence acting utterly apart from an exercise of the will. Experience may force upon us the consciousness of facts, but it cannot create that harmonious grasp and orderly representation of facts which we call artistic truth; and, therefore, diversity of moral outlook introduces, despite the objectiveness of the real world, a kind of relativity into art. It is this which explains the manifold differences between the extremes of what are called realism and romance. With these we are not concerned here; but it is evident that the creator of literature must be guided by principles, and the great conflict of criticism rages round what those principles are in practice and should be in theory. Statements concerning them are varied, but none seem on the whole more ample or more nearly correct than those set down by Matthew Arnold, whom we quote the more readily because he was not a Catholic.

In his essay on "The Function of Criticism at the Present Time," Arnold says: ". . . the elements with which the creative power works are ideas: the best ideas on every matter which literature touches, ·current at the time," and goes on to draw the inference that criticism is "a disinterested endeavour to learn and propagate the best that has been known and thought in the world." This statement appears to be substantially correct, although the emphasis is probably too strong on simple intelligence; surely there is some room also for the best that has been *felt* in the world. To the substantial elements of knowledge and insight the artist must add the less tangible but equally necessary forces of form and feeling, the vitamines of literature. Guided by the light of eternal verities, he will not forget the soil of the land through which he passes. Such a standard Catholic writing is ready to adopt and to practice faithfully, but the question naturally arises: What is the best, and what manner of expression is most befitting it? Arnold insisted upon the separation of the world of ideas from the 'lower' sphere of practical considerations and sectarian opinions. This is probably a Cartesian principle, but without criticizing it here, let us see whether great liberty and tolerant breadth are incompatible with the Catholic point of view.

II

Nothing could be more false than the impression that the Catholic creed acts as a curb upon thought. As a matter of fact, one of the foremost advantages to be gained from an acceptance of that creed is freedom. One can belong to the Church without being required to believe in any of the rigid specialties of the modern mind; one may be an evolutionist or none; a prohibi-

tionist or none; even, it might be added, a sinner or
none. The Catholic has not one rule of faith but two;
in a more earthly sphere he may be an employer or a
laborer, an Englishman or an Irishman, a pacifist or
a warrior. The Church has always most firmly opposed encroachments upon the rightful liberty of the
individual; she has denounced state monopolies such as
Socialism, religious sects which, like the Flagellantes,
stake everything upon an eccentric observance, and
movements within the fold which tend to sacrifice universality for nationalism. During the nineteenth century she was accused by Napoleon of being un-French;
by Bismarck of being un-German; by Gladstone of being un-British: in short, she has been steadfastly ar-
raigned for being too broad.

No other institution has ever made half so detailed
a provision for the divergent temperaments of men.
Her sacraments and rites reckon with every moment in
and every state of human life. She has created estab-
lishments for the mystic as well as for the active man,
which are so carefully individualized that they adjust
themselves spontaneously to every conceivable type of
soul. The very Calendar of the Saints is a study in
the differentiation of the human species. And Catholic society, which liberated woman from sexual bondage and made of the slave an owner of the land, has
also done most for the freedom of art. It made of the
artisan an artist; it raised masters of beauty beyond
number from the hovels of the poor. The coefficient
of its action for social emancipation was its eagerness
to expand the reign of intelligence. Historically it has
proved the only collective group that could thrive on
disputes and to it the distraught have come for settle-

ment. How many modern minds, egoistic in the face of surrounding mediocrity, have turned to Rome for solace! Brunetière went that road with Coppée, Patmore with Beardsley, Stoddard with Brownson. Men whose belligerent individualism was the root of their genius have thus come by scores into the most compact organization in history. They have discovered that a Catholic has a right to do his own thinking as Saint Thomas and Dun Scotus did theirs. They have found in the principles of belief the pathways to new horizons, to new continents of splendour and security. To sum up the matter, it may be said that if experience has proved anything thoroughly it is that the Catholic spirit has never interfered with the fullest liberty demanded by art.

What a different story this is from that of the sectarianism which marred the sacred structures of the older Christian time, or from that of modern industrialism which scorns the very name of beauty or its servitors! It is characteristic of our commercial civilization to be ignorant of the most simple artistic principles and at the same time to regard the whole matter with undisguised contempt. The conflict between art and the service of material results is irremediable. Our cities are huge villages of foreigners, not the victims of immigration, but the creatures of dissociation. The things that keep these people together are ugly, like the places in which they weave and spin. Society has vertigo from incessant turning in a dizzy treadmill, and, having been blinded by a delusion of progress, does not even realize that it is standing still. Art cannot be divorced from serenity of intellect, and we have lost that. From the literature of sentimentalism we have gone to the literature of sentimental cynicism, the ugliest expression of life that has ever been offered for worship.

The Catholic Spirit, however, has continued to insist upon one thing with all the vigour of its being. It has declared that there is a "best" among ideas and sentiments, that the premise of art is truth, and that truth (which is beauty also) lies in and above what the intelligence perceives as existing in the world. The senses have their usefulness and the appearances presented to them have their allurement, but it is often a deceptive allurement. Only a rational treatment of the garment of the universe will reveal the reality and preserve the beauty of the raiment. And here is where the service of religion to art becomes important. By reason of its faith in and communication with a world that is higher than nature, by reason of the revealed truth which it manifests, the religious spirit is successful in keeping the mind on a level higher than matter, in rescuing the hand of the artist from the iridescent pools that form in the mud of life. There is, indeed, a terrible beauty for the depraved soul of man in the ways of evil, a beauty that seduces the spirit so easily cajoled from the beginning by the powers of Darkness.

It need scarcely be added that in practice Christianity is the only force which can save art and life from the decay of the flesh. "Always and everywhere," says Taine the skeptic, "for eighteen hundred years, wherever those wings fail or are broken, public and private morals are degraded. In Italy during the Renaissance, in England under the Restoration, in France under the National Convention, man seemed to become as pagan as in the first century; he became at once as he was in the times of Augustus and Tiberius, voluptuous and hard-hearted; he misused others and himself; brutal or calculating egoism regained ascendancy, cruelty and sensuality were openly paraded, and society became the abode of ruffians and the haunt of evil." [1]

To save art from ruin is one service; to provide it with a new world is another. In the wide rooms of the spirit, as they are unfolded to the·Catholic vision, there are far-reaching vistas which have their influence on the reading of life. The symbolism that has distinguished Christian art is simply an attempt to visualize that portion of the unseen world which is manifest to the spirit. Whether we term this effort mystical or not, its sponsors vouch bravely for its reality. Their discovery has been bought too dearly to be termed a delusion, and its results are too worthy to be scorned. Anyone who derides it as untrue, or rejects it without earnest personal investigation, is emphatically not a seeker for the "best that has been known and thought in the world." He is simply a person with prejudices. Practically, then, the Catholic Spirit in art is both a regulative and a widening power: it is conservative in its human aspects and radical in its superhuman aspects. But it never forgets the soul or the body, the reality or the symbol.

III

It is particularly necessary to insist upon the dignity of art at this time when unusual efforts are being

---

[1] Quoted by A. Baudrillart, "The Church, the Renaissance, and Protestantism."

made in English-speaking countries to ignore it. The authors who are upheld as masters of contemporary writing are almost generally men with very little appreciation of the soul or of those things in which it is vitally interested. Naturalistic motivation in fiction, the drama of emotional revolt, impressionistic poetry that has been begotten sensuously, are acclaimed with surprising enthusiasm. George Moore, D. H. Lawrence, Gilbert Cannan, with a hundred lesser individuals, are literary gods before whom much incense is uproariously burned. In America the name before which we are bidden to make obeisance is Theodore Dreiser. Every adjective adapted to convey the impression of virility, of rugged honesty, of unique beauty, is made part of the vocabulary of a school of critics that seems to have gathered expressly to advertise naturalism. The coveted goal of expression appears to be visualization, and this is achieved principally in regions where the human race is "at its damndest," as Patmore would have said. New departments of "science" —psycho-analysis and spiritism—are invoked to justify the cloudiness of intelligence which seems to have conquered the world. The whole of this business has been admirably organized to drive away the faintest trace of a spiritual idea from the minds of those whose course in modern reading has been sufficiently thorough.

We are not attempting here any defense of squeamishness nor do we wish to imply that naturalistic art is without value. It is probable that the romantic and yet fleshly "innocence" in which so many modern fictionists have steeped their plots has been more baneful than plain speaking would have been; certainly it has given a distorted view of life, has occasioned a sentimentalism that wraps the most serious affairs of existence in flimsy pink gauze, and has induced puerile reveries that kill honest thought. Assuredly Saint Francis de Sales was a modest man; and yet his discussion of sex in the "Introduction to a Devout Life" does not shun reality. It was Saint John Chrysostom, the denouncer of kings and profligates, who thundered against prudery as a heresy. And in so far as intense, even squalid, realism is concerned, it may very well be true that modern industrialism has given abundant excuse for the terrible portrait of life which men like Balzac and Gissing have provided.

But it is a different matter to assert that literature is privileged to sponsor any principle so long as the form in which that principle is couched happens to be *à la mode*. It may be untrue, it may even be the product of a diseased mind. No sepulcher can ever be more than a whitened sepulcher; no literary grace can cloak the thing that is a lie. Dreary volumes of sordid detail will never manage, either, to be art, if the idea which they are written to express is some cheap falsity of pseudo-science, some hectic justification of brutish instinct. Every sane man in this world realizes the perverse fascination of the obscene; and it is the task of art, as it is of thought and religion, to transfix the demon that is without and within us. The great danger for an age which is the prey of advertising lies in the fact that the appeal of books which glorify the animal in man can be artificially stimulated to give them a literary prominence which the common sense of humanity would ordinarily refuse. Subtle philosophers are not average readers; and volumes that are utterly gaudy, useless, and vile can be set before the public as "great art" and "epoch-making," can be grounded on some mad æsthetic system, and can thus be made to aid in the subversion, now so nearly accomplished, of the sense of the true and the beautiful.

The forces which used to oppose paganism have weakened considerably. There can be no doubt that as Protestantism decays in America, other systems of thought based upon some vagrant species of mysticism will take its place. The mind of man is hungry and, it might be added, his nerves are weak. Centuries of individualism have pushed him close to the precipice which is license. What does the multitude know today of the true and the beautiful? What does it know of God? These realities, which formed the pillars of Christendom, are scarcely more than ruins to a large part of our society. But men do cling to the Messianic dream, to the Jewish delusion that the king shall rule on earth. And one after another social Utopias are being made into religions, Utopias which proceed upon the basis of some mechanistic interpretation of the world and in the hope that out of material welfare peace of heart may be born. Demagogue follows fanatic and their number is legion; all sense of the solidarity of human effort, of human destiny, of human dignity, disappears. The poor are either invariably virtuous or the rich are above reproach. Man is no longer measured as man, but by the riches he possesses or by the industrial function which he chances to fulfill. The degradation of art is a necessary consequence; for if the vocation of the artist is to conserve anything like concern with beauty, with aspiration, with ecstasy, it must deal first of all with man.

However much we should like to apply to this or

that feverishly acclaimed author the words which Joseph de Maistre threw at Voltaire, *"Paris le couronna: Sodome l'eut banni,"* the ghost will not be downed in that way. The battle must settle into a contest between conceptions of life; it must be won on the ancient alignments of right and wrong. The service of honest criticism is, therefore, of the greatest value, and we shall try to outline briefly the organized opposition in America to the cult of literary sensism. Most important, perhaps, is the humanistic position as defended principally by Irving Babbitt and Paul E. More. Professor Babbitt's principles are strikingly evident from two able books, "The New Laokoon" and "Rousseau and Romanticism"; and these may be permitted to represent the movement to aid which they were written. Babbitt's criticism, ably documented and based upon very wide reading in many literatures, is concerned chiefly with modern romanticism. The substance of his doctrine is apparently to be found in this statement: "The romantic error has been to make of revery the serious substance of life instead of its occasional solace; to set up the things that are below the reason as a substitute for those that are above it; in short, to turn the nature cult into a religion." He teaches that the true humanist is he who mediates between prosaic sensibleness and imaginative illusion, who satisfies "the standards of poetry without offending the standards of prose."

With so much of his doctrine we are in accord. Unfortunately, however, there is not wanting evidence to show that he tends to be what Ruskin would have called "a short-sighted Protestant person." One does not mean to be ungenerous, but it is clear that Babbitt has not taken into account many things which happened between the Aristotle whom he deifies and the Luther whom he admires. He does not realize that to the reasoned naturalism of the Greeks Christianity added the supernaturalism, to proclaim which it had been born into this world; he does not see that in Saint Thomas and other scholars of the mediæval time a synthesis of the two elements was effected that changed forever the intellectual complexion of Europe. Of course Mr. Babbitt has not stopped with Luther. The innate quietism and the ethical preoccupations of his spirit are interestingly shown by the fact that he has taken refuge in Buddhism. In like manner his æsthetic system is based upon the Greeks and the Renaissance; he cannot understand Christian society because he has skipped fifteen centuries. To this twist can be traced the manifold narrownesses of a critical system to which, in many respects, we may bow with admiration. Its chief concern is the arraignment of Rousseau, who is pilloried as the father of modern ills, but its author does not take into account either the fact that Rousseau may occasionally have been posing or the no less indubitable truth that Luther was guilty of the same superlative individualism, the same repudiation of intellectual "bondage," and the same reliance on states of mind that are divorced from action. In other words, he does not find the source of what he knows is the trouble with modern literature. But taken all in all, his system seems much more solid and helpful than, for instance, the idealistic views of Benedetto Croce, whose modified Hegelianism, fruitful of novelty, is gaining influence among us. That is quite too subtle and simple for life.

Professor Babbitt's humanistic—or classic—principles are ably accepted and defended, with modifications, by at least two exceptionally brilliant women, Agnes Repplier and Katherine Fullerton Gerould. Their writing has poise, wit, and acid, and there are few men amongst us who could safely risk a passage with either. But both are frankly aristocratic, disdainful of the vulgarity of the horde, and intent upon conserving the culture of the chosen few: Mrs. Gerould says bluntly, "I am cynical enough to believe that, if a generation feels like stepping down, it will do so." [1] And she seems quite right. How impossible it is either to stem the current of a popular movement or to inaugurate a new one by the simple expedient of creating a doctrine, especially a high-brow doctrine! Babbitt, as a matter of fact, has generally been either derided or ignored. The people who read Gautier will not accept his authority and those who do not are scarcely inclined to attribute to literary criticism the lofty position claimed for it in "Rousseau and Romanticism." The only influence that can elevate the trend of literature is a correct and generally accepted standard of life, a collective grasp of the sources from which art springs. More individualism is not calculated to remedy the excessive concern with the Ego which has unbalanced modern thought. And it is instructive to note in this connection exactly what has happened in France where the conflict has raged fiercest, where, as Arnold has affirmed, "the people are most alive," and where in spite of the tumult, Catholic tradition is still influential.

The nineteenth century opened, indeed, with the ro-

[1] "The Movies," *Atlantic Monthly*, July, 1921.

mantic revival of Chateaubriand, but its basis was still
the intellectual position that had antedated the Revolution. Rousseau who dreamed of a beatific return to
nature, and Voltaire who scorned with the full bitterness of an unbeliever the institutions which had upheld
society, had disturbed the minds of modern men too
violently for the acceptance of a moderate philosophy.
The author of "Emile" had professed to believe that
thought is criminal; his disciples simply did not think.
Delicacy of sense-perception, satiety of sense-experi-
ence, were set up as the guiding principles in art.
"Whatever is realized is right," said Oscar Wilde, who
was an excellent pupil, though the English jailed him
for being in earnest. Literature was divorced from intelligence, from morals, from every faculty of man except his animal instincts and his abnormalities. For
the first time, it was maintained, the artist was entirely
free; he existed for no other purpose than to dream,
"beautifully" perhaps, but differently at all costs.

And yet literature had never been so sternly bound
by fantastic and impossible theories. With Zola the
art of fiction became an experiment in the discovery of
laws that (supposedly) govern humanity with scientific
rigidity; his books are enormous wastes across which
move primitive men, characters formed and driven according to the iron rules of heredity, environment, and
the necessities of existence. For all his wealth of detail, he was interested in large, crude theses and not in
facts. Whenever the actual world ran counter to his
hypothesis, he denied the existence of the world. But
Zola was not an anomaly. He had learned his manner in the company of George Sand, whose theories were
ample, vague, often viciously sentimental; of Victor

Hugo, who preached long but engaging sermons in the interests of humanitarianism; of Gautier, for whom life was a piquant series of adventures—or experiments —in sex; and of Flaubert and the Goncourts who sought the *word* that would conjure up a musty odour for an inordinate sensibility. Not one of all these but was generously gifted, all had talent, and all were lasting and vivid demonstrations of the truth that literature cannot be divorced from reality and a sound philosophy of the world.

This was an era, too, of skeptic speculation, when the already unsettled souls of men were further shaken by the phrases of Saint-Simon, by the subtle irreligion of Renan, and by the dark Positivism of Taine. The old, solid traditions of Christian France were attacked by the intelligence just as they had been undermined by the romantic appeal to the emotions. It seemed true, indeed, that modern life had pitilessly made impossible the dogmas of the past. Well might Augustin Cochin cry out, *"Seigneur, il est bien temps de nous voir."* French artistic endeavour slowly poisoned itself with sensism. "Present French society," wrote Julien Benda a few years ago, "demands of works of art that they should arouse emotion and stimulate sensation; it does not any longer seek to reach through them any sort of intellectual pleasure." [1] Emile Clermont observed clearly that moderns ask of art the intoxication which the Greeks sought from wine or the celebration of their mysteries.

It cannot be denied that this attitude persists to a considerable extent today. The emotional derangement of the French mind is still great, but common

[1] "Belphegor," by Julien Benda.

sense and tradition have gained a victory. It began with the conversion of Huysmans, the "eye" of French naturalism; with the return of Baudelaire the nostolgiac and Coppée the humanitarian; with the sudden arousal of interest in Joseph de Maistre and Ernest Hello. The classic literature of France, with its admirable depth and serenity, had after all not lost its influence—the influence of Pascal, Racine, Bossuet. More and more forcefully criticism insisted upon the norm of reason, and later on the norm of faith. Brunetière, Lemaître, Bremond, Giraud, Doumic, Wyzewa, Strowski—in every instance the intellect was rounded out by religion, the scientific man learned credence. The tide of battle that had been desperate, turned.

Gazing upon modern France from across the ruins of four years, one beholds a civilization that has been shaken to the core, but the ancient traditions of which have stood firm. We intend no such thing as a generalization or classification of so mobile and differentiated a world as French letters. Nevertheless, it seems correct to say that two strong forces are now plainly in evidence: a concern with the morals of life and an interest in the ideal. The novels of Paul Bourget, Maurice Barrès, René Bazin, Henri Bordeaux, and of younger artists like François Mauriac, Alexandre Arnoux, and Edmond Jaloux, are resolute in presenting the spiritual ideas sternly taught by life; strong French women like Colette Yver and Leontine Zanta are stripping feminism of emotional excess; and a gallant host of poets like Paul Claudel, Francis Jammes, Henri Ghéon, and Maurice Brillant carry to dizzy heights the splendour of Christian song. And, lost in the mists of the war, how many goodly names there are! Charles Péguy, Ernest Psichari, Paul Drouot, and Émile Clermont, and older men like Joseph Lotte and the Count de Mun. With these stand a multitude of shining names in every department of literature— history, philosophy, criticism, journalism. To press the matter would make of this essay a catalogue.

We do not entertain the delusion that paganism has been banished from France. It does not even fear exile. But the disdain with which the generation of Zola looked upon ideas that expressed confidence in the reality of the unseen is no longer in vogue. Instead, the art of Zola has been turned to definitely religious uses in the widely read novels of Émile Baumann, whose "La Fer sur l'Enclume" is a story which the master of the naturalists would have considered dubious, to say the least. The same change is noticeable in many other arts. "There has not been," says Maurice Denis, "for a long time an epoch more passionately devoted to sacred art than our own." [1] The very spokesmen of the Church have recovered the majesty and serenity of the style of Bossuet. We are not interested here, however, in setting forth the victories of the Church: we wish merely to point out the success of Christian, of moral and idealistic art. It must be remembered always that, as Mr. Howells once said, Catholicism is the natural form of religion in France. And the success which the expression of the religious spirit has achieved there is also a succession; it has been the reborn voice of a France reborn, with her heroic breast to the enemy and her shield in front of the sanctuary of the world.

[1] "Theories," by Maurice Denis, Paris.

IV

Enough has been said to indicate not only that there is a place for standards in art, but that these have been contested with varying success by the leading schools of the past century. No man can write without a philosophy, because no man can exist without a philosophy; the very technique of an artist may be dependent upon his view of miracles. Now the Catholic standard in art is traditional, or rather the Catholic tradition is a standard. We are humanists in the sense that we do not believe that such and such a professor or critic has been born to give the world its first glimpse of truth and beauty. We are sufficiently conservative to agree with Pascal that "all the good rules have been laid down, and it remains necessary only to put them into practice"; the visions which humanity has entertained in its highest moods will probably not, we think, be improved upon by some small-chested dilettante who knows Baudelaire by rote, no matter how "young" he may be. But the Catholic spirit is above all radical: it has roots which it believes are vital, it will not separate art either from life to-day or from life in the past. One need not state here that the artistic era to which the Catholic mind naturally and joyfully reverts is that of the Middle Ages. This implies reverence for classical culture as a matter of course, for whatever elements of pagan grandeur were known to the mediæval artist or thinker became vigorous germs, seeds that burst open under the light of a newly risen sun.

The Middle Ages were distinguished from other periods of history by many things, but by nothing more clearly than the universal prevalence of the artistic mood. "That the end of life is not action," says Walter Pater, "but contemplation—*being* as distinct from *doing*—a certain disposition of the mind: is in some shape or other, the principle of all the higher morality. In poetry, in art, if you enter into their true spirit at all, you touch this Principle, in a measure; these, by their very sterility, are a type of beholding for the mere joy of beholding. To treat life in the spirit of art is to make of life a thing in which means and end are identified; to encourage such treatment, the true moral significance of art and poetry." The identification of means and end, as suggested by Pater, was achieved with happy results for art in the mediæval synthesis. Then, if ever, nature and human life were viewed as inseparable from the Source of truth and beauty; the smallest creature that hid from the scrutiny of man reflected the splendour of the Creator. Action became contemplation, and the slightest utensil as well as the most ordinary service were endowed with a grace, a comeliness, which our modern world cannot quite understand. Art was indeed inspired utility, uniting in its manifold forms a rigid reasonableness with exuberant fancy.[1]

For the only time in the history of mankind the collective soul, which is just as real and energetic as the individual spirit, functioned harmoniously. It moved staunchly forward along a path of reason that seldom wandered astray from the actual into regions of subjective idealism, or sank to the marshlands of sense.

[1] Cf. Chap. VIII on Francis Thompson.

With an admirable persistence the mediæval mind, though in the end it did expend itself in useless subtlety, continued for a long period of time on the broad level where harmonious coöperation of minds is possible. There Saint Thomas developed the doctrine of Aristotle, while others expounded with supreme originality and concreteness the teachings of Plato. There the science of building, the science of poetry, and the science of music were envested with a perfect vitality that is still the wonder of the world. Never did the din of argument rise higher, and never either was the voice of reason more equitable and discerning. The collective mind was guided in its aspirations by the light of Christ, by a firm and intuitive faith which cast its radiance over the pathway of reason and made the footing easy. No doubt mediæval men were proud, irascible, lustful even, with violence, but they were always men who knew that the robes of their destiny were about them.

More interesting even than this activity of the intellect among the chosen few, was that great popular experiment of the Middle Ages, the spiritualization of Democracy. The common man really and truly became a man, free in the disposition of his lot, the undisputed possessor of rights which society might violate but which it must recognize as inalienable. It was this man who set into movement the coöperative economic bodies known as the guilds; who undertook the expeditions of mystic conquest called the Crusades; whose menial tasks were so illumined by the glory of his spiritual inheritance that they became beautiful almost of necessity; who made of his handiwork a human firmament in which there are set a countless multitude of stars. The popular voice was not, as a rule, literary —that would have demanded writing—but it was more. It was artistic. A wealth of saints' legends and of fairy tales; the universal prevalence of a somewhat uncouth but vigorous and thoughtful drama; the kindly satire which we moderns can only repeat and sharpen; the breath of poetry which was shaken like spikenard over the passing throng: all this was alive with the voice of the people, who were creative because they were free and blessed with unity, because the earth upon which they walked was good.

Necessarily the coöperative effort of the Middle Ages was based on discipline, but it was as far as possible removed from coercion. Europe, which often seems to have been a riot of individual notions, was cast into a mould that was nothing less than a state of mind. The great motive power of Christendom was a full recognition of the freedom of the will and of individual responsibility, based upon belief in personal immortality. The sanctions of society were less than nothing on paper, but written upon the human heart they were immutable, irrefragable. Here was a law which none could escape, but which, properly understood, would become a burden of delight.

We are fully conscious of having said very little about the infirmities of the time. It was not paradise, and it did hear the voice of woe. Nobody need overlook the fact that there were no bathtubs and no automobiles, no newspapers or congressmen. But the men of the Middle Ages proved the human success of their social life by creating one mighty and unforgettable monument to happiness—laughter. The hale mirth of Christian Europe broke from the lips of the multi-

tude. It looked serenely from the lofty pinnacles of
the cathedral, it was discernible on every gate in Christendom. It was lusty in the throats of singers and
actors, it was sharp in the derision of the street-seer.
It was the blissful virtue that Brother Juniper caught
from his superior, and it was the legacy of Sir Thomas
More. Nothing ever appeared so spontaneously or
unexpectedly. In comparison with the laughter of
Christendom, Aristophanes and Mark Twain alike are
savage. Here was no deadly acid, but instead salt,
which saved the popular spirit from excess of fervour
and kept it wholesome even while it itself was the product of wholesomeness. The civilization of the Middle
Ages needs no further defense.

Thus a healthy communal philosophy that could not
conceive of existence as anything but a noble and conse-
quently beautiful enterprise constructed a society that
expressed itself fully, consciously, artistically. Now
literature is of necessity more individual than the
rest of the arts; it is, in fact, always a blend of the
subjective and the objective, of the mind and the world.
Nobody ever proved this better than Flaubert, who
denied it. Nevertheless, to revert once more to the
keen statement of Matthew Arnold, the gift of literary
genius "lies in the faculty of being happily inspired
by a certain intellectual and spiritual atmosphere."
Art is always, secondarily at least, the product of an
artistic society. The masters of mediæval beauty are
often nameless because they were absorbed in the mob
—the mob that rose from the soil of France to build
the miracle shrines of Chartres and Amiens; the mob
that made every city from Bruges to Saragossa an image of the New Jerusalem; the mob out of which came

living, immortal poems like Saint Jeanne d'Arc and Godfrey de Bouillon.

It is characteristic of the leaders of "those incomparable times, when an unsophisticated people had been formed in Beauty without themselves being aware of it," as Jacques Maritain says,[1] that they should have summed up the best energy of the world around them. We shall name as typical of the literary standards of the time three men, one of whom was, indeed, not very literary, but whose influence on literature, particularly in our own time, has been very great. Saint Francis of Assisi won over life because he loved it. There was in his thought no worship of the light within, but instead a wholehearted surrender to the Light Who is above, Whose reflection is upon all things. Francis smiled at learning, but sought truth and found that it was beautiful. His teaching was done by means of symbols, the common alphabet of all poets, and his religion got expression through them also. It was the secret of his success that he should have come close to simple things by renouncing them, that the Wolf of Gubbio walked by his side, tamed by an instinctive perception of unselfish brotherhood. The multitude that followed him lovingly did so because he had been called to represent, like some radiant metaphor, the things which they saw were good. He was the incarnation of the common spiritual quest of the time. Art could seek no better master, for art is not concerned with atoms or microbes, but with the soul that inspires the least of things with a memorable power. No spiritual interest of our own time is more hopeful than the growing love for the Franciscan mood.

[1] "Art et Scholastique," Paris, Librarie de l'art Catholique.

Francis was a saint, but the greatest mediæval writer, the keystone of literature, is Dante Alighieri. One may read the "Divina Commedia" for its revelation of the poet's mind and heart, for its religious fervour and theological science, or for its allegorical wealth. All three views have their value, as one may learn from respectively Ozanam, Moore, and Croce. The poem is the perfect poetic wedding of matter and form, of truth and beauty, of mankind and its aspirations to the knowledge of God. And yet Dante is not a solitary figure looming in solitary stateliness from the wastes of a lowly age. How much he owed to the poets who went before him, to the philosophers like Saint Thomas at whose feet he sat, and to the saints of the Church is not easy to determine, but assuredly he owed much. He was not afraid either to make his poem a realistic picture of society, or to incorporate into it the best that had been known and thought by that society. Dante wished also to do things; he did not seek to divorce the practical from the speculative, the will from the intelligence. Feeling that the life of man is a serious business, he took it sternly; and there is no realism that is darker than the terrible fires of the Inferno. But the nature of his genius made him also a contemplative and his convictions were Catholic, so that the Purgatorio, rich with brooding over the Ideal, with consciousness of man's painful advance to happiness, is a better poem than, as well as a complement to, the philosophy of the Inferno. Dante the mystic is at home also in the inaccessible regions of heaven, and like all true mystics he does not disdain the minute details of the finite world. The Ptolemaic astronomy in the Paradiso is not a blemish but a demonstration of the poet's constant concern with the real world. He knew that heaven would stand when the last star had fallen; but he realized as well that the only highway thither for the mortal poet leads athwart the stars. Nor was he guilty of the modern romantic confusion of revery with contemplation; he knew that the watches of the spirit are kindled by desire. And that impulse, that longing, for the goal of God was the profound motive of mediæval society, which viewed the Saviour not only with Saint Francis as a child in the manger, but also with Dante as the King whose brow is a throne of thorns.

What the art of the Middle Ages gained and lost by the infusion of humanism may be learned from a study of Shakespeare, who marks the passing of that art and also represents most successfully the nature of the English genius. He was the descendant of Chaucer as well as of the Renaissance, and Chaucer had none of the Latin *élan* or ecstasy, but instead the fresh kindliness of another race. His world was more earthly because his people were less abstract, more dramatic; and the spiritual concern of his poems lay with the forces that modify character in ordinary life. He gave body to the spirit and put its principles into action. That is the genius of the English race. That is what Shakespeare, too, has done, in a series of moral discourses which are almost as rigorous as the sermons of Saint Jerome. His drama is great, solid, marvelously beautiful, but it is also composite. The materials came from other artists, the philosophy is that which the time accepted. Shakespeare may have known comparatively little of the classics, but he stood at the center of life—a vigorous, all-seeing artist, whose man-

liness conquered both pit and gallery. This masculine
character of his thought and diction ought never to be
lost sight of; men are needed to speak his lines, no matter whether they storm or are tender. On the other
hand, all that is needed for the male rôles in decadent
drama is a "perfect thirty-six."

The standards which underlay, and to some extent were responsible for, the creative power of mediæval art were vitality, a recognition of social solidarity,
and a firm grasp of the things of the spirit. The masters of that time were not egoists; they worked for,
were members of, a free society which would not have
understood a pose of effeminate disdain. But neither
were they formalists, restrained from spontaneity by
gratuitous conventions. The character of Shakespeare
is merged in the general creative exuberance of the time,
as the character of the sculptor who wrought the miracle transept of Reims is merged. Nothing that the
Christian past has to tell us is more important than
that art at its best is a collective endeavour; that
sense, that understanding, is still strong at the end of
the Middle Ages with Rabelais in France and Cervantes
in Spain. These men would have scorned anything but
fellowship with their neighbours, and a tower of ivory
would have seemed to them suitable only for a lady's
boudoir. Let us be firmly assured that we shall have
no great art until that spirit of collective endeavour is
restored, until beauty is made to rise spontaneously
from a free society in which the fundamental principles
of life are agreed upon. For beauty cannot be distilled
in secret or spun from the sensibilities of the shirker;
it is the common delight of men that springs into being
in the common light of day.

V

How, then, modern life being what it is, can the Catholic Spirit in art become effective? It is quite true that it cannot exercise its power to the fullest extent. The connection between us and the mediæval tradition has been broken, and we could not go back if we would. The reasonable man everywhere is a lover of his time. He may see its manysided error, its engulfing materialism, the weakness and the sin of its institutional life; he may even believe that the whole structure of modern civilization is built upon injustice, that it cannot create beauty because it was conceived in ugliness. But he will not, unless he is blind, overlook the patient striving for light and loveliness of which our world is full. Living in an age that has been shaped ruthlessly by war, all of us have witnessed the surging idealism, the courage, of the multitude, and have seen, too, their bitter disillusionment in the outcome of the struggle. It is not so far from earth to Sirius as it is from Péguy and even Brooke to cynical books on the Peace Conference. For better or for worse, our world has dreamed of a crusade; you cannot satisfy it with a protective tariff.

Now the great value of the Catholic Spirit under present circumstances lies in its exact balancing of conservative and radical tendencies. It has saved the best that was known and thought in the past and it has refused to accept the results of a break with that past. Nowhere else is there a power which so bridges the difference between us and our forefathers. Unfortunately, the Catholic Spirit is not always alive and active. Unfortunately it, too, has been isolated in practice from the large hopes that once caused the dawn to stand over the Western world. Here in America we have as yet failed to understand fully the bonds which link us to the tradition of Christendom: the memories which Columbus strove to carry to the ends of the earth, memories of the beauty of a society that still rested secure under the dominion of the Fisherman's ring when men first began to wonder whether there might be a continent to the westward sea. For this we are not quite to blame. During several centuries the Church has been living in a state of siege, has heard the din of a tumultuous attack upon her ancient walls. Only today when the opposing forces have been weakened by the disintegration of their morale, when the giant dream of modern society has been shattered, has she, too, been liberated.

But the freedom of the Catholic Spirit has been restored in the midst of darkness. Shall we venture to dream of beauty and peace, of holiness and ecstasy, while the cauldron seethes? Often enough, indeed, one is inclined to accept the opinion that the disintegration of intelligence must proceed further; that only the ignominy of having been driven to its knees will arouse the multitude to fury with the base ideals that it has adored. Be that as it may, the truths and the energy of Christendom are eternal, as is its mastery of the heart. And nothing has been more perennially characteristic of the missionary work of the Catholic Spirit than the recognition of the sacred appeal of art. The beauty inspired by Greece was national, even local, but the creative power of Christendom denied the existence of frontiers. Wherever the Church set her foot, whether upon the coast of England or in the magnificent city of Constantine, the spirit sought expression in matter. Whatever the people into whose midst she came might have been, they grew into artists. To use a homely metaphor, she was the great gong that stirred the rhythm of the music of the world.

If, then, the Catholic Spirit in America can comprehend the cohesiveness of its traditions, can rise to the appreciation of its inheritance, artistic expression is almost certain to follow. Surely it is time for us to understand that life is not all utility or even all morality; that in the ordered union of matter and form is written the very alphabet of God. Our final task here, therefore, shall be to enumerate a few things which the circumstances of our environment would seem to suggest earnestly. The Catholic literature which we have surveyed has been written with full consciousness of the miracle of Christendom, but it has been the work of a comparative handful of men who have felt the constant pressure of isolation and have been forced to overlook the general indifference of their public. The attitude of that public has even in some measure been responsible for the limitations which our letters show.

In the first place, have we been interested in reality, which means life taken as life and not under the form of a palliative, highly edifying in some ways, but on the whole viciously untrue? It is indisputable that the fundamental quality of art must be sincerity, which does not mean realistic banality but does most emphatically mean reality. The dilettantism, the anæmia, so evident in our letters, will make no headway against the spirit of our time, which is based on business. The commercial mind may be dubious in its ethics, but it is sound in its estimate of the actual state of affairs. It examines conditions to find out what they really are, it knows the field and bases none of its calculations upon sugary illusion. Moreover, it prosecutes its purpose with overwhelming energy, with the full verve of the intellect. We know that it is shortsighted and materialistic, that it does not deal with or understand the whole man. But that is not its affair. That is the *raison d'etre* of literature. And until the art of writing becomes once more a masculine art, strong, courageous, thoroughly alive, it will not learn to speak the words for which this generation is waiting.

Just as soon as literature becomes more than a venal proffering of mental stick-candy, it will regain its position among the forces that mould men. This elevation will not be accomplished by the school of ultra-realism, of pessimistic individualism, now gaining vogue. That is no more honest than the hyper-sentimentalism against which we have protested. The great books that reveal truth believe in facts, but they are essentially not catalogs bound in gloom. "Color," said Ingres, "is the animal part of art." It is the stroke that reveals the master, and not the paintpots of verbal imagery or "statistics" with which he may cover his work. For interpretation, which is the goal of the creative spirit, is the product of the artist's intelligence and will, not merely of his eyes. It will be coloured, indeed, by his temperament and his state of mind; it may legitimately be as pessimistic as Pascal, as optimistic as Dickens. But it cannot honestly be as pink as "Pollyana" or as dirty as "Esther Waters." After all, Meredith has made the point here: "Philosophy bids us to see that we are not so pretty as rose-pink, not so repulsive as dirty drab; and that, instead of everlastingly shifting those barren aspects, the sight of ourselves is wholesome, bearable, fructifying, finally a delight. Do but perceive that we are coming to philosophy and the stride towards it will be a giant's—a century a day. And imagine the celestial refreshment of having a pure decency in the place of sham; real flesh; a soul born active, wind-beaten, but ascending." [1]

And that philosophy cannot any longer be effective if marred by an excessive individualism. "Never," says Palacio Valdes, "have men of letters been so much preoccupied with originality as at present and never have they been less original than at present." [2] We simply cannot afford to ignore the lessons that have been taught by the civilizations of the past, or to believe that the imagination of a single man can over-shadow the collective experience of the race. Again, if our art is not to be a vain and fruitless endeavour, it must take into account the ordinary lives of men, it must deal with the problems, the joys, and the sorrows of the universal mood. Its dealing must be sober, honest, beautiful.

The literature of the Catholic Spirit can safely trust the wings of its tradition. Let there be a deepening concern with the things of the spirit in the light of reason; convince men once more of the truth of the kingdom of God, teach them the beauty and responsibility of their human inheritance, make them feel the magnificence of the divine adventure into which they are born. The renewal of the face of the earth must begin

---

[1] Preface to "Diana of the Crossways."
[2] Address to the Spanish Academy, 1921.

with the soul of man. When the point of view of the multitude has been weaned from the glitter that distracts it, when the hale solidity of its spiritual heritage has been understood again, our task shall have been done. Until then we shall labour in the light of the past, strong with the strength of our fathers, in the gilded harness of undying kings.

BOOK NOTE

The literature on the subject considered in this chapter is, of course, very extensive. For the mediæval background see especially: "L'Art religieux en France au XIIIme siècle," by Emile Mâle; "The Mediæval Mind," by H. O. Taylor; "Chartres and Saint Michel," by Henry Adams; "The Substance of Gothic Art," by Ralph A. Cram; "Mores Catholici," by Kenelm Digby; and the standard works on mediæval literature, such as those by P. de Julleville, Gaston Paris, Karl Kantzius, L. Clédat, etc. In addition, consult "Dante" and "The Franciscan Poets," by Frederick Ozanam, and "Thomas v. Aquin," by M. Grabman. The controversy on literary standards may be studied in: "L'Art et Scholastique," by J. Maritain; "Théories," by Maurice Denis; "Le Romantisme Français," by P. Lasserre, and the same author's later "Chapelles Litteraires"; "The New Laokoon" and "Rousseau and Romanticism," by Irving Babbitt; "The Drift of Romanticism," by P. E. More; "On Contemporary Literature," by S. P. Sherman; "The Æsthetic as Science of Expression," by Benedetto Croce; "Belphegor," by Julien Benda; "Standards," by Professor Brownell; "Beyond Life," by J. B. Cabell; "Prejudices," by H. L. Mencken; "Essays," by Alice Meynell; "Les Maîtres de l'Heure," by Victor Giraud. Among older books see: "Lectures on Art," by John Ruskin; "Principle in Art," by C. Patmore; "Essays," by Matthew Arnold; "Heretics" and "Orthodoxy," by G. K. Chesterton; "Le Roman Naturaliste," by F. Brunetière; "Le Disciple," by Paul Bourget, and the same author's introduction to "Le Demon de Midi"; "L'Homme," by E. Hello; and, of course, Sainte-Beuve. Among a host of German books on the subject, it may be interesting to see in this connection, "Die Romantik," by Ricarda Huch; "Die Wiedergeburt der Dichtung," by Karl Muth; and a criticism, by Dr. Max Ettlinger, of Deutinger's teaching.

ADDENDA

IT is manifestly impossible to give, within the limits of a single book, anything like adequate treatment of the ramifications of a great movement. To the famous men who have been recalled, there might be added dozens of others whose work has been fruitful, generous, and amiable. But we shall have to content ourselves here with the briefest possible mention of a score or two of writers whose efforts in behalf of the Catholic Spirit have been distinctly worth while. Some of these have attained considerable fame, and others are not so well known; but surely all of them have found readers who will not indifferently permit their names to die.

Modern Catholic poetry, for example, cannot spare the name of Mrs. Hamilton King, one of the most interesting accessions to the Church from among the verse-writers of England. She was like Mrs. Browning both in feebleness of body and in a passionate concern with the national politics of Italy; but her poems largely antedate her relation with the Catholic Spirit. "The Disciples" is eager verse written out of a fondness for the aspirations of Mazzini, but it has mood-quality as well. "The Ballad of the Midnight Sun" is saga-like in its narrative skill and brusque colour of scene. Mrs. King's technique is always quite unconventional but seldom eccentric, and her devotional poems have flavour as well as piety. This cannot be said so truly of the verse of Augusta T. Drane, or of the poems of Armael and Violet O'Connor, though these do not lack fervour and some insight. Father E. Garesché, S. J., is an American religious poet of ability: if there is something too formal about his stanzas, they do possess on the other hand a suggestiveness that is the result of delicate spiritual feeling.

In fiction one does not like to overlook the present-day novels of Compton Mackenzie, whose adoption of the Catholic faith has not, indeed, meant any great accession to the wealth of specifically Catholic fiction, but whose virtues are even yet active. There is no better "threshold to belief" than "Sinister Street," despite its baffling passages. "The Golden Rose," a novel by Mrs. Hugh Fraser, is altogether admirable; its author is also a notable writer of memoirs, "A Diplomat's Wife in Many Lands," for instance. No other American Catholic teller of short stories has the dramatic power or the psychological finesse of Mary Synon, whose tales of French Canadian life are particularly well done.

We did not include in our survey of fiction one novelist who belonged to the "old school" and another who is quite new and deserving of the friendliest attention. Mrs. Elizabeth Inchbald's once famous novel, "A Simple Story," is no longer much read, but it seems to have impressed, by a candid realism and a genuine vigour, the great story-tellers of its time and to have inspired "Jane Eyre." Mrs. Inchbald was an actress of charming personality and deep faith, whose own life was a romance. Our newest novelist is that very uneven gentleman, Ernest Oldmeadow. Being a converted Non-conformist minister, he bids his stories deal with the Faith as a goal to be struggled for, but keeps them fairly human and lovable by means of honest humour. "Antonio," "The Hare," "Coggin," Mr. Oldmeadow's published works, reveal great ability in characterization and mastery of atmosphere. Coggin, who appears in the book bearing his name and in "The Hare," a sequel, is expected to show up once more in the third volume of a trilogy. His creator, endowed with a gift for romance and a shrewd interest in the Latin civilization of Portugal, bears a certain semblance to Mr. Compton Mackenzie. Fiction readers must take hopeful note of him and, meanwhile, be entertained.

It is after all only a step from the art of fiction to the art of narrating the truth, and Sir William Butler, traveler and raconteur, has a bright novelist's entire charm. Such books as "The Wild North Land," "The Great Lone Land," and "Far Out" remain among the most picturesque and compelling volumes of travel. Sir William was Irish and witty, but knew the worth of a sonorous and entrancing English style. His pictures of life in the Canadian Northwest are particularly fascinating. The "Autobiography," too, will continue to win delighted readers. A long and exceptionally active life led him into many places, but he remained to the end a man of hearty honour.

Sir William Butler was a public figure; there are other men who—may the pun be forgiven!—figure as publicists. In none of these was logic, clarity of statement, and sincere concern with social issues more evident than in Cecil Chesterton (1879-1916). He lacked the poetic genius, the verve of insight and expression, which have made his brother a man for the world to note; but he was, perhaps, a better journalist, a more rigid thinker, and he accepted the Catholic tradition in its entirety. None of his books may prove of lasting value—"A History of the United States," "The Party System," "The Prussian Hath Said in His Heart"—but they have done good and have shown forth a memorable man.

Cecil Chesterton was a democrat who often found himself at odds with another distinguished Catholic writer on social matters, William Samuel Lilly (1840-1920). Mr. Lilly was conservative in the sense that he was a close, almost too close, student of Aristotle, and believed firmly in the value of an aristocracy. His books, "A Century of Revolution," "Idola Fori," "The Great Enigma," and "Renaissance Types," are distinguished by sincerity of conviction, eloquence, and diligent scholarship. It is not out of place to rank with him a man who is not a Catholic but who has defended certain Catholic views with talent and industry, W. H. Mallock. "Is Life Worth Living?" was a challenge alike to sensists and positivists that gained the approval of a large public. "The New Republic," a famous satire, taught much the same lesson by insinuation. In other books, notably "Religion as a Credible Doctrine" and "Social Reform," he has shown an intimate acquaintance with the most diverse forms of modern thought. Mr. Mallock is likewise a successful novelist and poet.

No form of literature has a wider appeal to the discerning public of today than the whimsical, personal essay. We recall with great pleasure the work of

Thomas Longueville, a convert journalist, most of whose books were published under the pseudonym, "The Prig." "The Life of a Prig" and "How to Make a Saint" are delightful satires that are never mordant and are very nearly as urbane as the best of Charles Lamb. Mr. Longueville was also the author of a "Life of Sir Kenelm Digby." Another name that one loves to remember is that of an American, Charles Bullard Fairbanks (1827-1859), who signed himself, "Aguecheek." His principal work, "Memorials of the Blessed," breathes the perfume of the past and is at the same time the monument of an exceptionally lovable personality.

One ought not to conclude a consideration of the work of the Catholic Spirit without giving some attention to the writers whose concern has lain primarily with scholarship. Philosophy and the social sciences have profited much from a clear restatement of Catholic principles. "The Metaphysics of the Schools," by the learned Jesuit, Father Harper, is a notable work. To this must be added such well-known books as Cronin's "Ethics," Maher's "Psychology," Coffey's "Ontology," Zahm's "Evolution and Dogma," and Ryan's "Distributive Justice." Nor is the work of such able Jesuits as Father Rickaby, Father Slater, and Father Thurston at all negligible. It has been thought best to make but a cursory mention here of Father George Tyrrell, S. J., whose brilliant career ended darkly.

From the point of view of history, recent years have done much to awaken interest in the story of Christendom. One notes in passing the remarkable genius of David Urquhart, about whom Gertrude Robinson has published an interesting volume. In the United States "A Political and Social History of Western Europe," by Carlton J. Hayes, has won merited attention for its impartial account of the development of our civilization. The research of Henry Adams brought him to the threshold of Catholicism, and "Chartres and St. Michel" is a genuinely original study of mediæval life. Proceeding from the architect's interest in Gothic structure, Ralph Adams Cram, though an Anglican, has set forth admirably the significance of the Christian tradition in such books as "The Substance of Gothic Art" and "The Nemesis of Mediocrity."

In the domain of science, English Catholicism has done comparatively little of outstanding value. Sir Bertram C. A. Windle has set forth the Christian view on many subjects with clarity and authority. The earlier work of St. George Mivart is not forgotten by many students of the origin of species; and the able popularizing of James J. Walsh has earned merited renown. In addition there are many occasional treatises, like "Thoughts of a Catholic Anatomist," by Dr. Dwight, which we must pass by here.

Finally, there is the towering figure of Bishop John Lancaster Spalding (1840-1916), whose polished and incisive essays on the subject of education contain much of the best that has been written in this field. Bishop Spalding was an eager if quite realistic student of life, and his keen appraisal of human intelligence made of him almost a great reformer. There is in his work not a little of that lapidary quality which distinguishes Emerson, and it displays an ability to sustain a chain of reasoning which the Concord seer never possessed.

It is our earnest hope that the literature of Catholic scholarship will increase and develop influence. With the rise to greater power of Catholic institutions of learning, with the growth of a Catholic press, the authoritative voice of our thought cannot fail to make itself more distinctly heard.

INDEX

Acton, John Emerich Lord, (1834-1902), 194, 198.
Æsthetic Movement, The, 166, 167, 180.
Alighieri, Dante, (1265-1321), 343.
Allies, T. W., (1813-1903), 94, 191, 192.
American Environment, The, 294-297.
Angel in the House, The, 108.
Apologia pro Vita Sua, 52, 58, 63, 82.
Aquinas, St. Thomas, (1225-1274), 61, 339.
Arnold, Matthew, (1822-1888), 11, 321, 322, 341.
Art of Thomas Hardy, The, 177.
Assisi, St. Francis of, (1182-1226), 342.
Aurea Dicta, 144.
Autobiography of Archbishop Ullathorne, The, 99-101.
Ayscough, John, (see Bickerstaffe-Drew).

Babbitt, Irving, (1865-), 330-332.
Ballad of the White Horse, The, 233.
Banim, John, (1798-1842), 274.
Banim, Michael, (1796-1874), 274.
Barry, William, (1849-), 17, 71, 73, 197, 206, 226.
Baudelaire, Charles, (1821-1867), 16, 290, 335, 337.
Beardsley, Aubrey, (1872-1898), 159.

Beati Mortui, 157.
Belloc, Hilaire, (1870-), 243, 249-267. Individuality of, 249 ff; views of, 252 ff; historical work of, 255 ff; social outlook of, 259 ff; position of, 265 ff; style of, 262.
Benda, Julien, 334.
Benson, Robert Hugh, (1871-1915), 211-218.
Bickerstaffe-Drew, Mgr. Francis, (1858-), 219-222.
Biography, 199, 200.
Birt, Dom Henry Norbert, 197.
Blunt, Wilfrid Scawen, (1840-), 152-154.
Book Notes, 14, 32, 86, 103, 125, 146, 165, 186, 207, 222, 248, 268, 292, 316, 351.
Bourget, Paul, (1852-), 171.
Bread and Circuses, 163.
Broad Stone of Honour, The, 24, ff.
Brownson, Orestes A., (1803-1876), 302.
Brunetière, Ferdinand, (1849-1906), 324, 335.
Bunker, John, 314.
Butler, Alban, (1710-1763), 200-202.
Butler, Samuel, (1835-1902), 253, 257.
Butler, Sir William, (1838-1910), 354.

Callanan, Jeremiah Joseph, (1795-1825), 275.
Callista, 81.

359

Camm, Dom Bede, (1884–   ),
197.
Carberry, Ethna, (Anna Mc-
Manus), 281, 287.
Carleton, William, (1794-1869),
273.
Carlyle, Thomas, (1795-1881),
11.
Cathedrale, La, 21, 212.
Catholic Poetry, 106, 165.
Catholic Spirit, The, (Defini-
tion), 1-3, 13, 325.
Cervantes, Miguel de, (1547-
1616), 345.
Chapman, Dom J. H., (1865-
), 197.
Chateaubriand, F. R. de, (1768-
1848), 8, 15, 16, 333.
Chaucer, Geoffrey, (1340-1400),
55, 344.
Chesterton, Cecil, (1879-1917),
354.
Chesterton, Gilbert Keith,
(1874–   ), 98, 229-248.
Career of, 231; work of,
232 ff; purpose of, 238 ff;
position of, 241 ff; paradox
as used by, 243; style of,
245.
Christian Year, The, 89, 109.
Chrysostom, St. John, (347-
407), 328.
Circle and the Sword, The, 283.
Clarke, Isabel, 353.
Clemens, Samuel, (Mark
Twain), (1835-1910), 300,
341.
Clermont, Émile, 334.
Cobbett, William, (1762-1835),
9.
Cochin, Augustin, 334.
Colum, Padraic, (1881–   ),
282.
Compitum, 26.
Coppèe, François, (1842-1908),
324, 335.
Corkery, Daniel, 287-289.
Corymbus for Autumn, 136.
Cram, Ralph Adams, 295, 357.

Crashaw, Richard, (1613-1649),
12, 143.
Crawford, Francis Marion,
(1854-1909), 208, 224-226.
Croce, Benedetto, (1866–   ),
331, 343.

Daly, T. A., (1871–   ), 314.
Davis, Thomas, (1814-1845),
276.
Denis, Maurice, 336.
De Profundis, 159.
De Vere, Aubrey Thomas,
(1814-1902), 121.
Dickens, Charles, (1812-1870),
10, 158, 349.
Digby, Kenelm Henry, (1797-
1880) 15-32, 33. Personality
of, 17 ff; style of, 20 ff; work
of, 22ff; position of, 30 ff.
Dolben, Digby, (1848-1867),
157, 158.
Douglas, Alfred, (1870–   ),
159, 160.
Downey, Edward, 353.
Downing, Ellen, (1828-1869),
277.
Dowson, Ernest, (1867-1900),
159.
Dream of Gerontius, The, 84.
Dreiser, Theodore, (1871–   ),
327.
Dublin University, Newman at,
48, 49.
Duffy, Charles Gavan, (1816-
1903), 276.

Earls, Michael, S.J., 314.
Eden, Helen Parry, (1852–   ),
163, 164.
Egan, Maurice Francis,
(1852–   ), 310.
Eighteenth Century, The, 4-9.
Eirenicon, The, 90.
Emerson, Ralph Waldo, (1803-
1882), 149, 294, 297.
England and Ireland in Let-
ters, 268-270.
En Route, 212.

Essay on the Development of Christian Doctrine, 44, 68, 78.
Essay on Winckelmann, 172.
Europe and the Faith, 262, 263.
Eve of the Reformation, The, 195.
Evenings on the Thames, 28.

Faber, Frederick William, (1814-1863), 93, 94.
Fabiola, 99.
Fairbanks, Charles Bullard, (1827-1859), 356.
Fernando, 220.
Fiction, The Characteristics of Modern, 208-210.
Franciscan Spirit, The, 342.
Francis, M. E. (Mrs. Frances Blundell), 287.
Freedom and the Catholic Mind, 322-324.
French Letters, Modern, 332-336.
French Revolution, The, (Belloc), 255.
Froude, Hurrell, (1802-1836), 38, 40, 89.
Fullerton, Georgiana, (1814-1885), 211.
Function of Criticism at the Present Time, The, 346-351.

Garesché, E., S.J., 353.
Gasquet, Francis Aidan Cardinal, (1846-   ), 194-197.
Genie du Christianisme, La, 16.
Gerould, Gordon Hall, 201.
Gerould, Katherine Fullerton, (1879-   ), 332.
Gibbon, Edward, (1737-1794), 6.
Goddess of Ghosts, The, 218.
Goethe, J. W. von, (1749-1832), 5.
Goldsmith, Oliver, (1728-1774), 6, 7, 270.
Gracechurch, 220.
Grammar of Assent, 52, 62, 64, 65, 66, 67, 79, 174.

Griffin, Gerald, (1803-1840), 274.
Growth of English Catholicism, 95, 102.
Guiney, Louise Imogen, (1861-1920), 154-157, 179, 277.

Harris, Joel Chandler, (1848-1908), 309.
Harte, Bret, (1839-1902), 300.
Hawthorne, Nathaniel, (1804-1864), 297.
Hecker, Isaac, (1819-1888), 302.
Hello, Ernest, (1828-1885), 149.
Henry VIII. and the English Monasteries, 196.
Heretics, 236.
Hinkson, Mrs. (see Katherine Tynan)
History, Catholic Stress Upon, 188-190, 207.
History, Importance of, 187, 188.
History, The Writing of, 189, 249.
Hobbes, John Oliver, (1867-1906), 226.
Holland, Bernard, 18, 206.
Hopkins, Gerard, (1844-1889), 115-121.
Hound of Heaven, The, 134, 136.
Howells, William Dean, (1837-1920), 300, 336.
Hueffer, Ford Madox, 183, 185.
Hughes, Thomas A., S.J., 197.
Huneker, James Gibbons, (1860-1921), 311.
Huysmans, Joris Karl, (1848-1907), 115, 212, 335.

Idea of a University, 60, 70, 78, 80.
Imaginary Portraits, 175.
Inchbald, Elizabeth, (1753-1821), 353.
Initiation, 216.

Ireland, John Archbishop, (1838-1918), 310.
Irish Catholicism and Art, 271-273, 291, 292.
Irish Dominicans, The, 197.

John Inglesant, 211.
Johnson, Lionel, (1867-1902), 176-179, 279.
Johnson, Samuel, (1709-1784), 6, 7.
Journalism and Literature, 229.
Journals of Cardinal Manning, The, 97.
Joyce, James, (1882-   ), 290.

Kavanagh, Rose, (1859-1891), 280.
Keble, John, (1792-1866), 38, 41, 89-91.
Keon, Miles Gerald, (1821-1875), 211.
Kettle, T. M., (1880-1916), 284, 292.
Kilmer, Aline, 314.
Kilmer, Joyce, (1886-1918), 313.
King, Mrs. Hamilton, 352.
Kingsley, Charles, (1819-1875), 51, 52.

Lanier, Sidney, (1842-1881), 299.
Lawrence, D. H., 210, 330.
Ledwidge, Francis, 282.
Leslie, Shane, (1885-   ), 100, 153, 204-206, 268.
Life of Cardinal Manning, The, 204.
Life of Cardinal Newman, The, 203.
Life of Francis Thompson, The, 206.
Lilly, W. S., (1840-1921), 319, 355.
Lingard, John, (1771-1851), 192-194.
Lisle, Ambrose Philips de, 17, 24, 206.

Lives of the Saints, (Butler), 200-202.
Longfellow, Henry Wadsworth, (1807-1882), 298.
Longueville, Thomas, 356.
Love Sonnets of Proteus, 153.

Macaulay, Thomas Babington, (1800-1859), 10.
MacDonagh, Thomas, (1875-1916), 270, 283.
MacGill, Patrick, 291.
MacLeod, Fiorna, (1855-1905), 289.
MacManus, Seumas, (1870-   ), 286.
Magic, 236.
Maher, Richard Aumerle, 312.
Maistre Joseph de, (1754-1821), 330.
Mallock, W. H., 355.
Mangan, James Clarence, (1803-1849), 277-279.
Manning, Henry Edward, (1808-1892), 50, 95-98.
Marie Antoinette, 256.
Maritain, Jacques, 342.
Marius the Epicurean, 173.
Martindale, C. C., S. J., (1879-   ), 206, 218.
Mary Tudor, 122.
Masefield, John, (1875-   ), 161, 185.
Maynard, Theodore, 162, 163.
McNamara, Brinsly, 291.
Mediæval Outlook, The, 240, 337-345.
Meredith, George, (1828-1909), 11, 349.
Merry England, 127.
Meynell, Alice, (1850-1923), 115, 137, 149-152.
Meynell, Everard, (1882-1925), 138, 206.
Meynell, Wilfrid, (1852-   ), 127.
Miller, J. Corson, 314.
Monsieur Henri, 155.

Moore, George, (1857-), 290, 327.

Moore, Leslie, 226.

Moore, Thomas, (1779-1852), 274, 275.

More, Paul Elmer, (1864-), 58, 330.

More, Sir Thomas, (1478-1535), 3, 341.

Mores Catholici, 21 ff.

Mulholland, Rosa, (1869-1921), 287.

Murray, Amy, 289.

My New Curate, 286.

Napoleon of Notting Hill, The, 235.

Nation, The, 276.

Naturalism in Literature, 326-330.

Newman, John Henry Cardinal, (1801-1890), 33-86. General characteristics of, 34 ff; early life of, 36 ff; at Oxford, 39 ff; Catholic life of, 44 ff; failure of, 49 ff; inner spirit of, 54 ff; thought of, 56 ff; system of, 69; philosophical significance of, 70; art of, 73 ff; controversial manner of, 74 ff; style of, 75 ff; sermons of, 76 ff; versatility of, 80 ff; poetry of, 84; literary genius of, 85 ff; historical work of, 190-191.

New Jerusalem, The, 238.

O'Connell, Daniel, (1775-1847), 276.

O'Connor, Armael, (1880-), 353.

O'Donnell, Charles Leo, (1884-), 314.

O'Duffy, Eimar, 291.

O'Hagan, John, (1822-1890), 277.

O'Neill, Moira, 281.

O'Reilly, John Boyle, (1844-1890), 309.

O'Riordan, Conal, 291.

Oddsfish, 214.

Oldmeadow, Ernest, 354.

One Poor Scruple, 223.

Orthodoxy, 237.

Oxford Movement, The, 37-44, 88, 89.

Oxford Sermons, The, 39, 77.

Paganism: Old and New, 141.

Pascal, Blaise, (1623-1662), 71, 337, 349.

Pater, Walter Horatio, (1839-1894), 168-176, 338.

Path to Rome, The, 257.

Patmore, Coventry, (1823-1896), 108-115, 124, 139, 144, 161, 242.

Paul, C. Kegan, (1856-1902), 95, 122.

Pearse, Padraic, 283, 284.

Plunkett, George Noble, (1851-), 285.

Plunkett, Joseph Mary, (1887-1916), 283.

Poe, Edgar Allan, (1809-1849), 299.

Poetry, Modern, 160, 161.

Poetry, The Nature of, 104-106, 147-149.

Pre-Raphaelites, The, 180.

Proctor, Adelaide, (1825-1864), 158, 159.

Prout, Father, (1804-1866), 275.

Puritan Influence in America, The, 297, 298, 303, 305, 314.

Pusey, Edward, (1800-1882), 91.

Ramona, (H. H. Jackson), 313.

Reid, Christian, (Mrs. Frances Tiernan), (1846-1920), 312.

Renaissance, The, 172.

Renan, Ernest, (1823-1892), 71.

Repplier, Agnes, (1857-), 311.

Rhythm of Life, The, 115.

Rod, Root and Flower, 114.
Rossetti, Christina, (1830-1894), 182-185.
Rossetti, Dante Gabriel, (1828-1882), 181, 182.
Rousseau, Jean Jacques, (1712-1778), 4, 7, 331, 333.
Rousseau and Romanticism, 330.
Ruskin, John, (1819-1900), 11, 31, 167-169, 330.
Ryan, Abram, (1839-1886), 309.

Sales, St. Francis de, 21, 328.
San Celestino, 219.
Saracinesca, 225.
Scott, Sir Walter, (1771-1832), 8, 15, 208.
Search after Proserpine, 121.
Second Spring, The, 77.
Sentimentalists, The, 216.
Servile State, The, 259.
Shairp, J. C., (1819-1885), 36.
Shakespeare, William, (1564-1616), 243, 344, 345.
Shea, John Gilmary, (1824-1892), 198, 199.
Sheehan, Patrick Canon, (1852-1913), 286.
Shelley, Percy Bysshe, (1792-1822), 8, 141.
Shelley, 141, 142.
Shorter, Mrs. Clement, (see Sigerson, Dora).
Shorthouse, Joseph Henry, (1834-1903), 211.
Sigerson, Dora, 281.
Sight and Insight, 139.
Sister Songs, 135.
Smith, John Talbot, (1855-), 312.
Snead-Cox, H. G., 204.
Southern Influence in American Letters, The, 298.
South Sea Idyls, 303.
Spalding, John Lancaster Bishop, (1840-1916), 357.
Spearman, Frank, (1859-), 312.

St. John, Ambrose, (1815-1875), 54, 82.
St. Peter's Chains, 121.
Standards in Art, 319-322, 325, 345.
Stoddard, Charles Warren, (1843-1909), 303-306.
Strickland, Agnes, (1796-1874), 206.
Synon, Mary, 353.

Tabb, John Bannister, (1845-1909), 306-308.
Taine, Hippolyte, (1828-1892), 325, 334.
Thompson, Francis, (1859-1907), 127-146. Life of, 128 ff; poetry of, 132 ff; prose of, 140 ff; position of, 145.
Tracts for the Times, 42.
Tynan, Katherine, (1861-), 279, 280, 287.

Ullathorne, Archbishop, (1806-1889), 100, 101.
Unknown Eros, The, 112.

Valdès, Palacio, (1853-), 350.
Vaughn, Herbert, (1832-1903), 99.
Victorian Age, The, 9-12.

Walsh, Thomas, (1875-), 314.
Ward, Mrs. Wilfrid, (1861-), 222-224.
Ward, Wilfrid, (1856-1916), 75, 85, 202-204.
Ward, William George, (1812-1882), 43, 50, 76, 92, 93.
Waters of Twilight, The, 218.
Western Influence in American Letters, The, 300.
Whitman, Walt, (1819-1892), 298.
Wilde, Oscar, (1856-1900), 159, 179, 292.
Wiseman, Nicholas Cardinal, (1802-1865), 43, 98, 99.

Yeats, William Butler, (1865-
), 282, 285.
Yellow Bittern, The, 288.

Zola, Émile, (1840-1902), 66,
333, 336.